Quest of the Magic Wells - Síonna

Malcolm James Griffin

First published in paperback by
Michael Terence Publishing in 2021
www.mtp.agency

ISBN 9781800942462

Cover illustration
by Dómhnal Ó Bric

To Allen Ernest H Martiensen

Grá mo chroí
This splendorous love is our unifier

Síonna, an Irish Goddess of great beauty went seeking the hazelnuts of wisdom. She knew that hazelnuts contained the secret of poetry that was called éigse, learning. She found a deep pool with hazel trees growing around it. The trees were ripe with hazelnuts and Síonna watched as the nuts fell from the branches and dropped into the pool breaking open to reveal a rich purple stain. The salmon of wisdom feasted on these hazelnuts causing dark red freckles to appear on their silvery skin. With a deep desire to catch the hazelnuts, she leaned forward, lost her footing and toppled into the pool. The hazelnuts entangled, twisted and matted her long flowing hair like the eddies and currents of the pool. The unstoppable had happened once the mirror of the pool's surface had been broken. The terrible beauty of the Goddess Síonna shimmered and pulsated across the pool driving into the red earth and throwing up banks on either side as she reached across the sacred land of Eiru towards the sea creating the great river that bears her name.

Scriptist Kinney.

Chapter 1
Aisling
The Soul knows the true wish

It is a custom amongst the people of Fir Bolg, men of the bag, that on every full moon cycle, the children gather in Grandmother's roundhouse to listen to her tales by the fireside. A crackling and sparking of logs fill the hut with familiar sounds. The sound of winter and Grandmother's dreamy voice gift a journey of wonderment.

An orange glow dances on the walls. Her crooked form shadows over them. The earthy aroma of sage sweeps to their noses as she smudges the smouldering herb around the roundhouse with her hawk feather. Her pointed nose protrudes from her sunken, bony cheeks. A bun of silver braids sits a-swirly upon her head like passages of her long wondrous years humbly spent. Her capturing smile and the glint of her warm green eyes lift the joy in their hearts, mirroring the flames as sparks rise, twirling in the smoke and fly out a hole in the straw roof reaching to the stars with their wishes.

They listen for the subtle inhale of her breath and for the draíocht, magic, to begin.

"My wise children, with a sweetness of honeyed tongues let us speak the truth for we the Fir Bolg are the great weavers of lore. The wise shamans knew that Goddesses of wells, streams and rivers have particular powers and that the wild salmon was an ancient symbol of this power. They also knew that the elements of fire and water are traditionally associated with women. Quieten your minds and hear the whispers of our people echo in this sacred dwelling. As our fire burns, we unite it with fires of old, awakening the same streams of light that connect us through time; for this is a place of power, ho.

"Chew on these acorns of the sacred oak and join me on a mystical path of thoughts. Form a wish. Cast them into the transforming fire. See your wishes weave into the dance of flames ascending with the smoke. Forth they go sparkling through the roof like a silken thread across the sky, glittering amongst the blanket of stars, cultivating a new beginning as the beginning when we took birth on this sacred land with a great purpose, to fulfil the prophecy of the shaman.

"The Fir Bolg, acquiring the name from once having been enslaved in another land by a sallow-skinned race and ruled by a dark King who made them carry bags of clay and soil to build his empires. Our ancestors received a vision in Dreamtime telling them to flee from this life. They took heed of the sign and sailed the oceans arriving at Eriu led by the five chieftains of the Mac Dela, clan who divided the lands into five provinces: Sengann took North Mumhan, Gann took South Mumhan, Genann took Connachta, Rudraige took Ulaidh, and Sláine took Laigin.

"Establishing the High Kingship, our spioradálta, spiritual, ancestors lived in great relation with the cycles of nature honouring the visions of the gods and deities. They became keepers of our rich traditions nurturing each other while harvesting the lands and oceans of Eriu with a deep passion. Let us now delve into the wonders and myths of our ancestors, unveiling the story of our ancestral Goddess, Síonna."

Chapter 2
Síonna, The Goddess

She roams the rolling hills around the Valley of the Stags carrying with her a cauldron of dreams and desires. Born with inherent gifts she slowly unravels them within the movements and cycles of the surrounding nature. She still only bears the equivalent of six inner rings of the bark of a tree but embodies a fearless strength and bravery like nothing the elders have seen at this stage of youth.

She hears a sudden rumpus and growling of animals beyond a near hill. She scrambles over the mound to see wild hounds surrounding an abandoned fox cub. She picks up a stick from a nearby hazel and leaps into the thick of the beasts, beating the pack off with just the stick. Then she quietly coaxes the cub until she gains her trust and gathers special leaves making a leigheas, cure, that a druid taught her and wraps it around the animal's wound.

Within her safe grasp she brings the fox to a stream where she drinks. Given the baby vixen's astounding cuteness with her distinctive four white socks and a white streak that separates the soft sandstone fur on her forehead, Síonna names her Ríonach, the queenly one.

From that day forth the cunning little creature grows to become Síonna's best friend always remembering how she saved her life. They wander each day further into the woods and valleys beyond the Valley of the Stags, exploring together new secrets of nature.

Síonna learns the finer skills of hunting following Ríonach's lead as though seeing through the vixen's crystal-like hazel eyes a glimpse of the otherworldliness, the sixth sense. The young warrior observes the fox stalking as she homes in on her prey; how she crawls lightly placing her white legs tentatively upon the sward, her white-streaked tail swinging back and forth; sensing, her nose cocked sniffing rhythmically. How she lifts one paw and stills like a pelican fishing a stream waiting for that moment, for the inner confirmation. And she pounces or sprints or salmon-leaps upon her prize.

The red-skinned one and the young warrior venture everywhere together. She guards Síonna while she sits for long periods of time dreaming beneath trees, listening to the whispers of the winds and rivers, pondering on the clouds searching for the faces of the gods or deities to appear while listening for the voices of her ancestors to gift guidance from the spioradálta realms.

Daydreaming beneath an oak she is suddenly woken by a wailing of the women in the valley. Alerted she swiftly returns to see her grandfather standing at the edge of the enclosure with tears dripping from his chin, waiting. That humble joyful glint that warms her soul is now dulled and veiled in his eyes. A heavy knot clinches her stomach. Her heartbeat races. She slowly approaches feeling the concentric rings of his grief reaching out and cloaking her with a heaviness like an unwanted otherworldly veil.

He opens his arms wide cuddling her into his safe space and delivers the news of the drowning of both her parents and her grandmother. She feels a sudden wound open in her chest and begins to squeal uncontrollably like Ríonach that day beneath the ravaging mouths of the hounds. He grips her tightly. She feels a drowning in her own tears.

"Shush, shush, Síonna, their spirits now soar across that sacred veil and they watch over us, protecting us and helping to heal our torn hearts while we endure their loss. Shush little one, for you are destined with a great purpose and this is one of the biggest challenges you will overcome."

Waves of pain and sorrow surge through her being. He strokes the back of her head and begins singing, trying to ease their shock. She feels suffocated with her face buried into his stomach that hops and trembles as he quietly wails for his own loss but tries to conceal it from her. Sweat pours from her brow. The elders and others come showering them in blessings, trying to comfort them.

A band of women approach burning sage and mugwort ritually, capturing their grief and turn wailing in rhythmic voices, walking sunwise around the enclosure as though taking the grief to a safe distance to lessen their hurt.

Sionna spends many cycles of the moon cocooned in Grandfather's love who sings to her each night and tells stories uniting her with her parents just as she slips into Dreamtime so that she can meet them in the spioradálta worlds. But a deep sense of been abandoned by them floods her mind. She becomes angry at everyone, even questioning the gods and deities while hitting out at those around her. An inner struggle begins as she desperately searches for her loved ones in the furthest reaches of her mind. Grandfather allows her through the natural processes of the grieving cycle, offering his honeyed guiding tongue when she needs it.

Every member of the tribe nurtures her while allowing her to slowly grow into acceptance. Sengann and his wife, Aibhlín, care for her in a way considering her as one of their blood.

Born with that gift of seeing and listening and divining, and the warriors will to survive, after some time her urge to delve into the other realms returns. One day she decides to venture again beyond the enclosure and approaches Grandfather to get approval.

"Grandfather, I might take Ríonach today to explore a little."

His cheeks redden with the rush of inner excitement, hearing she is finally willing to step beyond the valley after so many moon cycles of grieving.

"Granddaughter, go, ramble further and return to the sounds and movements where you first began to hone your skills. And remember, the soul knows the true wish."

She smiles and whistles for Ríonach who comes blazing through the enclosure and they take to the hills and valleys. She looks back at his silver hair crowning his humble head, his eyes following her tracks while he puffs on his dúidín, pipe, that's almost dancing in his mouth with the happiness, watching her form until she fades into the rhythms of the valley. She strays further each day and wanders from the other children for a long-time, acquiring skills that a fully grown warrior would strive to embody.

After many seasons of ventures with her vixen, she begins to mix with her equals again. The other children, recognising something within her, come to tell Síonna their secrets, share their worries and fears with her while somehow feeling soothed by just one word she utters or finding relief by just happily been in her presence. Intuitively, she knows how to enliven them with just one sparkle from her crystal eyes, or a mere whisper wrapped with care in her all-loving voice.

Despite her skills, Síonna still holds her own fears. She grows knowing that she is somehow different because of the gift. Bumblebees begin to follow her everywhere, a sure sign of one who is chosen, for the bumblebee represents the Goddess. The shamans know it and carefully give her subtle signals that she has a great purpose as her grandfather told her that day. She soon gains the ability to hear what others don't. Voices of those who passed beyond the veil whisper to her. The subtle worlds peel open before her eyes.

She sees events in her Wonder-Eye before they occur and reads the movements of the elementals, telling the elders of incoming storms and drought. Her prophecies manifest as foreseen. Despite the gifts, she feels a certain weight carrying the burden of expectation as the one-bestowed-with-a-gift and duty to follow in the footsteps of past shaman and sage. Throughout time in Eriu, the sorcerer of the Underworld has stalked the Fir Bolg, enchanting those who fall weak to his delusions. Síonna, knowing from the druids and Grandfather that stepping into the quest of the sage, she would become a beacon of light for the dark forces like a fire drawing an eclipse of moth.

But also coming to know through Grandfather that change is the one thing life would present. She strives to accept her role and quench the fears of what could occur. Instead of seeing her destiny as a curse that could weigh her down helplessly, she chooses to grasp it and use it as a force to seek freedom in the unknown, ever-inevitable cycles of change.

She develops the warrior, discovering all kinds of magic and tricks, mimicking the movements of the animals, the elementals and the older warriors. To compensate for the loss of that bond between mother and daughter she feels drawn to the opposite of everything feminine, finding some peace in developing all that is considered for the men of the clan.

She masters the sword and the bataireacht, stick-fighting, in a way that no warrior has ever seen. She contests the young warriors her equal and many much older than her, winning the children's samildánach, Master of all the arts, challenge yearly. She strays from the usual girly hobbies such as basket weaving, jewellery making, craft and play, making cooking implements, or the simple daily chores of preparing food, helping with the animals or nurturing the young or washing the furs and hides in the rivers with the older women.

Nor does she attend the ceremonial counsels of the Mother or gatherings with the other children. She chooses to solely venture into forbidden places. Places of power and mystery.

This day tracking through the Valley of the Boars far beyond the barony of her own valley, she discovers a passage tomb hidden in a mound grown over with trees. Having heard the stories from the elders trying to ward off the children, telling how sorcerers or brown bears can sometimes dwell in these untouched places. Birthed with such courage she fearlessly crawls in through the dark, narrow entrance that runs deep beneath the passage tombs. She ducks beneath the huge boulders crawling on all limbs. Ríonach darts by. She trails the passageway using the other sight of the Wonder-Eye, seeing in the dark as though in daylight to emerge into a huge cavern where a shaft of light shaves the back wall.

"A Suncatcher," she whispers, knowing that the ancestors used their wisdom of the solar cycles to capture the alignment of the Sun God on certain days of the seasons for many purposes.

She walks to the shaft of light to see it illuminating the rock paintings of her ancestors etched upon the back wall. Her eyes flicker, owl-like in awe of the magical sight.

She quietens her mind and whispers, asking the place of power to reveal its soul to her. And there on the etchings, she sees the depictions of the spioradálta worlds and how her forefathers lived and worshipped. Awed at the sheer skill and size of the paintings, she ponders on what they used to create the vast array of colours and how they managed to work at such height as some reach the roof of the cavern.

Her eyes track over the lines of the many power animals, spirals and triskeles, three legs, following the symbols in the direction of the sun, seeing through her ancestors' eyes the images that surfaced within their minds that they brought to life here. She envisages the strokes of their hands, how relaxed they held their wrists flicking them just as she holds her sword to swipe or stab. Hearing their whispers, she captures the insights that poured through their creative minds, the wishes of the gods and deities leading them. She arches her head and rhythmically sniffs, receiving the same cold peat scent that they would have smelt.

She closes her eyes sharing their great moments of silence as they opened their souls to the pulse of this place of power while unveiling their magic onto these great sheets of basalt, beautifully adorned with sparkling layers of quartz.

She goes to her deepest inwardness feeling-their-way and taking a deep breath, she envisages the breath taking all the etchings through her Wonder-Eye to be mapped on an inner slab of basalt within her mind. She whistles for Ríonach who leaps from the darkness. Síonna springs from the earth racing after the vixen through the passageway with a surge of excitement pushing her to get back to Grandfather before the sun sits at its full height and reveal her day's findings.

She tumbles in the door almost tripping over the stone slab.

"Grandfather, I saw the paintings deep in the burial tombs beyond the river in the Valley of the Boars. I saw deities and bears and the gods and medicine wheels and, and…" she stutters with the urge to describe everything all at once.

"Calm the belongings that you brought in your mind and allow the moonlight to cool the moving waters. Allow the images to come alive one by one and let the ancestors do the talking."

She is always owl-eyed at the teachings he gives when she brings something new to share with him.

"You must ask yourself, who is revealing the secrets? Is it you or the ancestors wishing to speak through you?"

She smiles, never thinking of it in that way and calms her racing thoughts, watching him tapping his lower lip, a trait he is known for throughout the land when he is ruminating to reveal his spioradálta wisdom or to bestow one with a spontaneous riddling of magical words; having acquired the title of an Ollamh and the worthy holder of the golden hazel branch through his spioradálta quest, that saw him travel the lands meeting sages and druids and other Ollamh where they shared insights and teachings of everything worldly and otherworldly.

Despite his many journeys and inner gatherings and sharing with the wise ones of the land, it was a near-death experience that truly opened his Wonder-Eye to soar to the summits of the sacred where he merged with his soul and acquired and embodied the highly sought-after Rainbow Body, the highest known spioradálta achievement of the sage, shaman or druid.

Recognising his true merit within his actions, the Ard Druí, High Druids, of Eriu bestowed on him the title of the great High King of Consciousness and he became known to everyone as Grandfather.

"Sionna, within the intricate drawings of our ancients' art is how they symbolize the motion of our actions, cycles and the progress in one's life and what tasks are held in the destiny of one's future."

Grandfather sometimes uses words he wouldn't share with any of the other children knowing Síonna has the understanding of someone much older. She smiles repeating, "intricate", loving his use of the new word and repeats it,

"Intricate like the infinite formations of the stars that sparkle in your cornflower eyes."

"Yes granddaughter, you have it," he humbly responds, smiling at her éigse ability.

"Now let us pick the ancient triskele from the map of your mind as a worthy example. Being the oldest of the symbols found in many of our places of power, it represents the three stages of life: life, death and rebirth. The three elements: The Father, the Son, and the Great Spirit. And the three domains: earth, sea and sky, past, present and future."

He yawns and takes another puff and sweeps a ring of smoke between.

"Let's take another: the medicine wheel. The wheel represents life's mystery as a never ending circle, constantly turning like the cycles, the seasons and everything that we are interconnected with, the power animals such as the bear you saw, and what position we are in the cycles of our lives. As we grow, we change like the seasons. Much of nature moves in circular patterns."

Grandfather stills and rolls his eyes sunwise and begins to twirl the opposite direction shuffling his feet at great speed while puffing on his dúidín, rising a veil of smoke that encloses his body. As dizziness grows, he comes to a sudden stop chuckling wildly trying to regain his balance and continues.

"Ah gaja, dizzy as a frog I am, balancing on a lily pad shaken by a solar storm. Now let us enter the godly direction of the North, where the start of the growing season begins at Samhain, November. The veils between the worlds are thin. Here we walk the path to find the wisdom of An Bradán, the salmon, the oldest symbolic creature of our tradition, teaching us to fearlessly Salmon-leap into the unknown shadows of Geimhreadh, Winter. There we meet the ancestors. The elder time on the wheel teaches us of the Deasghnátha, the ceremonial rites of the shaman, how to use the senses, bringing outward, the inner journeys."

Grandfather takes a deep breath and exhales raising his hazel branch whispering a blessing and points it easterly.

"The direction of East, where Lugh, the Sun God, casts his Suncatchers gifting all things to begin, the path of opening the way for the dawning of new souls. Where we summon courage. Youth and prosperity are brought through on the Suncatcher rays of the rising sun. It is the realm of An Iolar, the Eagle, who soars higher than any bird perceiving life from a higher plain who can shape-shift into a lightning being teaching us to let go and be unfettered by the physical body. Where Death has no longer a fearful hold on us." Grandfather takes another couple of puffs before hissing like a serpent much to Síonna's amusement and continues.

"South, is where we shed the old skins, and renew, like the Nathair, the serpent, learning the way of the warrior while coming into Being growing with the season of Bealtaine, May. We witness the great illumination of Summer Solstice, where the fire of the sun is at its highest. Here we become the leigheasóir, and find healing, a playfulness, and learn patience and the understanding that we are part of the interconnectedness of all things. Granddaughter, soar like the most wondrous sunflower like a Suncatcher spear cast by Lugh, and learn in the South that Death illuminates the new beginnings we gained in the east."

Síonna laughs at his humorous ways of teaching. He takes the short-stemmed dúidín from his mouth and taps his lip ruminating before heading to the final direction on the wheel.

"West, the direction of destiny, where the sun sets giving way for a new day. Where we slow down as the animals hibernate. We go inward on the path to grow and gain strength from the wisdom we acquired, and come to understand the messages of the ancestors, and the visions from the gobbly deities we receive in the darkness of Geimhreadh. Granddaughter, learn to harvest the essence of all life given to you, and complete the wheel to arrive in the centre. There you stand finding balance within, bringing the values and teachings of each position to be rooted like the great oak into the Mother. With this balanced state, stretch your little robin cheeks with a great smile while chirping a new tongue, only a clever Goddess would acquire."

Her rosy cheeks peel back with the laughter and the humorous praise he bestows upon her, and he delves deeper.

"Our people knew that without a well, life has no source. The medicine wheel also represents the wheels that spin on the body also known as the Wells. These Wells withhold the same essence and teachings telling of what position we occupy in life and about our inner spioradálta values and how we relate to the seasonal time measured in cycles; they can help us map out how we can live and create the life-slab onto which we too can paint our stories."

He pauses taking another few puffs before completing this day's teaching.

"The dolmens, the tombs, the Faery forts, the Suncatchers and all our sacred stone workings have something to teach us. So, you see, there is a depth withheld within these etchings for us to unveil thousands of years of teachings, stories, myths and great lore. Go and explore, Síonna. Sit within these sacred spaces and go to your most inwardness. And remember, while doing so allow the moving tides to calm down and the elementals will shine on the surface of your beautiful godly being. And as they do, let your laughter spread your smile so wide until it wrinkles your nose; then go through this world passing this shamanic joy onto others, making life shiny for you and those around you."

She chuckles at his riddling ways, always the wise, opening her mind anew each time like a spring flower stretching its petals towards the warming sun for the first time.

Chapter 3
Grandfather

The familiar, sweet, oaky smell of his pipe hooks her nostrils as smoke furrows before him on the wind. She hears the soft touch of his feet approaching; a wonderful presence she could never fully describe to others, one of joy, peace, a sense of true happiness more beautiful than the most majestic rainbow, more beautiful than the sparkling waterfalls of the land; such pure love that every time she feels it a beautiful warmth floods her being even when he is at a great distance from her.

It's as though his light reaches through the air like a string of golden nectar that envelopes her entire being with the sweet enchantment of his wondrous, glowing heart.

His shadow stretches over the ground bending around her legs. Feeling the peaceful warmth, she turns and looks upon his soft, soothing face.

"Grandfather," she whispers.

His silver hair glistens like his silken, sallow skin as he pushes his black, curly eyebrows into a dance above his light blue eyes that gaze wondrously upon her whilst he taps his lower lip with his chubby, hairy finger, a distinguishing trait he carries out before he delivers a magical verse.

Known for his healing abilities and having acquired the status of an Ollamh, Master-poet, and the title of High King of Consciousness, many come to hear his soothing wisdom or be blessed beneath his golden hazel branch.

"Éist le mo ghuí, listen to my prayer."

Grandfather first greets her soul in the teanga dhúchais, mother tongue of the land and then switches to the foreign tongue that came to Eriu by way of raiders and traders. And over time through the interaction with these people, this new tongue grew like a leech upon the people of Eriu.

"To know your true self is to live your life and relationships from the level of the soul. Síonna, the years have grown wondrously and mysteriously upon you, disappearing beyond veils like the many cycles of the sun and moon. So, robin red are those locks you wear. I see the fires of Eriu lit within each strand withholding an ancient power. I see the lakes and rivers of Eriu mirror the éigse in those hazel star-like eyes. I hear the voices and wishes of the gods and ancestors waiting to sing within that jewel-like heart you vigorously protect. You must one day lay down your shields to truly walk the secret path of the Rainbow One. To go beyond all thought and emotion and sing from the heart a music like the birds, chirping while perched on the royal seat of your soul raising the flowery crown of a Goddess."

They stand before the waters of Abhna na t-Sionainne, River Shannon, reflecting on the many journeys that have brought them to this joyful time in their lives.

He gazes into her hazel amber eyes, her fire-red locks sway on the subtle wind twirling around her shoulders, shining with a shave of the sun's orange glow that turns her yellow brat golden. Her skin glistens with youthful radiance. Admiring her distinctive brown birth mark sitting on the summit of her left cheek just below her eye; the mark of one-who-is-chosen for a noble purpose as the elders have long foreseen, he puffs on the dúidín.

Smoke circles her face as she reaches out her hand. Her soft skin enters the firm grasp of his brown, calloused, earthy skin, like an ocean meeting the land churning a new tide of events they bind the light traces of their souls for a great purpose.

He recalls how spirited she was in youth. Her once little red dimples for cheeks now sit like two blazing suns. How her orange ringlets danced at waist height with a string of buttercups woven into one strand as she darted by with Ríonach always on her trail. How she strayed from the usual girly skills to exchange them by showing her physical prowess, her skills at wrestling and fighting with the boys. She learned the finer movements of the sword and would enact battle scenes with the strongest of the young warriors.

"Granddaughter, take a breath and know that before the next one lies all possibility. It is our connection to the sacred, something that we must strive to make each day."

As he has her attention, he sticks out his tongue and flickers it three times sunwise before letting out a riddling verse of praise.

"Your eyes throw stars furrowing magical paths for rising dawns and sinking dusks that carry the wondrous moons of a wandering womb. Your soul sears the plains of Dreamtime, cast by the ancestors who colour your soul to form the walk of a wondrous Goddess. An ancient turtle tribe chants in majestic temples of afar, pulling together strings of magical tunes so Eriu hums a name in an enchanting drone that echoes over her mountains and lands. Three times it can be heard like a conversation of the gods pronouncing this chosen warrior's name: Síonna, Goddess of Eriu."

Glowing like an open flower stilled beneath the approaching drone of a bumble bee, mesmerised by his mysterious riddling tongue, her radiance glistens like the morning dew wearing rays of the rising sun. He opens his arms and she falls into his warm embrace.

"Grandfather, always churning your wondrous wisdom," she whispers.

He wraps her beneath the fold of his arms like a wise owl enclosing her young within a clutch of feathers. Ríonach stands on her hind legs, sniffing and moving her whiskers before leaping and butting the back of Grandfather's legs. He turns, stooping to one knee.

"I am not forgetting you, gobbly little furry one wrapped within all that mystery with those beady dreaming eyes gazing so cunning."

The vixen rolls onto her back, pushing her paws into the air. He strokes her belly and cups his hand over each of her four white socks. Zara swoops down with her wings spread, showing her beautiful white plumage, her yellow beak letting out a shrilling call.

"Ah, Zara, jealous of my attention to the little belly one," he says, recalling the day when the mysterious bird not native to Eriu came to him when he had been attacked and badly wounded by a crazed warrior from an overseas tribe.

As death stalked, the gods sent this winged deity to guide and accompany Grandfather home. She has stayed by his side ever since. He scrunches his lips around the dúidín, puffing out circles of smoke. Síonna looks upon his greying moustache that lightly dances beneath his nose as he puffs. A veil of smoke swirls between them. She twirls her index finger creating a circle in the smoke seeing the blue of his eyes peering through. She feels captured by the light blue spheres as though she sees the entire meaning of life glowing within them.

Dragonfly glide by. Now grown into a young warrior after all these years, she is still held within his enchantment.

"Lest we forget the dancing fly taking the whispers of our wish to the gods," Grandfather whispers. "Soon, we will take to the hills and valleys across Eriu, south-west to the Kingdoms of Light that will lead us to the roaring belly of the Atlantach ocean and into the perils of the sea to the magical Rainbow Isles."

Her eyes light up. Síonna watches him spin three times while blowing three circles of smoke.

"Quest," he whispers, swinging his Ollamh branch in an arc.

A sacred moment unfolds. A veil suddenly opens and whisks their consciousness along a path of living links to another world where they witness a glow of golden trees brighten. Animals, insects, mountains and rivers sing in witnessing wonder as though nature has lain in sleep waiting for the aligned action of their two souls to utter that very word, 'quest'. Celebrating in glorious dance, their feet glide parallel, swishing through the grass until they arrive at a grove of oaks in this magical world.

With fingers pinched and arms outstretched with his golden hazel, Grandfather raises his thick eyebrows, swirling his eyes and spins and spins as Síonna looks at the embers from his dúidín furrow like a trail of sparkling stars behind his dancing form. She joins him leaping into a twirling movement and coils downwards to the earth before springing into a series of salmon-leaping. Blossoms and leaves stir around their feet like two winds meeting in a great celebration.

"Síonna, write your name with your feet upon the earth, pronouncing your light trace."

She creates her name with a swirl of footsteps leaving her wish in the dark earth with delight pouring out as she roars from expanded lungs, her name. Aloud, her voice fills this subtle realm followed by Grandfather pronouncing his birth-given title. Ríonach races in circles. Zara sweeps down in great swirls so fast her yellow beak looks like a spear cast through the air.

They witness green fields stretching to distant horizons. Some have crops of waving, silken corn that sway on the wind. Cotton spindles flutter by amongst pollen and winged seeds. An abundant world is in flow about them as they merge with the music of it.

After a long passage of expressing their heightened joy, they slow to a gentle swaying matching the calming wind. A light suddenly flashes veiling their sight.

They are returned to the Valley of the Stags bringing with them the rapture of what they experienced, knowing that a new living time in their lives has begun. To mark the event Grandfather unfurls a timely wondrous tongue,

"When two kindred spirits meet, we are upholding the privilege of our birth upon this Earth. This splendorous love is our unifier. We have great work before us, Síonna. Such as the curling wind that unfurls a golden strand of sparkle from your Dreamtime eyes that glint of another world's beauty, mirroring a wondrous, mysterious, unknown depth."

She laughs with a delight that she hasn't felt for many years. She thinks back to how joy was like a distant cloud being swept away from her by a constant wind when her parents and grandmother drowned when a sudden storm blew torrential rains forcing them to cross a river where they met their fate after visiting relations in another province.

Feeling empty and abandoned, how she retreated into unknown depths of herself where she searched and searched, imagining where she could find them in the forest and mountains, in caves and passages tombs of darkness, in the deep of the river; depths to where she could hear their voices calling them from landscapes and seascapes afar. How she gazed at the stars to see their faces dotted in the sky or mirrored upon lakes or held in some unseen realm within the soft whispers of the trees, she searched leaving no realm uncovered.

After all her searching, she recalls the day she sat with Grandfather who with his Ollamh understanding knew that she was reaching a time of transition and cocooned her wounded soul to allow for expansion. She gazed into his dreamy cornflower eyes and suddenly realised that her loved ones were never far away from her all that time; they were there in a realm just beyond her reach. As Grandfather held her within the love and compassion of his heart, she saw the eyes of her loved ones reflected on the surface of his being.

She remembers venturing afar with Ríonach, observing the animal wisdom. How they survived and recovered from wounds and long journeys, learning from them, how to breathe, to rest, to hunt and feed. How she slept beneath the stars and moon, in caves, on mountain tops, anywhere that she could find that sense of inner calmness. And how she became adept at blending with her surroundings while listening to the subtle signs of the forests and woods when a disturbance entered. She would map the movements of every beast and crawler, distinguishing their presence through the unique concentric rings each one created.

How she sat for long passages in boughs of oak, hawthorn, rowan and hazel, inwardly gazing, developing her senses to heightened levels, going to depths where mankind may not have gone before and entered the Dreamtime of the trees. It was there beneath their calming grace that she developed the skills to fully open her Wonder-Eye and listening to the wise riddles of Grandfather, she began to feel that inner power to see the spioradálta realms having no separation with those of the visible world.

She stands before him now feeling honoured, casting great gratitude for all that she has learned and all that he has guided her through.

"A bit of a past wobble there or should we say a gobbly dream, Granddaughter? As everything we encounter is but a dream we manifest."

She smiles nodding her head and asks him,

"Grandfather, gift me in the wise ways of the Rainbow sages, a way that will bring Oneness to my skills to become a leader of our people."

He places his hand on her heart, giving a blessing with a draíocht-of-the-fingertips.

"With every wonder and moment that my gobblied heart will pulse, I will accompany you, for we will dance together like river and ocean blazing a wondrous feeling-of-our-way. Others will follow as mysterious stars never born of a twilight sky will shine within the tributaries of your blood that will race to an ocean guided by the hands of a wizard's spin, and swirl they will a new dream where a wondrous leaping salmon will enclose the land within its enchanted Wonder-Eye."

She follows the trail of his words in imaginative leaps, listening with such intensity as though she captures the essence before it is magically formed on his honeyed tongue.

"I am ready," she replies, "for I truly believe that our magical way is lit!"

The shamans hold many councils discussing the task bestowed upon Síonna. Word soon spreads around the enclosure. She stands with Grandfather before the waters of Abhna na t-Sionainne where he bestows more insights.

"Síonna, allow the moving waters of the mind to calm and the sun and moon and stars will shine on your being like the glowing of your soul that sparkles within. You wear this great sparkle on the windows of your eyes. Share it Granddaughter. It is your time to voyage, your time to make your life shine. Remember, this is your destiny. Now make a wish and cast it upon the silver sparkle of this ancient salmon weaving river."

Overjoyed and gazing into his cornflower eyes, she forms her wish and turns casting it into the eddies and currents, asking the spirit of the waters to take her task to the gods to where it will be woven and churned into manifestation.

Grandfather turns to her.

"Allow me to say a few more things," he says. "First and foremost, be kind to yourself and do not let your emotions control you. Cultivate the love in your heart and gift it to whomever you will come across as you journey through this life. Remember, laughter is the sparkle that kindles the fire in the soul. Above all, offer humour and thanksgiving to everyone and in everything that you do, even as you meet the most challenging obstacles. And lastly, if I was only to say one thing of importance to you, it would be to know that you owe nothing to anyone but respect."

As she grasps his golden words, the children spring from the rushes and swarm around them having heard the story of the prophecy circling the enclosure.

"You are going to the far distant lands into kingdoms of the druids, to the mystical mountains of the great Cúroí, visiting the wise ones in the Kingdom of Light."

Their high-pitched voices ring out in unison. Grandfather beckons them to sit on the riverbank and join hands to form a wish. He taps each one upon the Wonder-Eye with his golden branch summoning the magic while they watch the sun cast yellow streaks through the sky, then green, blue, weaving into gold and copper before turning red as they follow the glowing furrow until it bows to begin its sleep behind a cluster of twilight stars.

They hear the sudden drone of horns from the enclosure. They make their way back and join the shaman, druids, bards, ovate, scholáire, scholar, and the wise elders who assemble beneath the old oak at the centre of the enclosure.

Ceremonial fires are burning; the uplifting scent of sage sweeps through the enclosure. The High King Sengann approaches bearing the crown of the encannach, bird-headdress, the symbol of his bird-vision and his Kingship. The mighty King raises his sword to each direction summoning the elementals of the south, the east, the north and the west before he crouches, laying a kiss on the earth and rises again with his hands outstretched to the sky, summoning the gods and spirits of the ancestors for the task ahead.

He delivers the wisdom received from his night of Bull-Dreaming.

"Éist le mo ghuí, upon the rising of a new dawn, as prophesied, Síonna and our wise High King of Consciousness Grandfather will journey to the Rainbow Isles. Chosen and so worthy they are for this magical quest."

Cheers echo through the enclosure. Dúidín are passed and in ritual smoke, they pray to the task ahead. Celebrations begin. They feast and play games into the oncoming darkness of the night. The shamans summon shape-shifting states while the children and elders dance around the transforming flames. Cauldrons are emptied, horns full of Poitín and honey-infused mead are drained, a wondrous journeying of consciousness unfolds.

Chapter 4
Stag-vision

Grandfather is awake before dawn. Loving the síochán, peace, that sits over the enclosure at this time of day as the flowers stretch their petals for the Suncatchers, he walks to the river and prays up to the sun with his golden hazel raised to the sky. Forming a task, he throws a wishful gaze over the stilled surface, seeing his heart-shaped lips mirrored as he casts his wish. His form suddenly becomes shadowed; he turns to see a deity looming behind him. He sees the blue of the sky filling the space between mighty antlers that reach like branches on either side of the Stag-headed one who stares from large, rounded, glinting eyes.

A hide that reaches to the ground sits pinned by a bronze brooch over one side of the beast's breast. Grandfather glances down at the hoofed feet.

"I am Cernunnos, Horned God of the forest," the drone of the stag's voice seems to fill the entire valley. "Grandfather, you have been called forth by the gods as the one who has stag medicine to guide the future Goddess of Eriu upon this Quest."

Grandfather looks to the beady eyes of the deity, seeing them narrow and events suddenly stream through the Wonder-Eye of his mind. He sees rivers and oceans swirling into a mighty charge. Great sheets of ice cloak the lands growing luminously until the entire sod is covered from one horizon to the next. A scorching sun arcs through the sky and quickly melts the snow, sending mud and mountains climbing high. Plants and rock-beings emerge fed by the Water Spirits. Mystical luminous mermaids appear and out pour wells and rivers and oceans sprouting life, creating everything that makes up Eriu, her wondrous Dreamtime seascapes and landscapes.

Horses, stags, elks, boars, bears and an array of four-legged species and crawlers trot the trails in a great stampede. Lightning-beings bounce and arc through the racing clouds, squeezing torrents of silken rain upon the earth. Thunder beings rumble; the moon throws her pale light to meet the sun that lights a fire while decorating itself in woad and colours the clouds, as the stars cast a glitter that reaches the surface of the waters. He witnesses the elementals merging, creating what we now know as wondrous life.

"As a Leigheasóir, Healer, and one who took the throne as the High King of Consciousness, you understand the Creator and his creations. It is just for this stag-vision that you are chosen to accompany Síonna," the deep voice of the stag brings his wandering mind back.

He looks again into the beast's big brown eyes listening attentively.

"Síonna is worthy of this quest but you must take heed for the sorcerer will spring from the shadows of her mind to enchant the future Goddess."

The Horned Stag crouches forward and sweeps his hand over Grandfather's brow as though gifting him the wisdom of eternity, and then places it upon his Wonder-Eye. Images rush through his mind and he opens his eyes to discover that the antlered deity has vanished.

Grandfather sits on the riverbank ruminating on the importance of the message. A murmuration of swallows swoops down and flies parallel to the water as he forms a verse,

"Your rivers run free. glens sprout flowers and trees in magical boughs beneath stooping, wise oaks as a swirling hand of the wind plucks otherworldly acorns, carrying old bile lore whispering into Faery groves. A salmon leaps shining like sunflower petals, spinning a golden dream as she races to the spawning pools, leaping over mighty rocks and falls. The eddies leap alongside her upstream until she reaches the forbidden Well of Connla where she spins her glittering scales mysteriously giving birth to an otherworldly éigse!"

No sooner has his honeyed riddle left his mouth than a beautiful kingfisher darts by, leaving its luminous blue image mirrored upon the surface. He listens to the great humming of the mountains that reach to every horizon, still wearing caps of snow while a mist drifts ghost-like over the sod. The meadows are coated with swards of flowers; snowdrops sway luminously alongside the graceful daffodil that yellow the riverbank. Animals are stretching the cold of winter from their backs. Grandfather kindles his dúidín and releases a generous puff of smoke that swirls like his wandering thoughts, ruminating on the great task ahead.

He rests against a rock and slips into rock-dreaming as his skin warms upon the sun-hot surface whilst observing the rushing river, dancing peacefully across the land. Schools of baby trout sparkle, filling the water with shimmers of their light as they dart back and forth, glittering silver. He sees an otter sitting on the riverbank waiting to pounce through the surface. A sudden leap and her paws part the surface with equal softness; two concentric rings spread out and in one gulp some trout fills its empty belly.

Further ahead, a line of rocks breaks the rushing waters leaving a pool mirroring the purple-blue sky. In an explosive motion, a salmon leaps. Grandfather watches as her magnificent silver scales, speckled with orange, pink and purple sparkle in mid-air as a wave runs through her body propelling her over rocks to a great height and into the rushing waters against an upstream current, towards her sacred spawning grounds.

Enchanted, he looks upon Mother Mountain in the distance, seeing speckles of deer and wolves and hounds running upon her slopes, hearing the hunting call of the eagle and hawk. The mountain whispers to him,

"Come home Grandfather."

A great sense of síochán pours over his boyish smile peeling back his handsome face, lifting his chubby rosy cheeks. To celebrate, he leaps into a dance holding both hands outstretched, his hazel grasped in one. With fingers pinched, turning with a shuffling of his feet he twirls while bursting into laughter. Tapping his lower lip, he sends out an Ollamhs dán, offering.

'Éist le mo ghuí
Oh, where to roam thy heart
To a people, in wondrous Valleys and Oceans
Wholeheartedly whispering
An enchanting otherness tongue
Knowing
O, body, we touch another
O, mind, we interact with another
O, soul, we merge our light and shine as one
With ever-growing love, between the mountains and the sea.'

Grandfather returns to the enclosure. The tribe are awake ahead of the two sages' noble journey. The young warriors are running about with excitement playing battles of bataireacht showing the skilled fighting art of the stick. The cracking of their furze clashing echoes around the enclosure. Yelps ring out from those who suffer a blow. Others are gathering beneath the old oak. The elders bring waters from the wells for a blessing of Síonna and Grandfather. The horns lift a great drone calling all to assemble beneath the oak.

Fires are dancing. Sage smoulders sending a minty fragrance through the enclosure. Warriors prepare the horses. Women and children wear their ceremonial attire, tunics decorated with symbols and deities and belted at the waist displaying a woven array of colours. Riverbed shells adorn their ankles and wrists, copper and golden torques glitter on their arms, amulets hang. Sacred symbols are painted on their faces and torsos. They begin chanting ancient incantations summoning protection for their sages.

Horns and trumpets ring out from the centre of the valley. The tribe form a circle around Grandfather and Síonna beneath the great oak. A warrior sounds a bodhrán. The drone of the drum is felt within their chests. He continues beating a steady rhythm that soon matches that of the tribe's heartbeats, inducing a trance-like desire to dance. Thunder-beings suddenly leap and fork through the sky, flashing from horizon to horizon, sending signs that the gods and deities are observing.

The warriors dance, clad in their full ceremonial attire. Grandfather admires the fearsome young men towering as they encircle him and Síonna. Their muscled torsos spin bearing spiked and braided hair dyed with lime. They gnarl as though they are fanged like the wolf and ready for battle. With a ferocious sense of strength mirroring from their eyes they cast out their swords and spears that spiral through the air. Skulls of slaughtered foe hang from their mighty shields.

Torques and lunulae, gold bands, glitter. Some are clad in tartan, pinned over one side of the breast and decorated with brooches and golden sun disks. Others dwell naked with symbols painted on their skin. Battle scars trail their faces. Some of the roundhouses display the revered rewards of battle with skulls of their foe impaled on sticks. Cauldrons are steaming, spits spin with game skewed roasting.

The younger girls bear shells from the riverbeds sewn into the hems of their brats, adorned around their ankles and wrists. They catch the courting eyes of the young warriors, rattling enchanting sounds, intoning them with magical incantations. Síonna is in awe with pride looking at the nobleness of their clan.

They spin and leap chanting to the gods until Sengann raises his sword beckoning silence.

"My great people, make a wish and close your eyes as we create a new time of life for a sacred path to unfold and guide our worthy sages. Upon enduring this great quest and acquiring the ancient wisdom, bring them safely home to the Valley of the Stags, ho."

The tribe acknowledge his wish with a mighty roar. They repeat the word several times 'Ho', it echoes afar. Drums and horns and trumpets loudly announce the wish of the High King as Grandfather taps his lip. Everyone knows it to be the familiar trait he carries out before casting a riddle of his great wisdom. They wait in silence for the clever guidance of their High King of Consciousness.

"A black beetle waddles through faraway oceans, swaying through golden veils to reach his brother snake who leaps into another worldly sky, climbing stairs while shedding his scales and shape-shifts into a wondrous winged one who takes a silver flight around the sun and the moon, sunwise, three times, announcing,

"Eternal Ones of the Aisling are dreaming a journey of a Rainbow-Headed one, of a luminous daffodil-beaked one and of the trot of four paws of a cunning fox who will all lead a young warrior to emerge as the Goddess of Eriu. Hear this rainbow-filled wish."

The clan bathe in his joyous, tongue-weaving riddles. Síonna pinches her two fingers and lets out a piercing whistle. Toirneach Bán darts through making music with her thundering trot. Her snow-white being leaps the height of two warriors before she comes to a stop at Síonna's feet and lowers her snout, munching on a handful of oats from her cupped hand. The horses silken hair is groomed showing the white streaks running through it like lightning-beings said to charge her mighty gait. A strand of hair with a string of buttercups hangs to the left of her shoulder matching Síonna's. The beast beautiful green eyes are crowned by a white star formed in the hair of her forehead.

Sengann raises his sword in an arc signalling the warriors to release Silent Galloper. The horse canters forth with great bulging shoulders and light blue eyes that glitter as though holding the mysteries of the universe. He trots past the applauding tribe with his ears and black and white tail cocked. Also bearing a star shape within the hair on his forehead, his body hair is dark wearing four white anklets like those of Ríonach. The horse stops beneath the raised blade of the High King.

Sengann casts his divining eyes over the clans. Grandfather's eyes trail the scar that runs the course of the left side of the King's forehead that joins the crevasse of his smile on the right of his inner cheek, his silken white braided hair that reaches to his waist. The King arches his neck giving out a screaming howl like that of a wolf. Silent Galloper rises onto his hind legs, neighing as though acknowledging his role in the task.

"Grandfather, accept this horse from the great draíodóir, Magician, Cúroí Mac Daire. Galloper will walk paths that others cannot and see into realms beyond those of earthly eyes and run in the dark of night, tracking far beyond the senses of man."

Fionn, the son of the High King, then steps up holding a robe of white wolf's fur in his hands. He walks to Grandfather and wraps it around his broad shoulders calling out in a ceremonial tone,

"Gods of the North, wolf brother, guide Grandfather with the wisdom of the ancestors so that he will track with ease through the shadows and lead Síonna along a path of Happiness."

Grandfather receives the gift and bows before the tribe. He lifts his gaze into the light blue eyes of the King's son knowing the secret he shares with Síonna and makes a silent wish that their love may one day flourish into fruition. He then pinches his fingers in one hand and imitating a dance as though he is at a banquet hall at the hill of Tara, he leaps into a spinning charge holding one hand over his head while sweeping an imaginary kilt before him with the other.

Great laughter rises as they watch his form graciously move across the green sward. He makes a series of bows before their thunderous applause.

Aibhlin, wife of Sengann comes with green eyes glistening like emeralds, bearing the most beautiful golden locks. In her hand she holds is a multi-coloured críos, belt, decorated and woven with godly symbols. She takes Síonna's hand beckoning Grandfather and wraps the críos around both their wrists, wishing,

"Spirit bind our sages as though you are tying the hearts-filled wishes of our people around them. Embrace them with the protection of our ancestors, and allow Síonna to acquire the gifts and bring them both safely back to the hills and glens of the Valley of the Stags, ho."

The clans bang the butts of their shields against their swords and chant aloud as a great drone of horns and trumpets rise. Grandfather places his hand on the muzzle of Silent Galloper, gazing into his eyes and whispers,

"I have seen you in Aisling, Galloper, thundering those hooves of sun lightning making medicine songs."

He runs his hazel over the horse's spine. Zara swoops down and perches on the animal's back.

Amid the celebration, Síonna's eyes tear up seeing the saddened frown etched across Fionn's face. Her heart leaps, separated from him by the dance of flames as she thinks of his imminent marriage to the daughter of the High King of Laigin Sláine.

Fionn lifts a bronze horn to his mouth to signal the beginning of the noble quest. He stands kingly, like his father with long golden hair. His blue eyes are fixed on the distant horizon as he honours the clans, slowly inhaling, filling his belly. His chest rises. With lips pursed, he releases a fierce wind into the horn. A faint bellow gathers and grows as a wave motion runs through his belly, pumping air into the instrument in rhythmic bursts.

The drone echoes across valleys afar as though reaching into the distant kingdoms their sages will pass.

He blows three times, turning sunwise honouring the cycle of the sun. As the humming of the horn settles, and the chanting of their voices and the last bellow rests upon their ears, they erupt with cries of thanksgiving, showering Grandfather and Síonna invisibly with their thoughts, opening safe trails before our sages' brave march.

Chapter 5
The Quest

They canter from the Valley of the Stags to the sounds of the cheering tribe. For days they cross barren plains and mountains. Sionna still hears the drone of the horn as they left the enclosure. Seeing the round of robin that trailed the path before them as she held onto the tone. She carries it in her Heart-Well like a magical shield to guide her as they follow the waters of Abhna na t-Sionainne, leading them south-westerly.

She dreams of reaching the Kingdoms of Light and the Rainbow Isles in the great Atlantach ocean. Envisaging herself collecting the great wisdom of the Wells, like a golden pollen she will bring back to the people. She forms an image of the day when she and Fionn will be united without the secret.

She returns her mind to the task as they approach the barony that marks the entrance into the province of Gann of South Mumhan. They see great valleys flowered with an abundance of heather and trees that stretch afar. Herbs of all colour shiver and dapple beside fawn rushes that sway on the wind, wearing the golden spears of the midday sun. Herds of cows and bulls roam; gorse speckles the mountainside in a golden yellow. They see great herds of doe, elk, boar and stag grazing and the silhouettes of wolves on the edge of the horizon between the mountain and the sky.

Rabbits leap following each other's tails before darting into burrows. Butterflies glide through the air flapping wings of silver and gold with rainbow-like beauty. They observe paired swans soaring over the silver waters of the river. Síonna imagines she and Fionn shapeshifting into the mystical birds and taking to the skies from dawn till dusk. The chorus of a pack of geese wakes her from her daydream. Pointed like an arrow in unison, they watch them go south west towards the far distant ocean.

Grandfather senses a sudden movement in the undergrowth and dismounts Silent Galloper. Síonna sees the glitter of a snake's scales slithering through the grass. It stops by grandfather's feet. They watch the transformation as the serpent begins sliding from its old skins, shedding what is no longer needed, symbolically leaving the past behind it.

Grandfather taps his lower lip recalling words once gifted to him by a wise elder,

"Sage, shed the otherworldly skins in the direction of the South as all journeys begin with one step, and one steppingstone shines into the next. There are two paths in life, the path-of-happiness, and the path-of-danger. One is a feeling of comfort, the path-of-happiness, and the other, a feeling of discomfort, the path-of-danger. But remember, that you have a choice, and there are lessons to be learned from both."

He kindles his dúidín and begins to sweep the smoke over his body and draws it over Síonna while wording a wish.

"Spirit give us a mouth of whale singing wisdom to give sweetly to all ears while tickling the hearts of all whom we encounter with a gobbly delight. A Dhia, os na Déithe, God before the Gods, shroud us with clear senses like those awakened in a state of infancy to sow our wishful seeds."

Sharing a wondrous smile, he follows the prayer with a riddle.

"A spark kindles within my dancing Heart as our ancestors stand around us, walking about in the sun silver dew upon the paths of our thoughts while lifting great fire spears and casting them through the Otherness of an Aisling sky that curls into a serpent's golden eye, gazing from a soul of great light entrapped in a darkness, waiting for the destined blade of a Goddess to set him free upon a way that is lit!"

His words flutter around her mind like a beautiful flower bathing her senses. She can almost smell and taste the teachings within them. A sudden inspiration floods her being. And from her honeyed lips comes a riddle of her own.

"Sunlit spear vision
Where the edges of light and darkness assemble
In the web of a great battle
Where
The Druidess
Gods
And the Goddess
Awaken."

He smiles, knowing she is slowly unravelling her gifts. They look to the branches of a nearby oak seeing the glisten of a spider's thread floating on the gentle breeze. They step forth observing the tiny creature hanging by way of its silken thread anchored between two branches. The many-legged one reels in and tightens the first strand before it walks, strengthening it with a second and then dangles down to form a Y-shaped netting, followed by working from the centre to the outer frame, and lastly to the outer rings inward, completing the mysterious aligned structure.

"What a perfect little creature, weaving a magical dwelling like the birds with such a timed thrusting of those tiny limbs. Granddaughter, in the ordinariness of this spider, in the mystical nature of this crawler, a tiny little heart pumps blood throughout, flooding those tiny legs to weave like a spinning wheel. O' my dear Síonna, what great mystery your own spidery eyes have yet to see. Soon, we will peer into the otherworldly gaze of another mystical one that dwells high in those mountains."

Grandfather points his Ollamh branch to the Slieve Mish range in the distance where waits the mighty fortress of Cathair Conrí.

Chapter 6
Cúroí Mac Daire
The Fortress of Light

After journeying through the cycle of a full moon, they reach the foothills of the great mountain. The sward glows luminous beneath their gallop. They know that they have entered a sacred place. A rainbow arches over the trail. Grandfather raises his hazel, halting their canter. They pass through the glow of rays knowing that they cross the invisible barony into the Kingdoms of Light. The mountains wear crystal waterfalls that reach down like silver veins and course through the soul of the Valley of the Wizard.

The bands of the rainbow brighten. Síonna gazes to the summit, observing like a distant eagle the wondrous stronghold etched against the blue pane of the sky. In one glance, it fulfils all her expectations.

Grandfather takes a golden bell gifted to him by a wise elder and closes his eyes, whispering,

"Make a wish as we enter the barony of the wizard. Go inward. Do not wait and do not doubt. Use the inner power that you took birth with and remember; that the soul knows the true wish, ho."

He shakes the bell. The tone carries their unified wish like a great hawk to reach the summit.

They ascend, as though following an invisible path created by the tinkle of his bell. Ríonach trails, sniffing for a hunt while Zara soars in the sky above them. A sudden mist falls and quickly encloses the entire fortress.

The children of Cúroí, seeing their distant approach, run towards them. Gathering about them they are curious about Grandfather's golden hazel and of the flame-red hair of Síonna, and the strange hawk and the fox leaping in and out of rabbit burrows. Grandfather fondly greets them,

"Sit with us, gracious children, and let us make a wish for magical and happy events to occur. Let me give you a gift that opens the wonders of those little minds. Together, let us bring something new to the world through a churning of our honeyed tongues, magical verses that will invoke the gods within us. Children, you are the carriers of the glow. Cast your wishes into the movement of a riddle and create something that didn't exist in the world. With a great leap of your imagination spill magical verses evoking an enchantment upon others. Close your eyes and take a breath and form it like a silver wind that reaches to the Guiding stars that already sparkle with your wishes. And listen deep within the bough of your souls, where all these stars meet and give you the signs."

Síonna smiles, observing their little faces so engaged in his ritual. He lights his dúidín, puffing three times and sweeps the smoke around them letting out a tongue-twisting example.

"Our chorus sings of a living breath that fills the womb of the Mother's wish and churns the breasts of golden milk for leaping lambs to jump bravely outside the herd! With twinkling eyes and a stern boldness, strangely rooted feet will trot new paths as the earthworm spins her swivelling nose, so silken, emerging with neither neck nor limb, she spins a dream skywards to crest on the wandering tongues of those who summon little golden droplets to magically word a gifted wish."

They giggle at his tongue-twisting verse, examining his humble face as he swirls his eyes owl-like. He gives them further clarity.

"My little dreamers, this is a way of the sages, of the Ollamh, of the seer, and the Rainbow Ones. We-who-form-a-task, a wish to create a new living time of life through a verse of imaginative riddles, or through the movement of spontaneous dance. The gods and elementals hear our wishes and merge with our motions. Our inner cauldrons come alive gifting realisation to the task and the gods deliver. Remember, the most important part of this is to feel joy and delight while doing so and capturing that which you wished for. Bestow this joy upon others and leap beautifully together to a place of freedom where all your desires are granted. Who wants to try?"

"Me, please!"

"And what is your gobbly name?"

"Éanna Mac Daire."

"Ok so, little wise dandelion-face, begin."

"A mysterious one comes wandering, gazing silver in eye, scaled asa salmon of an otherworldly Well's river, speaking the secret tongue of the éigse who is sent by an Eagle white-haired wizard who soars in a silken flight from an otherworldly sky."

"Éanna, you are cleverer than all the sages of Eriu that ever-got-lived'd. Who's next?"

"Me, please. I am Cronin. He drove lightning before his steps, striking the eyes of the mountains and trees, twirling silver boughs before him forming steppingstones that laughed with otherworldly verses as a Goddess walked the-feeling-of-the-way."

"And you are wise beyond the blonde locks that twirl and nest upon your cotton head, Cronin."

The child giggles at Grandfather's unusual praise.

"It is so glorious to be amongst your curious manifesting minds, children of Cúroí," chuckles Grandfather, tapping his lower lip and lifting his moustache into a dance almost in disbelief at their abilities. He looks to the twin brother of Cronin, asking,

"And what is your name?"

"I am Conall, the youngest Ollamh of these lands."

"An Ollamh so young. Could this possibly be? And how did you acquire this title, little knowing squirrel of the gods?"

The children giggle. Grandfather winks at Conall allowing him the silence and mystique of his self-elected title and moves the focus forward.

"Let us now take all this magic to your wizard and elders, as there is much to do and not enough moons passing the arc of the sky in time to achieve everything today."

They merrily chuckle at his riddling and begin walking with our sages towards the summit.

The tribe have gathered at the edge of the mountain observing as a herd of roaming stag approach our sages and the children. Grandfather takes acorns from his bag, hands some to the children and they gift the antlered beasts who feed from their open hands.

Some warriors who ran to the outer edge of the fortress and raised spears, lower them knowing that a man of great power is approaching when they recognize him as Grandfather, he who bears the unique, twirling golden hazel of the Ollamh. Smoke trails rise above the summit. The faint laughter of other children and a distant barking of dogs reaches their ears.

Men are tending crops in the surrounding fields and ploughing furrows, churning up veins of great, dark earth. Fine, fierce-looking warriors ride out upon horses from the west side of the enclosure, hunting, driving and roving livestock.

"As we step into this realm, feel the state of otherness grow upon you for there is a magic here like no other," Grandfather informs Síonna. "We have journeyed well and our journey has been truly kind."

Circling his hand on his belly and with the other, he drags down his lower lip and taps it in contemplation before the great fortress. He releases his finger, forming the shape of a heart with his lips and sticks his tongue out while circling his eyes, evoking much laughter from Síonna and the children.

Clouds hang like a great shawl over the fortress. They look to the distant fields divided into squares by walls of stone bearded with lichen. Hedgerows resemble the multi-coloured patchwork of the master weavers.

The meadows are dotted with grazing cattle and bulls. Bluebells, cowslip and buttercups sway, shivering with the wind that sweeps softly over the sward. The marshy land makes their final ascent difficult, but it was just for this that the great wizard had built his fortress at the summit of such a steep slope, gifting him an advantage over invading foe or livestock-stealing rovers.

They get their first glimpse of the western ocean and her turquoise waters on the far horizon. A sense of delight floods her heart. The clouds suddenly spin and spin as though the entire fortress spins with them.

"Do not be startled, he knows that we have approached. The ceo draíochta, magical mist, brings confusion upon those who try to enter without permission."

The winds calm. Another rainbow arcs down. The clouds part.

forming a sphere.

From it emerges a luminous bumblebee. Síonna reaches out to the creature that lands on her outstretched palm. She shares a smile with the children.

"Eoghan the-mighty-draíodóir."

The young boy steps up, pushing his chest out sending the others into a giggle. He glances at them throwing a glare and a great scowl. The bee takes flight back through the circle and the veil closes. Eoghan takes a half step, pulls back his shoulders and raises his voice,

"It is I who summons the bees from a magical hive in a deep bough guarded by the only brown bear left in Eriu, hidden in a far distant summit, a place where only I and the Faery wander."

Grandfather taps Eoghan on the Wonder-Eye with his golden branch and whispers,

"To imagine is truly to believe, draíodóir."

Grandfather's reply satisfies the young warrior and he folds his arms, standing mighty like a King before the others. Morough, the eldest of the children who has been silent, suddenly takes into song and beckons our sages on the final path. They follow his paced march. The mist continues to swirl, veiling and unveiling the summit before it finally lifts, revealing the huge fortress in all its might reaching godly into the clouds.

Síonna is in awe looking at the huge boulders that sit wedged into each other, forming the thick walls spread across the summit. She feels so small approaching the highest dwelling place of power in all Eriu. Suddenly his mysterious form arrests their eyes. A white brat adorns his body. Cúroí stands beneath a huge boulder as though he is holding it up with an otherworldly strength. His white hair swirls on either side of his broad shoulders. He gazes with penetrating, wolf-like eyes, capped with black bushy eyebrows that curl into spirals. A huge sword adorns his waist. He waves a staff of white birch, beckoning our sages forth.

As they near, Síonna looks at his white puffy beard, matching his silver locks that curl over his strong cheekbones, at his silken skin said to be a result of special milk he drinks from a sacred cow. In a commanding voice, he welcomes them,

"Daoine d'anam, people of the soul, come truthfully for I have foreseen your visit."

The wizard wraps his huge hands around Grandfather almost squeezing the air from his lungs before embracing Síonna more gracefully and whispering in her ear,

"Daughter of Sengann, I have heard tales of your great skills. Rovers that have travelled to your land speak of you with great admiration. I graciously welcome your queenly presence."

He stoops to one knee, taking her hand and placing a kiss of gratitude upon her soft knuckles, whispering,

"Goddess to be, there is a lot at stake for our people and the future tribes of Eriu but you have the wise Leigheasóir guiding you."

He winks at Grandfather then rises and leads them through an entrance cut from two huge boulders.

Beyond is a huge oak door which he pushes aside. They follow him through a dark passageway that runs beneath the fortress, leading to another door. He leans heavily against it with both hands and it opens, revealing the inside of the vast fortress.

Stone walls rise in circles, climbing into a spiral formation meeting the roof that is layered with thick wooden beams resembling the webwork of a spider. Built on the symbol of a triangle, the fortress sits on the south westerly shoulder of the summit with protection from steep cliff edges on all three sides. The fourth side is defended by huge, dry-stone walls, a sight honouring the great work of the skilled tradesmen. And north stands the long, narrow mountain of Gearhane.

A huge fire burns at the centre of the open court; cauldrons are steaming with wine and honey-infused mead and broth that fill the air with sweet aromas. Game is rotating on spits. The Mac Daire erupt into a huge cheer for our sages who bow in respect as they enter to a wondrous drone of carnyx horns. Children are running around, wrestling and sword playing. The young warriors give a display of their hair-raising bataireacht, their furze sticks arcing through the air.

They swing and sweep and roll on the earth trying to hit each other's limbs. Yelping and grunting and the crack of sticks give our sages a real treat of their adept skills.

Young girls are awed at Síonna's beauty. They blush in wonderment at her Goddess looks and are equally silenced by the radiant Ollamh presence of Grandfather. Cúroí leads them up a spiralling stair of huge steps. Little doors sit under archways looking westerly to the blue ocean cresting the horizon.

Emerging at the top of the fortress, they look to see the vast span of lands stretching in all four directions. They see scholáire teaching young sages, reciting ancient writings on scripts.

Cúroí speaks proudly of the learning of his young poets,

"Some are in training for the Bardic title of the Ollamh. Those who acquire the status of a master-poet must remember and recite over two hundred and fifty stories of the druids and poems of the lands. First, they receive the bronze branch of hazel, then the silver and finally, the golden jewel like Grandfather's."

Grandfather taps his lower lip.

"In my youthful days," he says, "a wise seer once said: 'Words before anything else were sound.' In my training as an Ollamh, I recited thousands of words a day and memorised hundreds. But one winter's night just before I was to receive my title, I sat beneath a rowan, pondering and gazing at a full moon's light mirrored on the surface of a river when I finally unveiled the jewel. I heard the music of my soul and that of the earth, the moon and the mountains. Nature sang to me in an otherworldly whisper. It was the most wondrous sound my old, crispy owl ears have ever heard."

They laugh at his humour as he taps his lip and rolls his cornflower blue eyes before spouting more magic.

"So, my little Ollamhs, in time when you compose as master-poets, allow your souls to sing and unfurl such enchanting verses that you stretch the very boundaries of magic and enter into afar realms that we have not yet passed; realms to where magic lands and magic things occur, where ancient beings come alive in mystical mountain caves hidden far beyond the clouds of man's thoughts. And there they will lay golden eggs of another world's realm. And guarded by a band of otherworldly brown bear, from these eggs will grow the golden hazel trees that form the special wands of all future Ollamhs."

Bright smiles wreathe their faces, awed by his riddling verse. Síonna looks at a druid taking out the pith from fresh shoots of alder, binding them together. One end is plugged with wood as he trims the other to make the notes for a whistle.

The children pick up whistles already made from this alder and cast out a beautiful haunting drone from the shoots. The musicians in the open court answer the children, plucking golden harps and beating beautifully crafted drums of hide and goatskin. An undertone of bellowing trumpets and horns accompany them and soon rise into a mighty chorus.

Descending the spiralling stairway to the melody, they join the clan. As they enter, a sudden uneasy feeling grows upon Síonna. She senses a gazing eye. She looks up to see an old woman at the top of the fortress, hooded with a dark cloak like a raven glaring. It unsettles her. She nudges Grandfather knowing that he has visited this kingdom before. He looks up.

"Fear not," he says. "She is the oracle, She-who-walks-between-light-and-darkness. Do not meet her gaze with weak emotions for the eyes of a raven do peer and pluck the will of your soul; she may if wound or spell crosses her otherworldly sight. And from her frothing tongue, she may cast a frog bound to the swamps of dark desires."

Síonna feels a great unease but forces a smile on hearing Grandfather's riddle. Cúroí quickly shuffles his feet into a spin. His white brat creates a luminous-like pillar. He raises his voice,

"Eirnín, wise one of the Rainbow, and Síonna, warrior daughter of Sengann, welcome to our fruitful province."

Our sages bow before the applauding tribe. Grandfather raises his hand, pinching his fingers and with his other sweeps his imaginary kilt, leaps up and quotes a thought-provoking verse,

"As we fish the lagoons of our souls, seeking for every wish to come ashore, some glitter brighter, announced by a golden eagle's shrill and a dolphin's chuckling spin that churns in concentric rings, sending a lore to the meeting place of all sacred tongues."

Zara sweeps down and perches on his left shoulder, showing her fawn plumage and white headdress to the people, like a little godly deity. Cúroí elegantly strides across the courtyard to the centre where he raises his white birch staff, announcing,

"We gather to honour the presence of these two great sages."

A thunderous rapture of drums follows. His warriors strike the butts of their swords against their shields, gathering in a circle around our sages with a stamping of feet. The wizard summons a ritual, casting the protecting leaves of ash in each direction while turning three times sunwise.

He then casts Betony upon the flames, summoning more protection. The clan begin to tap the earth with their feet, instilling prayers into the sward while chanting incantations to prepare a great feast.

Great chunks of meat with the finest vegetables of the land spread upon wooden plates are brought through. Copper goblets filled with the wine of elderberry and elderflower and honey-fused mead are plenty. Horns full of Leigheas are passed between their lips. A nourishing bone broth follows, strengthening our sages' travel-weary bodies. Horns filled with Poitín, Home-distilled, are drained, kindling fires within their bellies.

The ceoltóirí, musicians begin to pour their spirits into instruments summoning up a great melody. The others yelp: "Hup!" evoking a dance that the gods would be proud of. Síonna feels the sound of the harp strings curve into her being as though the strings of her heart are being tickled and twisted. Her mind hops on the tones that quickly take her wandering back to the Valley of the Stags to see her secret lover.

Grandfather is at her side with eyes closed. The melody turns and twists and rises in rhythmic bursts, soothing and summoning like an incoming tide shuffling through a pebbled shoreline. They pluck the strings one last time and allow the drone to slowly fade.

Tricksters begin giving great displays, leaping through flames, chanting druidic incantations before taking knives and swords and swallowing the blades down their gullets. Others juggle copper rings whilst balancing barefoot on sharp swords. They bring in goats and doves and in a flash of fire and mist make the creatures disappear. Síonna is mystified.

Cúroí cheers on his men as some young warriors take to the centre and engage in furious swordplay. Sparks rise from the clashing of blades.

"Daughter of Sengann, grant us with your skills!" shouts the wizard.

She is reluctant at first until Grandfather encourages her. Síonna quickly draws her blade while summoning energy with her breath, up through the earth and takes flight with a warp spasm of strength. Holding an emotionless state, allowing the earth's power to flow through her, she breezes through the three men like a gust of wind.

Her subtle speed takes them by surprise as she swings her mighty weapon in a figure of eight. Leaping and crouching, changing levels with incredible swiftness, she leaves the young men in a haze of confusion. She darts by them in a blur. One of the men known to be the strongest warrior of the mountain, jealous of her skills, draws with huge force upon her blade. He soon learns that strength does not gain him control over the skill of the mind. Understanding the subtle processes required to redirect tension, Síonna captures his emotion and intention at a level where the sensation of movement is first formed in his mind knowing that the emotion gives the soul the wish of the move. He drives forth placing all his anger into the attack magnifying that sensation. She accepts his force and meets his blade with an unusual softness of a kind he has never felt.

He looks down to see his sword in two halves upon the ground. She dances around him, juggling her sword before bowing to one knee and whispering,

"Release the tensions of the body and mind. Open yourself to the charge of the earth and the sky, standing between them connecting and accepting this living thing, only then will you embody this inner knowing and sense everything that is outside of you through your own soul."

Laughter and cheers erupt as she bows in respect to the young men. Cúroí, hugely impressed, leans over to Grandfather.

"You have taught her well. She is fierce like the great Sláine of Laigin."

'It was not I, nor Sláine, that she acquired these skills from. She is self-taught through her determination to develop her most inward potential."

"A survival gift inherent within us all, my dear man," replies Cúroí.

"Certainly, but at different levels of knowledge for everyone," says Grandfather, knowing he does not practise the way of the sword.

The games continue.

Young warriors face each other and enact a battle scene. Swords and shields are raised. Torques and armlets adorn their necks and arms. Their hair is spiked or braided and whitened with lime, their faces and bodies painted with woad. They snarl and taunt each other waiting for Cúroí's signal.

"Begin!" he shouts.

Swords clash and war cries quickly fill the air. They play with great prowess, displaying competent sword and hand to hand skills. As one group advances, the front line of the other side stuns them with a sudden mist that lights up the battleground, veiling their position, the great skill acquired from their wise wizard and the very trait that makes him known as a fierce draíodóir throughout the lands.

They rain their blades down and leap through the air, somersaulting and rolling to the ground while clashing swords and wrestling hand to hand until sweat streams down their faces. The wizard calls a halt to the action and they bow before their guests to great applause.

After the games, Cúroí beckons Síonna and Grandfather to his clochán, beehive hut. A hefty fire flashes to their eyes and colours the corbelled floor and roof with an orange glow. He closes the door and they sit around the hearth of flames, waiting in silence for something. The door suddenly springs open and a shadow falls over them.

They look up to see the haggard-looking old woman from the summit. Brown, weather-scarred skin hangs like concentric ripples in an ocean upon her bony, pointed face. She circles, limping and crooked, holding a wand of ash and bearing a necklace made of black raven claws. A matching black cloak covers her skinny torso. Grandfather makes no eye contact.

Síonna follows his example, lowering her gaze upon the fire as the hag proceeds, drawing a circle with her stick on the floor around them. Cúroí welcomes the elder,

"Wise one, I call you to divine and give your solemn message to our guests."

She reaches into her pockets and throws fronds of fern tree upon the flames, evoking the gods. Sparks rise and dance around the roof. She begins murmuring beneath her flickering tongue, casting three bones upon the ground and spreading them with her shaky fingers. She holds her trembling hand over them whilst reading with the-draíocht-of-the-fingertips, a technique already known to our sages.

Her whole body begins to shake. Her eyelids flicker - divining. She makes a hissing sound twirling her tongue around her mouth. Her eyes suddenly spring open, she glares wildly and screams in a terrifying voice like a wild beast and reveals a mouth full of rotten teeth,

"Witch, witch, sorcerer, beware the hazel tree!"

Startled by her reaction, Síonna grasps Grandfather's hand. The hag pulls back from the fire, throwing a fearsome glance at Síonna as though possessed by an otherworldly spirit, before rushing out through the door in a flustered state. Cúroí explains,

"Do not fear. What she has seen may never come to pass but you must take heed of what she tells you, Síonna. Go to her quarters at the top of the fortress and hold counsel."

Síonna doesn't delay and pursues her up the stairs with trembling legs. She approaches the crone's den, recalling her devilish, moon-like eyes as she pushes aside the heavy door.

Shivers sprinkle down her spine as it creaks open. Smoke pours out, clouding her vision. She hears faint murmurs. Smouldering mugwort hooks her nostrils. The place feels cold and dark like a tomb. She searches in the shadows for the haggard face. A sudden burst of flames lights the dwelling, revealing her frightening glare. Síonna flinches.

"Sit down, child, you bear a great curse. A curse that you cannot run from. A curse that is embedded like your destiny."

She unveils the stark message while gazing into a rounded quartz stone, divining further and whispers,

"I see the hazel of an otherworld's sorcery calling you, calling you to a well that has its source in the underworld. It is the very eye of the dark beast. You must listen to Grandfather and see out your service to your people. Fear not, because all will not be taken. There will be a way to break this curse. The sorcery of Balor can be lifted by a great warrior who has neither desires nor temptations, a man devoid of the wish for power, a warrior who holds nothing but truth within his heart. He is already within your dreaming."

The old woman cups blessed water from a cauldron and casts it over Síonna then throws a handful of rosemary upon the flames.

"Take heed and journey lightly through the forest-of-the-nine-hags. Go forth to the Kingdoms of Light and onwards to the Magic Wells and there you will receive the gifts!"

Síonna hasn't felt fear like it since the day she heard of the tragic drowning of her loved ones. She reaches with her hand through the smoke and grasps the cold hand of the crone, giving thanksgiving for her warning and leaves the tomb-like hut with all sorts of stirred emotions shaken by the prophecy. She descends the stairs with a frown, leaning heavily into each step.

The first whispers infiltrate her mind,

"Seek the hazels, Síonna, and the éigse will be yours."

Goosebumps coat her spine. She searches the stairwell but finds it empty. A sensation grows in her belly as though an ancient burden is cast and she knows that a great inner challenge has begun.

"He will come when the time is right!" shouts the oracle from her den.

"Who is this warrior she speaks of? And how is he already in my dreaming? These whispers, what of them?" she asks, shaking it off as she walks down into the courtyard.

Grandfather sees the fear in her eyes and whispers,

"Do not be afraid. What the old hag sees or says is only one path. Like choice, there are many as we spin the wheels of life, Granddaughter."

She rests her mind on Grandfather's suggestion.

Cúroí approaches and beckons Síonna. She follows his quick pace, trailing through a passageway leading to chambers beneath the fortress. As she follows the sounds of his footsteps a light appears and she emerges into a huge cavern with a flaming fire burning at the centre. Pillars of quartz and stalactites weave down from the roof. Her eyes follow the light across the room to see an altar at the centre. She sees etchings painted on the walls like her secret cave in the Valley of the Boars.

"First we will carry out a laying-of-the-healing-blade," says the wizard.

He quietens his mind and opens a sacred space. Warming rolled mugwort root upon the fire, he spreads it over the altar and ushers Síonna to lie upon it. She feels soothed by the familiar scent of the herb that Grandfather smokes, as the wizard stands over her.

"We draw out the unwanted," he tells her.

Kindling a dúidín, he puffs, drawing a mouthful of the smoke and blows it over her body. Sweeping it with his hand over her Wells, he takes his sword from its scabbard and raises it above her.

She witnesses a furrow of light-beings suddenly emerging through a veil surrounding the wizard and they grasp the sword with him.

"Ancestors, guide me as a channel for this living light."

He lays the sword over her Wells, with the point directed downwards towards her feet to affect a calming sensation, chanting a druidic incantation. Síonna's body sways subtly at first and builds into a shaking charge as a spell is summoned to release the shadows. Tears well up. She becomes uneasy. Sweat pours from her skin as the wizard whispers,

"The path of the Ollamh, Shaman or Sage is not always easy. Distractions are a challenge that you must endure as many are tracking you, Síonna. I know that you have heard the whispers. Remember, find the strength to uphold truth at all times as you walk the path."

She begins growling like a beast as the sword evokes hidden tensions. Fears and emotions arise. Those of lust, envy, attachment, anger, shame, pride and desire all emerge as though shadows held deep within her mind and then peel back like the skins of an onion, unravelling the impulses stored in her lower Wells.

Cúroí raises his sword to the sky and calls out,

"A Dhia, os na Déithe, God before the Gods, through the realms of shadow I command my tracking sword to cut the desires of the beast that binds her in this darkened sleep. Peer not at her soul for her wounds I now fill with the healing edge of this blade. Come forth and fulfil your thirst in another world's veil for I cast you into the light of my ancestor's hands."

A sense of calm rushes over her mind. Images of the hazel and well appear. The glittering golden husks arrest her attention. A blood-red moon shines on the surface. The whispers follow,

"Come forth, Síonna. And the éigse will be yours."

She sees a wondrous salmon in all its glory appear, leaping from the surface. Cúroí quickly takes a knife and begins to cut at the space around her body, releasing threads that the sorcerers have cast.

Her mind darts back to the cavern. Her body begins to jerk up and down as though strings that were binding her are been lanced, releasing the hold of the curse.

The wizard sprinkles blessed waters over her while singing.

"Elementals, take this darkness from her soul and bring solace as the whispers of Balor fade from her ears. Draw the taste of the golden hazels from her mouth. Cast from her touch, the husks of this otherworldly tree. Deter from her nose, the smell of desire whilst expelling from her mind the inability to choose wisely to not fall and bear the salmon's skin."

Síonna feels a sudden awakening as though an invisible veil of lightness embraces her, freeing her of a great weight. She watches the ancestors of the wizard rise like a thread of light through the veil. He takes the sword from her body and runs it through flames while guiding her.

"Red hair, the eye of the beast haunts you. It is only you who can truly break this curse so that you can walk the path-of-happiness. Balor will not give up easily and will enter wounds you may not be aware you are carrying. I will teach you something that will prepare you for what you must endure. And you will need it going forth when you soon pass through the forest-of-the-nine-hags."

She stands lighter than she ever felt with a renewed energy surging through her veins like the trick of youth she learned to command.

"Let us carry out the finer mastery of the Blade. Draw your weapon," he commands, in a serious tone.

She unleashes her sword with one swipe of her right hand.

Silent and gazing, he stands. A strange feeling suddenly comes over her as she looks into his shining eyes. Without sensing his movement, she sees the light of his form suspended in mid-air and he plunges his blade deep into her chest. She feels a hot sensation burrowing inwards that spreads over her breast. She clenches into a painful knot giving out a huge sigh; the room spins, her eyes spring open, owl-eyed in horror as pressure fills her neck and head. Her chest lifts, her lungs squeal for air.

Tears drop from her chin. A terror grips her. A deafening silence lingers. He pulls the blade out. She drops lifeless to the floor with the essence draining from her being.

Cúroí stoops to one knee and whispers in her ear.

"Accept it. Do not fight it. Gather your breathing in quick bursts as the animals do after a hunt. You know this Síonna. Now gather this fear into a ball with your breath and as you build a rapid rhythm, capture this tension with a sharp inhale then exhale it sharper from your being. Do it!" he screams.

She struggles at first to pursue his suggestion but sees the wolf she observed that day puffing in quick succession recovering after a hunt.

As she weakens, waves of fear race through her as though some ghostly presence is drinking the essence of her soul.

"Cast it out, Síonna!" he roars louder.

She draws through her nose a mighty breath and exhales in sharp bursts. She feels a certain sense of hope enter as she builds a steady rhythm. The wizard breathes in unison with her, directing the pace with his hand. Together they gain speed. With one sharp inhale catching the pain and fear into an imaginary ball, she commands it from her being. He sweeps his hand holding a quartz crystal as though recapturing all the fears he first put into her.

She expels it out with a final breath. The wizard cups the crystal as though containing all her lower impulses. She sinks onto the floor emitting a huge sigh. A sense of peace washes through her mind. He stoops to one knee whispering,

"Now you are in acceptance, Síonna, your mortality is clearer. Grandfather experienced this detachment when death stalked him. It is for this very reason that he brought you here, to embody this state. Truly capture this feeling so you can recall it when you need it."

She slips deeper, nearing death as he raises his sword calling aloud,

"Daughter of Sengann, death demands us to leave everything behind, including fear. I have captured what fear was in your body in this crystal. Now let your doubts fade and everything will become possible. Spirit, gift her with the light for she is truly worthy."

A sudden warmth returns to her cold limbs, her pulse grows, a sense of power floods her veins. Regaining composure slowly, her legs and arms begin to twitch. With amazement, she sits up in wonderment, gazing at her chest that is devoid of any wound. She slowly raises her body as though a new being born to the world and cries out, releasing any remaining fears. Deities arc through a veil twirling around her as though lifting her, adjusting her lightbody to merge with her physical form.

Their shimmering forms spin and spin as her spine clicks bone by bone and she feels a sense of being taller than before. She watches the lights ascend to the roof in a swirling charge and disappear. Her eyes return to the wizard's gaze.

"How did you do that, Cúroí?"

"It is nothing but the magic that we are each born with. Do not question it, experience it. Catch the sensations and practise. You have just felt one of your greatest fears, death. Now go forth without this barrier in your mind and you will move mountains with your thoughts. This will be the gift of grace upon your path; when you face the nine hags and the dark sorcerer of the Underworld, summon this fearless state."

She takes a succession of deep breaths, commanding the energy of the earth to rise. A warp spasm floods her being. She stands before the wizard with veins bulging in her neck, ready. He raises the crystal to the sky murmuring an incantation and then sweeps it through the flames, cleansing the shadows. He turns and sharply calls out,

"Let us continue. Come forth with all your force; swing with full strength as though you are cutting off the very head of Balor."

"What?"

"Let there be no 'whats'. Do not attach doubt nor fear or I cannot teach you. Recall what you have just experienced and keep that sensation within as you strike."

A ferocious speed carries her blade, followed by a sharp clashing sound. She turns to see him standing behind her, smiling.

"You are brave, daughter of the east. Now defend as I try."

She holds her sword with a new sense of lightness and empties all thoughts, sending her senses out around her. She creates an illusion of support for his attack by giving him the sense of a position as she tracks his mind. She catches his intention just before he swings and watches the weight of his lead leg press into the earth and slips to the side, listening to the flow of his blade advancing. She circles. His blade meets emptiness and he tumbles to the floor. She stands over him smiling.

"I see you are already adept at the subtle skills, Síonna. Now let us try with eyes closed."

Blow after blow cracks out. Grandfather and the tribe hear the clashing of steel echoing as the two warriors prowl each other in fierce play, sensing each other's breath, intent, the sudden swish of a foot or a subtle movement of the belly. Using their hearts to sense, like a bat uses sound to move through the darkness. Capturing the wish of the move as it is formed.

"There is little more I can add to your skills, Síonna, you bear great bravery. Remember, let nothing dethrone you when you stand as Goddess. Do you hear me? Nothing, including your own desires," he says and without a flinch or intention, Cúroí swings his sword in an upward arc towards her head.

The clash rings out. He smiles as she swiftly redirects his attack.

"You hold a true mastery, warrior of the Fir Bolg."

"Cúroí, you have dutifully gifted me. I will remember this as I journey through the rest of my life. I am forever grateful. Thank you dearly, le grá, mo chara, le grá," with love, my friend, with love, she says in the ancient tongue, placing her hand upon his heart.

He returns the gesture with a smile.

They sheath their swords and warmly embrace before returning to loud applause from the tribe. Síonna walks to Grandfather and kisses him on the brow whispering,

"I have felt the sensation, in a way that is beyond words."

Grandfather curls his eyebrows feeling a tear run down his cheeks that filters through his moustache and sits on his lower lip. Síonna's eyes also well up and they share that look of deep knowing that they have shared since she was a young girl. He is so proud of her spioradálta attainment.

Sweet music fills the air; celebrations ensue. Golden harps are plucked, casting enchanting melodies across the fortress. Flaming spits are stacked with stags and boars. Cauldrons are steaming with vegetables and roots of all sorts from the mountains. A great cheer rises. They see a white cow with black patches scattered over her fat torso been led by the children to the centre.

Cúroí stoops to one knee and drags on her four udders withdrawing nourishing milk said to gift an otherworldly strength and beauty to those who drink it. Síonna, admiring the elegance of the beast, reaches out and strokes its head. The cow bellows and wraps her long, pink tongue around Síonna's hand, evoking a sense of great joy.

The wizard fills a horn with the milk and first offers it to our sages. They drink, offering sláinte, health. A sweet taste roams their palates like nothing they ever tasted. It soothes their throats as it slides down, filling them with a sense of invigoration.

"You have now doubled your strength and beauty with the milk of this sacred cow," the magician says, smiling.

He takes a sip himself and then passes it around the tribe who all drink from it.

A feast of mouth-watering game is had and washed down with goblets of elderberry wine and mead, fused with dandelion and honey. A special potion Cúroí acquired from a travelling rover is then presented, a juice made from the sacred crab apple, a symbol of eternity said to preserve one's life. Another horn of the leigheas is passed and they each sup from it. The potion is bitter, bursting on their tongues and roaring down their gullets like a fire filling their bellies, like the warming properties of Poitín.

Scents of frankincense, mugwort, sage and gorse trickle in on the wind as young girls smoulder the herbs, summoning a protective circle around the stronghold. A tall warrior wearing a white ceremonial tunic parts the clan in the centre. He approaches holding a silver plate bearing two sparkling triskele torques and a golden sun disk.

"Torques, worn by the noble and such an honour it is to be gifted by Cúroí," says an elder.

The mountain wizard steps forward for a passing-of-the-gifts.

"These jewels will protect you wherever you wander throughout Eriu, or into dark realms and lands beyond, to the four winds. Before the earth and sky gods and deities and ancestors of our people, accept these gifts with blessings, wise warriors," says the wizard.

Grandfather and Síonna bow before him. He wraps a triskele torque representing the trinity around each of their upper arms. The people erupt in rapturous applause and begin to play a heart-raising melody on their instruments, accompanied by a steady beat of drums.

"Mac Daire, it is our blessing to befriend you. Receive this in return as an appreciation of your kindness and for the great gifts you have given," says Síonna.

She hands him a dagger in a sheath adorned with precious stones she received from Sengann in her youth.

"With honoured pleasure, I accept, thank you future Goddess of Eriu."

The wizard then takes the golden sun disk from the silver plate and stands before Grandfather.

"Suns shine from your delightful being, bringing your honeyed gifts to us. We are so worthy of your visit, sage of the Rainbow wisdom. This will protect your sacred, ever-giving loving heart, ho."

Grandfather lowers his head. The wizard places the hide string of the relic around his neck. The sun disk sits centre on his Heart-Well.

Grandfather wraps his chubby hands around Cúroí and whispers in his ear,

"Agus buíochas, and thanks, for your gift of Silent Galloper."

The wizard nods smiling.

And our sages leave the open court to loud applause, bowing three times honouring the trinity of the triskele. Síonna's mind races back to the first time she saw the ancient symbol in the Valley of the Boars, beneath the passage tomb.

"Watch over her, Rainbow one, for the eye of Balor glares

strongly!" shouts Cúroí.

"That I will do. Go n-éirí an cosán leat, may the path rise to meet you." Grandfather honours the clan in the ancient tongue.

"Níl aon tinteán mar do thinteán féin, there is no hearth like your own hearth, ho," says Cúroí, returning an ancient blessing.

They follow the same trail down the steep path with their horses rested, groomed and fed by the mountain clan. They look back to see him standing and casting his protecting gaze over the valleys.

"Your way is lit! ho."

The magic returns as the ceo draíochta falls, veiling and spinning the great fortress once again.

'Mists of another worldly eye
Veils a great kingdom
Where waterfalls of mountain tears, race
Ushering a silent knowing to those in belief
We, as carriers of the light
See through the dark with pristine clarity.'

Grandfather unleashes a timely riddle.

"A flight of winged emeralds emerges, red-billed with sunburst breasts. Yellow, hawk-eyed, they peer bearing orange talons spreading light upon the foe so bright only the moon imagines it whilst a sky full of stars furrows through their breasts followed by a golden sun lighting their pale faces with rosy cheeks. Síonna, I sense the Wells of Wonder are bubbling beneath the earth, waiting for a wise leader to drink from their source to gift the people with a new dreaming. Do not walk in somebody else's dream of you. Quest, and you will find, Granddaughter. Such is the truth."

She smiles. He follows it with the humbling story from his childhood fitting to the event she experienced with Cúroí.

"With power comes responsibility. Like fire, your fear should cast no shadow. The only true fear that mankind has, is 'that of death'. One day a young man plunged a knife into my back fifteen times and I was taught the honour of playing life and death, not being far away from each other. Everything is a lot brighter when they are close, either one.

I have been able to balance the two. Granddaughter, if you fear death, you will fear change in life. Remember, death is practical and nobody can hurt you without finding a hurt from your past. And that balancing of life and death I began to do with great rhythm in my life."

Síonna still gets owl-eyed and distraught at the thought of anyone hurting her humble-hearted grandfather. He takes a deep breath, circling his eyes and twirling his ears, breaking the heaviness of the story. A peal of laughter spreads across her pale cheeks. He continues with lighter teachings as they stroll happily with their horses.

"Don't let one moment spoil the next. The moving waters are the tides of our emotions. If I was to say another thing of importance to you, Síonna, it would be to: grow balls that will make you shine from the inside out."

She bursts into laughter and through her happy state he reveals the deeper teaching.

"Death is in constant movement around us, as is life. It is as practical as birth, like night closing over day reminding us that each opposite has purpose. Remember, the enemy is not outside, it is within. Quieten your mind allowing these moving emotions to calm and there you will find clarity. Find the, who am I. And the, I am will follow. Do not wonder about the future because unease will enter. And do not respond from the past because disappointment will come."

He fills his dúidín with mugwort, lights it and puffs a veil of smoke over her allowing her to digest everything for a few moments before continuing,

"You hold a splendorous light within you, Granddaughter. Remember, non-forgiveness is a limitation to be thrown away at all costs. Forgive yourself and everything that you need will come. Accept your motionlessness and move within the caverns of your mind, seeking the unknown landscapes. As we journey, remember this for the rest of your life: Take every good thought in by others and you will move mountainous obstacles by your thinking! If I was to say one more thing of importance to you it would be: Nothing, nor can anybody hurt you unless you give them the power to do so; unless you give them the power to do so! And now let us lighten our way," he says, and crouches slowly onto his hands, sticking his legs in the air.

With the dúidín still alight in his mouth, he puffs upside down and spills out a riddle.

"I'm not a miracle man, just an ordinary man having the ability to think beyond the human side of us. Ho, woo so fickleness, and wickedness of beasts and foe, come wandering the valleys of your thoughts because you are the point of the mystical Goddess's spear. Darkness can never be total and will struggle in your shining beauty. Síonna, put the wish into the fish for the shoal to take it while gazing at the jewel within your navel, at the invisible glow as the caterpillar within the butterfly."

She repeats his colourful verse looking at his cornflower eyes.

"Now let us continue and have joy, for our way is lit!"

He finishes the teaching. Síonna quietens her mind. They reach flat land again, mount their horses and canter forth building into a gallop.

After a testing day's ride through marshy lands, they come upon a glen with a little river running through it and let the horses drink. Ríonach and Zara are the first to explore. Grandfather gathers kindling and dried grass and lights a fire. Síonna goes on a hunt and is quickly pursued by Ríonach. Rabbits fall to her adept skills providing them with an abundance of food. She returns with the game strung over her shoulders.

The horses lift their heads seeing her returning with the hunt and bow again, grazing on the lush grass of the meadows. Grandfather skins and prepares the meat and mounts it on the small spit he crafted. They sit sharing wisdom, nourishing their bodies with the smoked meat. Grandfather gives wisdom of the mind as the moon lights the sky while Síonna shares teachings of the warrior. Blessed by a glitter of stars, they rest their heads and welcome Dreamtime after a long day riding deeper into the Kingdoms of Light.

Sleep comes with ease. Síonna is soon visited by sorcerers and witches who surround her laughing, letting out piercing tones. Pointing at her with sharp, curled nails on long, bony fingers, they snarl and grunt roaring,

"The beautiful one, we will teach her, ha, ha, ha!"

She wakes in a sweat to see morning has arrived with the sun climbing out of the horizon. Seeing Grandfather's silhouette erect against a wall of light by the river, she approaches. He turns catching the worried expression etched on her face.

"Do not be frightened. Those who walk the path of the sage will be taunted by the shadows. You have already caught and overcome the chill of death, so go forth fearless."

She looks west, seeing the forest of darkness standing between them and the Kingdoms of Light. She envisages beyond, seeing the blue of the ocean in the afar horizon, soothing to her soul. She yearns to feel it splashing on her skin and to wade in and leap beneath a wave of white horses. But first, she must face the challenging task of the forest.

Chapter 7
The Dark Forest of the Nine Hags

"Sleeping wounds within will one day surface and emerge like a beast," says Grandfather, "and only by an invitation to the edge of the fearless blade of your mind, showing them the light, can we clear the disturbance to our glow. Spirit, guide us through the dark of the forest with great courage. Allow us to weave through this place silently like spiders weaving in a nightly spin, binding silken threads over our wounds so they cannot enter, and we will conquer this sorcery. Let us prepare."

He follows it with a riddle.

'Trickery, sorcery
Return your spell from where it fell
The snake has shed the skins
We hold strong
Our Guiding stars
A soul-light
The rainbow-light
A love-light
The snake has shed the skins
Return your spell to where it fell.'

Síonna shrouds herself in his blessing, wishing for safe passage. They mount their horses and ride swiftly. Reaching the boundary of the forest a sense of heaviness falls. The wind blows, scattering dead leaves and roots on the forest bed. The boundary is sharp, turning from a vigorous green into an instant mantle of blackness. The lifeless wood wears a murky mist that hangs heavily making visibility difficult. The scent of something rotting suddenly curls to their nostrils.

Ríonach cowers behind Síonna. Zara perches with her head snugged into Grandfather's back. The songbirds are silent.

The horses neigh in unfamiliar tones. Beneath the shadow of the leafless trees, the trails are empty. Nature seems drained. The sun retreats. They watch the last rays flee from the forest floor out past the boundary. Síonna rides with one hand on her sword, sensing. Grandfather never carries a weapon, but she leans over handing him a knife and winks.

"If nothing else, it will serve you to prepare game."

She scans the fruitless forest. They come upon a grove of apple trees, the only sign of life bearing a full blossom, enclosed in a green faery mound. Pink and white flowers swirl down and sit luminous upon the dark undergrowth. Grandfather, knowing the tree is out of season to blossom and fruit, takes heed.

"Do not eat from them, Granddaughter, they are not apples gifting divine light, eternal life, nor any wisdom light of our ancestors."

He leads them away down a narrow path. The undergrowth stretches tall on each side. Síonna flinches, sensing a presence and draws her sword. Tracking through the mass of thorns and branches she catches a sudden movement darting through the trees. The horses are startled and neigh wildly. She leaps from Toirneach Bán, diving over the undergrowth to see a beastly spider as tall as Grandfather with glaring, fire-lit eyes. The creature advances with huge legs bearing pinchers swinging wildly.

She runs to meet it, evoking a warp spasm and hurls herself to the ground, rolling and swinging her blade in a figure of eight, slicing through the spider's front legs. Its fangs spear forth like blades. With one swipe, she beheads it and plunges her weapon deep into the heart of the beast, to the hilt. A hissing sound fills the forest as the life drains from the beastly crawler. She rises, recalling the moment when Cúroí plunged the blade into her chest and hearing his words of warning. She knows she will be challenged by the hostile environment but fear it, she does not, recognising, thanks to Cúroí, that death no longer has a firm grasp over her.

She emerges with the creature's blood dripping from her blade.

"What is this place, Grandfather?"

"This is one of many tests, Granddaughter," he replies, with a wink.

She plunges her blade into a nearby river to cleanse it, then they mount the horses and trot forward tentatively. She suddenly hears a faint echo building into the most beautiful and enchanting music. A scent of gorse like that from the Valley of Stags roams to her nostrils. A trail opens to her left. She glances to see Fionn standing with his hands outstretched, beckoning her. Startled at first, her heart then fills with a sudden sense of delight.

A tear falls and drops from her lips. As it hits the sod, a flower mysteriously sprouts. She is suddenly overcome by emotion and jumps silently from her horse. She walks, stepping lightly on the undergrowth not to alert Grandfather who continues along the track while she recalls the day they parted to the drone of the horn. Ríonach leaps, hitting her on the backside with her front paws. She turns ushering her away with a silent pushing of her hands.

Spellbound, she gazes at his love-lit blue eyes. Yearning, she walks closer and reaches out to touch him. Grandfather's voice startles her,

"No, Síonna, it's a trap!"

She flinches, as strands of thorns swirl around her legs, crawling swiftly around her body and the unseen force binds her before she can draw her sword. Fionn vanishes. She is speedily dragged through the forest. Laughter fills the surroundings. Grandfather races with Silent Galloper, swiftly followed by Toirneach Bán and Ríonach.

"Zaz, find her!"

Grandfather watches his hawk part the heavy mist with her wings.

Síonna is brought to a cave and dragged deep into a lit-up cavern. She finally sees the mysterious foe who captured her, Darkelve, faery from the hidden veils of the Underworld. They throw her before the nine-hags-of-the-forest who surround her as she foresaw in her dream. They poke her with sticks and point with the same curled nails. So much darkness, so much anger and hatred surge through her as they pour their foul curses upon her with sticky saliva dripping from their pointy chins.

They laugh and taunt her as she foresaw.

"Balor, we have the beautiful princess-of-the-red-hair, ha, ha, ha!"

Síonna tries to scream to alert Grandfather but they quickly stuff her mouth with cotton. Steaming cauldron sits over fires, human skulls skewed on sticks are displayed throughout the cavern, thrones collected by the wretched hags. A stench of rotting flesh fills her nostrils. The Darkelve glare with horrid yellow eyes and little pointy faces, which she wishes to squeeze like a pimple with one hand.

The furious hags grunt and spit on her. She watches them throwing human skulls, crows, toads, hawks, limbs and claws of animals, followed by herbs and roots, all into the cauldron while they chant and squeal spells like wild beasts. Lancing their wrists, they allow blood to drip into the mix. The Darkelve dance around them thrusting wands and spears into the air.

The hags glare through dark, bushy eyebrows with their eyes turned inwards to the back of their heads, white-eyed, the look of madness mirrored. Pointed ears stick out above their harrowing wrinkled faces as they shout, exposing mouths full of rotten, black teeth, fanged like wolves possessed.

"Oh, so beautiful she is, beautiful and elegant. And where is your wise rainbow man now? Bring him to us, little princess or …"

They drag her to a pool of water in the cave. Mirrored upon the surface she sees Grandfather searching in the forest.

"Call him or we will cut out your tongue and boil it with the frogs," says one, grabbing her by the hair, then releasing her bound mouth and taking a blade to her throat. "I said, call him!" it screams.

Síonna casts her voice,

"Grandfather, look for a cave."

He hears her faint plea and closes his eyes, divining.

"You toad, we will feed you to the hounds of Balor and cast your limbs to every quarter of this land," roars the hag, hissing as the image of Grandfather vanishes.

Smoke and flames rise from the cauldron. They stand stirring with sticks and drinking from goblets containing their own blood while reciting spells backwards from a scripture. Síonna watches one of the hags approach a wild boar enclosed in a wooden cage, taking her blade and with one fierce swing beheads it and throws the spouting head into the cauldron.

Another approaches Síonna.

"Ah, what have we got here, a golden jewel, oh so beautifully adorning your princess-like arm. So innocently untouched and protected you are by the foolish minds of mankind."

The hag bows to one knee to take the torque from Síonna. As the edge of her blade meets the jewel, a surging glow bursts forth in arcs like Suncatchers of light through the cavern, sending the hag flying and screaming in pain. Grandfather feels a sensation through his triskele torque gifted by Cúroí and receives an image in his Wonder-Eye of the whereabouts of the cave. He pushes his legs into the sides of Silent Galloper, urging him forward with pace.

Zara is just ahead, parting the mist, tracking and sourcing a feeling-of-the-way to the entrance. The hags draw their knives and lunge at Síonna, their mouths frothing.

Zara spears through the cave entrance, swooping down, beak pointed and plunges into the back of the hag's neck as Silent Galloper thunders in, leaping like an arrow through the air, hitting the witch in the chest, then stands on his hind legs, releasing a terrifying battle neigh before leaping into a stampede, sending the hags and Darkelve fleeing.

"You little beauteous!" cries Grandfather, as he marches around the cavern on Silent Galloper.

Toirneach Bán plunges in, knocking the hags in all directions. Síonna unleashes the sword to blood her blade but they vanish like shadows into the darkness, followed by her curse,

"Damn you, and your illusion, hags."

"Do not be angry with yourself, Granddaughter; when emotions control the mind, you must search deeper."

The whispers return,

"Princess-of-the-Red-Hair, we will get you, bound you will be … ha … ha … ha!"

Síonna runs from the cave, screaming,

"Show yourselves, crones of Underworld. Come and I will give you the drink of death." Enraged, she shouts to the sky, "you pungent creatures, our paths will cross again. This I promise you."

The forest soaks her commanding voice. They hear a sudden thumping of the sod that grows into a deafening rhythm. Something is approaching at great speed. The undergrowth suddenly parts and packs of wild boars burst through.

"Boars-of-the-poisonous-bristles!" shouts Grandfather.

Síonna leaps, summoning a warp spasm of strength, sending her blades into a motion of mass slaughter. Blood pours around her as she unleashes her fury. Bristles advance like arrows which she deflects with her shield. The nine hags emerge from the undergrowth and lunge at her with knives and the claws of their poisonous fingers.

The Darkelve cast streams of arrows. She slices through the hags in an emotionless state. Her blade cuts deep and the hags crumble to ash and fall to the sod, only to form again whilst Síonna battles with a cluster of boars. Grandfather gallops around them with Silent Galloper stamping on the creatures.

One of the wretched beasts casts a bristle that gets through and embeds itself into Síonna's left forearm. She winces but the warp spasm drives her on as the hags approach. Her sword takes their heads with furious accuracy. As their headless forms tumble, they soon gather their bodies to rise again. Grandfather is sending clusters of them back with the magic of his golden branch when a spear gets through and impacts the golden sun disk on his chest. It falls to the sod. Unharmed, he smiles sending a blessing to Cúroí.

Síonna salmon-leaps, letting her blade and knife swing in unison, meeting their heads with savage accuracy. Dismembered, they come down in a heap around her.

As they try to reform, the forest suddenly comes alive from a magic Grandfather summons, reversing the spell of witchcraft they used. Thorns race across the ground, weaving around the hags, wrapping and strangling the shadows from their souls. A returning light floods the forest floor. A surge of essence emerges. Flowers spring forth. Buds grow sprouting on the trees as melodies of the birds return. Stags, wolves, elk, boar and all who crawl, come graciously galloping the trails. An ever-churning spring gushes from the earth and trickles through the forest like a silver snake gifting wondrous life back to the sanctuary of nature.

Butterflies and bumblebees and all sorts of winged creatures sweep through the sky like the coloured rays of a rainbow, dancing from flower to flower, droning like little horns spreading renewing nectars summoning back the beautiful whispers of life. Our sages rest knowing that the sorcery is conquered for now. Great beauty flourishes. The Forest-of-the-Nine-hags flowers again into a great place of power.

Grandfather gathers the makings of a fire and some medicinal plants. Soon a dance of flames comforts and warms them. He makes tea of comfrey and fireweed and crushes leaves of nettle to tend to Síonna's growing fever. He gathers the roots of Athair Talún, Yarrow, and prepares a poultice. She sits cross-legged before the fire as he slowly pulls the poisonous dart from her forearm. She squeals. He covers it with several layers of spider web to stop the bleeding before wrapping the medicine.

With tears bathing her cheeks, she asks,

"What about the poison?"

"You have received sorcery through the Cuisle do Croidhe, vein of the heart, Granddaughter. Do not let it disturb you. First, we will cleanse it from your blood and then you must rest."

For a quarter cycle of a moon, they shelter in the chamber of an old oak where Síonna slowly regains her health.

One night in Dreamtime, Grandfather receives a vision of a leighsasóir living deep in the forest that he must visit. Taking heed, he rides out the next morning before dawn, journeying into distant valleys and comes across a rover driving a herd of sheep across a river in a glen.

"Binn an cat ag crónán in aice na tine, the cat is purring beside the fire." He greets Grandfather at first in the ancient tongue.

Grandfather looks at his earthly cheeks stretched by a warm smile gazing from light blue eyes. He answers the rover in a riddling manner.

"Cleave the sward of the mind with a magical team of horses, ploughing and sowing new seeds. Like a magical taibhse, ghost, spreading a blossoming of life. A man of the earth will not stray far. His footsteps are firmly rooted; rooted like the blades of the plough that shiver through the green sward with crows and seagulls on the bough, waiting for the tip of his caipín, cap, to slant over his eyes. And beneath his stilled rest, they swoop in glorious chorus, plucking a silver fill of worms until the swift blades churn again behind the canter of eager hooves. And in the evening's dusk, as sweat rests upon his brow dutifully earned, he sweeps with the sleeve of his shirt the labour of his day beneath a forthcoming twilight sky."

"Oh, you hav' it, my dear man, my pleasure to meet you, I'm Jo."

"Eirnín, at your humble sharing, but call me Grandfather."

"You are here to see the man with the medicine?"

"Yes, he has called me in Dreamtime."

"Many hav' come the same way to sit with the great scholáire of an dTeampall Geal, the White Temple, and learn the Seanchas, old lore, from the máistir de an teanga dhúchais, master of the mother tongue. Go east and where the gorse parts the path, follow the stream into the next valley and there you will find the wise Leigheasóir," says Jo, pointing with his blackthorn stick and he throws a wink before walking after his herd. With a roar he lets off an old saying: "Hup, agus is ait an mac an saol, and such is life."

Grandfather watches the relaxed gait of the drover as he turns a final time sending another reminder,

"Remember, there's healing in the purr; the cat has it."

Grandfather mounts Silent Galloper and canters onwards to where the gorse divides the path. Veering east, he follows the stream that eventually leads into a bough in a valley wearing clusters of elm and oak. The stream winds to encircle a small wooden dwelling. Smoke billows from the chimney. Grandfather leaps from his horse and lights his dúidín, offering prayer to the forest around the hermit's humble dwelling.

He walks towards the door that slowly creaks open and as he steps through, steam curls around his face. When it clears, the elder is sitting before a glowing hearth with a dog by his side.

"Th'anam On Diabhal, tar isteach, agus le brí na taise, mo bhuachaill, your soul from the Devil, come in, and with the energy of compassion to you, my boy."

"Eirnín, Mac Conchúr, tá me ag lorg treoir, son of Connor, I am looking for guidance" replies Grandfather.

"Micheál "Toose" Mac Gearailt, tá tú lán d'anam, a bhuachaill, you are full of soul, boy" he continues in the old tongue, while running his fingers through his white, neatly groomed, curly hair that is thick upon his head.

Bushy black eyebrows sit over his shiny, soft brown eyes that gaze deeply. His puffy cheeks are parted with a generous smile. A white woollen geansaí, jumper, adorns his torso. A white cat with black-tipped ears and a brown curling tail sits upon his lap purring.

"Ah-ha, got you now, Jo," Grandfather whispers.

The dog is white and black, dappled with spots of grey and with the most turquoise eyes. Three of his paws are black and one is wrapped white. He raises his front paw and Grandfather cups it into his hand. The hearth bears brass pots steaming fed with water by an iron pipe coming in through the wall. The room is filled with a light mist. The scent reaches Grandfather's nostrils. He scrunches his face. His dúidín has gone cold in his lips. The unusual scent climbs and curls, opening his senses.

"Ó mo chroí, from the bottom of my heart, I tell you my dear scholáire. The future Goddess has taken poison from the witches of the sorcerer. I ask you, dear man, for your adept wisdom to help us."

Curious about the unknown brew, Grandfather asks,

"And what is this medicine that smells so strong?"

Toose fills a horn of the steaming liquid and puts it aside to cool. He then cups a wooden spoonful of it and hands it to Grandfather.

"A special Poitín, my dear man, drink and summon blessings for your own tír dhúchais, Mother Country."

Grandfather sups the brew which catches his throat, making him cough as it pours like a hot river down his chest. He takes a big breath and leaves out a sigh. Toose winks and leaves out a chuckling laugh.

"Completely recovered, daughter of Sengann will be when she drinks of this merrily leigheas. It will lift the very soul from one's body and light the eyes to leap spirited like a new lamb of Imbolc, spring. Made from spuds sown in the rich sod and the waters that are drawn from sacred wells, then mixed with the sweet of cane," he says, and hands Grandfather the bull's horn of the potent drink.

"Take this Slámíc, healing salve, and mix it with the nine waters of the wells and nectars of these valleys. Let the warrior drink of this draíocht and she will leap from the sod like a swirling wind. Now allow me to gift her. As she ventures on this quest, tell your Granddaughter to hold one value that will help her to embody the teachings, and that is A bheith ionraic, to be honest. With an inner honesty to herself, she will open paths she never knew imaginable. Journey forth and take my loving cat, Taibhse, with you. Let her rest upon Síonna's lap and after she will find her way back to me. Ride swiftly and let your anam, soul, take the ceol, music, of this forest with you. Téigh anois, agus, go mbeirimíd beo ar an t-am seo arís, go now, and, may we be alive this time next year."

With his hand spread upon the sun disk on his Heart-Well, saluting the old wise sage, Grandfather steps out the door. He takes one glance at the wooden hut warmly hugged within the flowery bough of dTeampeall Geal, and offers a prayer to the scholáire and rides onwards through the nine valleys with the purring Taibhse spread on the hind of the horse. He is intuitively led to a well within each valley where he gathers the waters and nine different nectars, as suggested by the cure-all.

Silent Galloper makes the journey back to Síonna short. Zara swoops through the sky to meet their oncoming canter. She hears the distant trod of hooves; opening her heavy eyes seeing the whiteness of Grandfathers hair shine like an oncoming light as he sways in upon the mighty horse.

"Ah gaja, the sleeping princess awakens as the horns of battle sing within. Oh, so magical is your amber gaze fixed upon my speedy return. And a new furry friend I have brought. Meet the little purring starry eyes, Taibhse."

"Oh, little pussy, come here," she says, as Ríonach barks, circling the cat, curious and jealous of the attention received from her master.

The cat tentatively puts one paw in front of the other and walks up Síonna's leg to rest in her grasp.

"My mind keeps wandering, hearing otherworldly sounds and seeing confusing images but I will be fine now beneath the wings of the wizened Rainbow one who has returned with a leigheas, won't I?" she asks, smiling while casting him a wink.

Grandfather wastes no time and goes to work gathering roots of yarrow, dandelion and mugwort and mixes the nectars with the waters and then the special leigheas. He applies it over her wound, withdrawing the curse and then hands her the horn to drink from.

"Gifted by a humble sage deep in the forest. Drink of this, Síonna."

She sups from the horn. She scrunches her forehead and squeezes her cheeks together, taking a sharp inhale followed by a splutter of coughs and silently sweeps her hand down her throat and over her chest, following the hot trail of the potion.

"The sage also gave me a spioradálta gift, Síonna. A value that people most honour in another, a bheith ionraic. There will come a time that will call for this honesty to yourself so that you can inwardly choose the correct path. Others will see this trait in you and be inspired and practise it too," Grandfather winks.

The cat's purr soon matches the pulse of Sionna's heart. The rhythmic sound lowers her into sleep as Grandfather sits reciting incantations. From his heart, he sends healing images into the waters of the wells so that when Síonna drinks, the charged crystals will fill her with the impressions holding that healed image. He knows that it will cleanse Síonna at a certain level but also knows that she has received sorcery at the level of the heart, and it will take more than this leigheas to truly conquer that.

The witch knew her target well. An indent on the inner forearm that connects to the inner tributary of the heart, that influences a flow within, the wretched hag directed the flow against nature slowly weakening her heart.

Grandfather ritually draws with his hazel branch an image of the witch upon the sod, sticking three Blackthorn thorns: one on the forehead; one on the heart and lastly, one upon the stomach whilst making a wish. Repeating it three times, he then draws a protective circle around Síonna before kneeling and softly stroking her forehead, whispering,

"The stars shine through you, Síonna. Remember, the untarnished spirit within cannot be harmed. You are a worthy warrior. Be aware of every image and feeling for tomorrow awaits your dreamed actions. As your blood runs clear of this sorcery, a new dawn will emerge in your belly furrowing a path-of-happiness."

Each night in her dreams, one by one the hags haunt her, screaming and laughing,

"We will bind you, beautiful one, ha, ha, ha!"

Grandfather places leaves of laurel beneath her head, countering the sorcery and carrying out several cleansing rituals. Sweeping smoke from his dúidín with three hawk feathers, he clears the light of her body. He sprinkles the waters of the wells and with his hazel draws symbols of power and spins her bodily Wells with the tip.

The more she drinks of the charged waters, the clearer things become. She slowly expels the poisons as her mind begins to control the nightly hauntings. The sorcery dissipates as each night, beneath the singing magical tinkle of his bell and his ancient incantations, the hags' voices fail to reach her in Dreamtime.

After many deep sleeps and wandering states, she returns with a sense of strength gleaming from her eyes. The essences awaken her being as she takes the horn and drains it of the last Poitín, feeling a warp spasm of energy flooding her veins. She strokes Taibhse and kisses her on the head for her healing purr, then with a sharp exhale, she lunges from the ground sending the cat racing back to her master. Síonna flips the horn of Poitín into Grandfather's grasp and gripping her sword, twirls into a celebration dance.

He smiles witnessing her move in a ghostly way like a wild wind just as Toose foresaw. Rising as though through a thousand petals upon a stream of air, he watches her beauty and radiance quickly return. She swirls and swirls laughing aloud while stamping on the sod with profound joy.

Grandfather lights his dúidín, blowing swirls of smoke and offering thanksgiving to the gods and the sage and forest for his wisdom and leigheas. He turns sunwise lifting his eyebrows joining Síonna in her dance of delight. After a long thanksgiving movement, Síonna is finally ready to venture further into the Kingdoms of Light.

Chapter 8
Crom Dubh
3 steps of the wish

"Sprinkling summer's pollen with a tip-tap of elvish feet that glisten before the edges of mystical blades, they dance the dance of a great battle between life and death, as Crom Dubh fills the battleground with lightning beings," Grandfather riddles up the beginning of another journey as they advance from a canter into a gallop and he soon follows the riddle with a teaching.

"Síonna, as we voyage to the depths of ourselves, we too must voyage to the heights and summits to where the lightning beings sleep."

Silence falls as they journey on until the high mounds of Cnoc Bréanainn, shrouded in clouds, appear in the distance.

"The mountain of the druid," whispers Grandfather.

A luminous rainbow arches over the summit. Through the coloured rays emerges a fly a flock of swans leaving their white furrow within the red shawl of the sun that sprinkles over the summit. They watch their magical forms drift distantly through the orange glow as ravens and crows caw mysteriously.

Across the sound to the north stands the An Triúr Dreifiúr, the Three Sisters, that merge with the headland of Ceann Sibéal, reaching westerly into the Atlantach ocean where the Rainbow Isles await.

Guarding the south is Cruagh Mhairtin, Hill of Martin, with Sliabh an Iolair, Mount Eagle, sitting easterly of it. Grandfather having seen the sacred Isles many times is still silenced by the surrounding sheer mystique of the mountains and headlands. Dappled by the sun they watch the patches of light on the rocks stretch and merge to form a misty-like shawl that encloses them in an otherworldly veil.

A rainbow arcs down before them on the sod. As magic has unveiled new secrets each day on the quest, a violet ray pours out in a great spin and from it steps the King of the elementals: Crom Dubh.

His luminosity captures their eyes.

"You have reached the rainbow bridge, the great passageway into the barony of the lands of Dovinia."

The little King points to a border formed by bright gorse that runs down the entire belly of the mountain, stretching into green pastures. Their eyes follow the yellow line as far as they can track.

Síonna observes the golden light emanating from his body, adorned in the hide of a wild boar; his chest is naked and painted with a spiralling symbol, the blue zigzag pattern of lightning that crosses his face and his curly black hair falling to his waist. The golden torques that glitter upon his chubby arms and neck and the magician's staff with a quartz tip, he holds in one hand with a rod of lightning held in the other. She notices the glitter on his eyes and how they first seem hazel, then yellow, gold, and silver. The bushiest white eyebrows crown these mystical eyes.

His chubby rose cheeks part with frequent smiles. Her eyes follow his ears that meet to a point with lobes pierced with two bronze pins. She tries to read the stories etched upon his skin that is cracked like the copper sward, folding over his face.

He stands forth with thick stumpy legs and raises his voice,

"Sages, of the Valley of the Stags, welcome to the Kingdoms of Light. You have reached the barony that can only be crossed by those possessing hearts full of love and compassion; those with the dúchas, heritage."

"We quest for the Magic Wells," says Grandfather, reaching out his hand to the noble who grasps it tightly and embraces him.

He hugs Síonna, his head only reaching her waist. As he does, he sees the great sword adorned with an emerald glowing to his eyes.

"Sages, you are no strangers for I have seen you Bull-Dreaming," he says, looking into Síonna's eyes. "The Emerald Eye has been foreseen and will soon take its rightful place within your worthy grasp."

His message leaves her puzzled.

"Daughter of Sengann, remember, the signs are sitting upon the surface, be aware. Now let us make fest; sit with me and share," he says.

With a sweep of his lightning hand, a steaming cauldron mystically appears over a flaming fire on the sod.

"Whist, agus éist le mo ghuí," he says and unravels a riddle like Grandfather.

"Where the Sun sleeps
I make fire in my head
In oak groves and woodland pools
I spread seeds of enchantment
Within the golden underfoot of the earth
I plant imaginings
Mountain-Dreaming
Sending lightning beings like stars
Sprinkling my wishes
Whilst
Behind the unknown course of the moon
I dream
The three magic steps."

Síonna tries to piece his riddle together as they feast on the finest meat, flavoured with herbs unknown to their palates, nurturing their tired bodies. And the mysterious sage unfolds his guidance before the dance of flames.

"Daughter of Sengann, I know what lies ahead. It is just for this that I will gift you. It is simple and keep it so. Tar isteach sa ríocht dhraíochta, come into the magical kingdom, and carry out the three steps of the wish:

Form a task, a wish
Act by giving it motion
And look for the signs."

Simplified into three steps, Síonna smiles as he continues,

"Bring a time of life to your wish. Moving forward the wish is important. Walk around the medicine wheel and know your place. The soul knows the way for a true desire. A feeling will be gifted to you by the great inner star, your Guiding Star. With all your senses of hearing, seeing, touch, smell, taste, the feeling of space and that of balance, bring a part of the outside world inside you. Like once you taste something, that taste remains forever. Sometimes we hear beautiful music that draws us; beware of an otherworldly melody you may hear and things that you may taste for otherworldly desires will weave unannounced upon your senses!"

Síonna suddenly feels the weight of the burden, sensing that the whole future of Eriu depends on her ability to complete this quest.

"Integrate all your senses and feelings into one place, as though you already stand in the centre of the medicine wheel having acquired the teachings of each direction, and raise them into that of the seventh Well that spins upon your head. Here you will catch the path-of-happiness, the feeling. Tune yourself as you bridge into the spioradálta. Bring and share something new and leave an aligned trace of light wherever you walk. It is important to remember; beware of the eclipsing mist that is veiling the true light of your soul. A person becomes noble only by developing the three steps: Wish, action, actualization. This is my gift to you warrior of the Fir Bolg. Now gaze to the Isles and make a wish!"

Síonna turns to the magical sight that seems to hold the entire western horizon under a spell and makes a wish. Music floods her being as though she can feel the pulse of each Isle merging with the beat and song of her heart, attuning, beckoning her journeying soul to place her footprints upon their magical hearths she wishes. She turns thanking the great wise seer embracing him warmly.

As before, a mysterious violet ray pours out of the rainbow. Mist descends, swirling around the luminous bands that whisk him from the earth like a shooting star.

Grandfather leaps singing his praise. With his fingers pinched and both hands outstretched, he raises his eyebrows and shouts,

"We come dancing, sensing through cunning fox eyes while gazing to the golden tooth of an eagle soaring high over the lagoon of a sea dragon's cave to reach the golden sands of a timeless memory while unravelling the otherness mysteries of the universe."

Chuckling at his verse, Síonna spins with him until dizziness halts their steps and they come to a still, gazing across the mountains into the Kingdoms of Light seeing white trails of smoke rise as though giants sit in the foothills, smoking.

"The burning of the gorse," says Grandfather, sending blessings to the people who are preparing the land for harvesting.

He rings his bell summoning movement to their journey and accompanies it with a riddle.

"Tumbling and rumbling with bellies rolling, leading our gracious walk we cross the gorse barony bridging who we leave behind with who we are becoming!"

Chapter 9
Chorca Dhuibhne
Dovinia

They gallop hills and through valleys, over rivers and around lakes and pass ancient gallán, Standing stones, and Faery Rings scattered over the land like deities. The sight Síonna has been wishing for suddenly captures her. Entranced by the luminous blue, she witnesses the silver-bellied ocean stretching as far west into the distant horizon as she can see.

An array of flowers dangles majestically on the hedgerows around them, beautifully dominated by Na Fiúsaíos and foxgloves. A faint moon peeks behind wispy clouds, raindrops fall on their brows. Grandfather senses the shift in Síonna entering the kingdom of Dovinia and offers it sound.

"If we have enough light within us and the will to share it, the universe will send a sign. The world will open the invisible to us and a deep informative image will be revealed in these places of power. Capture this and remember, we are not just looking, we are witnessing and influencing. What you are seeing reflects your inner world at this moment, observe it precisely flowering before you like these red teardrop blossoms of Na Fiúsaíos. Remember, those who dream awake from the soul are those who hold a power to see the potential in the miraculous emerging."

She keeps his words rolling about her tongue as they gallop westerly towards the coastline. They come to rolling hills that brings them into the golden góilín, inlet, of Ceann Bhaile Dháith where they let the horses roam. The four-legged guide them to a well beneath an Na Fiúsaíos flowered hedgerow. The red and purple petals float on the surface. Grandfather stoops and cups a handful of the fresh water that cools his palm. With a blessing of the draíocht-of-the-fingertips, he passes it to Síonna who drinks its essence.

She leans over to cup another and there on the surface the glistening sorcery eye of Balor first appears. Flinching, she pulls back and blinks in quick succession. Confusion and a sense of enchantment flood her being. Her eyes are drawn back. She looks again to see a wondrous hazel tree with golden husks sitting over what looks like the forbidden Conlla's well. They glitter as though belonging to the very jewel of her soul. A red moon floods the surface bathing her being with lunar sorcery.

A sense of power courses through her veins. Grandfather's voice startles her.

"Síonna, not everything is as you see. Remember what Crom Dubh said: 'beware of the eclipsing mist that is veiling the true light of your soul.' Remember, nothing, nor anybody can hurt you unless you give them the power to do so."

He winks allowing her time to collect herself, knowing that the sorcerer has begun the hunt. Startled, she feels a terrible weight has been cast upon her.

Grandfather leans into the well and fills a horn. Síonna looks on in fear but the stealing eye of Balor and the tree have vanished. He turns, noticing the desire left etched upon her eyes as the horses drink their fill.

A sudden neighing breaks their thoughts. An elder is sitting on the back of a hairy, fawn donkey, swaying from side to side with its droopy, glinting eyes lowered to the path. Grandfather recognises him as Breandán, Shéamuis, Pheaidi Ó Grífín, the renowned Ollamh. Síonna looks at his dark, earthen skin strung upon his chiselled cheekbones, a caipín slanted over his face as he puffs on a white dúidín that hangs to the side of his mouth, releasing swirls of smoke before him as though a dolphin casting magical crystal rings, his generous smile and glinting brown eyes arrest her.

"Ar ghnúis na gréine, na talún, on the face of the sun, of the earth, let us awaken and share something that will form a living thing upon the crest of your tongues to spread throughout the kingdoms you journey. Carry words like nectar and pollinate the tongues of all you encounter with their magic. Now with sweetness of the honey-mouth. Allow me to command a verse.

> "Our souls meet
> Like crystal granules of the stars
> Each shining

A Guiding light
To assemble into one Suncatcher
Bestowing upon all sentient beings
The ever-blossoming smile of the Creator."

Síonna feels the warmth and fuinneamh, energy, in the message of the Ollamh.

"Sages, accompany me to my clochán for warm broth waits."

They ramble with the Ollamh up a winding boíthirín, country lane. With each puff he takes, laughter leaves his mouth.

"A jolly, earthed man," Grandfather whispers.

They come to the headland overlooking the ocean to the western horizon. Stooks of fawn hay adorn the meadows around his clóchan where the horses delightfully roam. A grove of apple trees sits west of it. As the Ollamh pushes aside a heavy wooden door, warm air crawls to their nostrils from a steaming pot hanging above a blazing hearth.

"Sit, sages of Sengann, it is my great honour."

They gather around the glow of embers as he serves a warming broth, followed by a mystery of words.

"In the beginning, the stars sang in the infinite skies gleaming down guiding the darkness as the moon cast her lament, rustling the singing leaves of the White Willow. Goddess trees sang this lament churning the oceans, rivers and Wells into a great dance. The Earth answered with a swirling magic gifting nature wondrously with an awakened chorus of man."

Síonna inhales his descriptive verse which he follows with some guidance.

"Síonna, remember, the quality of your words will determine your thoughts. Speak words that gift compassion, love, thanksgiving and most of all forgiveness. Stiúraithe faoi do réalt, be guided by your star, and you can walk in darkness on the-path-of-happiness."

He puffs his dúidín three times and blows circles that curl around her nose. Laughter spills from her mouth as he continues,

"I have spent half the years upon my head learning rhythms, stories and the movements and the rhyming of words. Mastering the skill of the Ollamh like your wise Grandfather, we learned words to affect a magic or a charm; a sorcery if needed, An Áer, a backward spell. Be so wary of these otherworldly voices, daughter of Sengann, for many sorcerers are tracking behind the veils of daylight."

He lowers his earthy-looking head, peering beneath his eyebrows and takes his golden wand standing by the hearth and waves it over the fire. Sparks rise and the winds curl the flames into a dance. He stretches his eyes wide and warning words unfurl from his tongue.

"A murderous wolf call
Left my mouth
Whilst blood of the beast
Dripped from my lips
Casting a spear
Upon my killing word
Whose tip, pierces
Daring foe
O' cross not
The Áer
For not mountain nor cave
Will (hide) your ear."

His words summon up the image of Balor at the well. Breandán, reading her thoughts, breaks the image by chuckling and winking in quick succession, twirling his ears.

She looks to his dark bony face glowing beneath the dance of flames, to the roguery in his eyes.

"Síonna, remember, words can summon the magic of the gods or they can bring down the strongest warrior, or enchant a sense of madness upon the foe, or even stir the guiding stars of the night and turn the tides of a fierce ocean. So, no harm being in thought, word nor deed. Feel every word that rolls from your honeyed tongue; their intent, energy and what your wish for them is when they go out to the world. And ask yourself the most important question: is there hurt in my words? Words must not stab like a knife nor puncture like an arrow but melt lovingly into the heart of another, offering pure soulful joy."

She ruminates on his guidance and offers her grace.

"Breandán, le mo cuisle mo chroí, with the love of my heart, I truly thank you. I feel a great beauty is sown within me. With great merit, I will nurture your wisdom and mature it on my tongue to blossom like the most beautiful sunflower ever seen."

A smile lifts the dúidín between his lips.

The Ollamh rises and beckons our sages outside to the flowering apple tree where he plucks one of the precious fruits and offers it, giving lore.

"Síonna, taste this crab fruit that offers the eternity of the soul and form a wish, a task. Cast your look within and see another sense of yourself holding the same apple but is now golden and contains all the properties of your wish. Step forward and merge with this other self. Now taste the apple and taste your wish as you cast your Wonder-Eye out upon the Isles. Send forth the silken threads of your consciousness like a beacon of light across the sound bringing your dream ashore."

Following the sage's suggestions, she raises her energy and merges with her other self and looks to see the apple has truly turned golden. She takes a bite. A taste so wondrous and sweet swarms her mouth as the fruit releases an otherworldly juice. He smiles and speaks in a husky voice as though he is reciting an ancient prayer.

"Wise daughter of Sengann, you have now tasted your wish. Once this sensation enters, it will never leave. The pulse of those Isles is now within you. The Magic Wells are calling, ho."

Awed by the experience, she stands ruminating on the event as the two Ollamh share a smoke. Grandfather rings his bell to complete the ceremony.

The wise man of the west leads them back down the bóithrín to the golden shoreline of Trá na Feothanaigh where a beautifully crafted boat sits like an overturned beetle on the sandbank.

"Wondrous words tipped on an arrow of the druid's tongue spears skywards like a sharp glance of the sage. A swift, double-edged blade sweeps the stars from the sky with one arc of truth as swift as the toad's tongue leaps at the unbeknown fly. A blood moon salmon carries the burdens of the Earth upon her back, revealing the purple scales of regret while swimming in the otherworldly tributaries of Eriu."

Síonna picks up the constant reminding of this otherworldly salmon and warnings of regret and troubles in the words of Grandfather and the sages they are meeting on the quest.

Breandán tips his hat to slant over his eyes, knowing what is before her and ushers our sages onwards.

"Take this Sídóg to navigate the sound between here and the most westerly kingdoms. Your horses will be looked after. Go, sages, and do not doubt the importance of this voyage. Maireann an duine ar aoibhneas croí, agus is fad saoil dó an t-áthas, gladness of heart is the very life of man, cheerfulness prolongs his days."

Wishing thanksgiving by placing their hands on their hearts hearing the Ollamhs beautiful blessing, they turn and push the Sídóg upon the crest of an incoming wave, willing their exploring hearts to the ocean. Síonna whistles and Ríonach comes racing down the shoreline and leaps into the boat followed by Zara who sweeps down to perch on the bow.

"Síonna, remember, stiúraithe faoi do réalt, and you can walk in the darkness!"

They wave to the Ollamh and the swelling sound soon tests their strength. Pinnacles rise on the northern headland as they turn into torrent, north-eastern swells. They hug the coastline to their left passing the beautiful inlet of Doneen seen its fortress of basalt rock layered with quartz. Making pace they work hard curving around the headland through crunching waves into the open sea. They churn through the sound for a long measure of time before coming to realise that they will not make the first Isle before dusk, they agree to veer easterly towards the white sands of Cuan an Chaoil. As they pass the towering headland of Ard na Caithne bearing the trinity peaks of the Na Triúr Deirféar, the three sisters, the first sight of An Fearr Marbh, the Sleeping Giant, appears. Síonna is instantly enchanted looking at him sitting upon the edge of the horizon in the deep of the ocean.

Her eyes circle his huge form and outwards to the Isles spread westerly behind him. Three times sunwise she spreads her eyes around him forming a wish.

Reaching the shoreline of Cuan an Chaoil, they secure the Sídóg. Towering above the inlet is the huge rockface of Sybil Head. The first thing Síonna does is race back into the lapping waves dousing her being in the source of all waters. She dives into huge crashing waves sucking in their charge like a warp spasm from the earth. After several plunges beneath, she stands closing her eyes and allows herself to float. She begins to sway on the surface, feeling the cool waters caressing her skin. Embodying that lightness, she conjures up in her battle skills; the ocean intensifies it feeling as though she is bodiless. After some needed silence in relation to the sea, she returns to the shore.

"Ah gaja, the ancient mermaid of the west has come ashore amongst us mere mortals."

She falls beneath the spell of Grandfather's humour and chuckles wildly while describing her invigorating encounter with the Atlantach and they walk up towards the dunes to explore. On a grassy path that meets the dunes, they come to a ráth, circular earthwork, with a mossy Ogham stone standing in the middle. They walk to the ancient gallán and carved upon it is a druidic inscription in Ogham telling of the seed of Dovinia and the clans of Corcú Duibhne, tribe of Duibhne. Honouring all who previously dwelled there, the tribes and the voices that echo within the hollow of these hills, Grandfather rings his bell placing his hand on the stone and whispers,

"Síonna, close your eyes and journey the previously passed paths."

The winds lift, leaves spiral around their feet; a beam of light drops down hitting the gallán turning the moss a luminous green. Eyes form on the surface, soon followed by a stream of lights that merge to form into a magical deity. A towering Goddess, cloaked in a green moss shawl with two mighty wolf hounds standing by her side, emerges.

Long black hair curls around her slender shoulders bearing the most beautiful headdress of laurel, intertwined with the red and purple blossoms of Na fiúsaíos. Her skin is silken, copper-like from the evening's dusk that falls, lighting a glittering gold upon her eyelids as her green-yellow eyes mirror the landscape to their backs.

She smiles, holding a sword decorated with an emerald jewel upon its sheath and a nine-fold bronze shield adorned with gemstones held in the other. As though the very stars sing from the twilight of her voice it sounds.

"Sages, by the rays of the same sun that shone a thousand years ago, Eriu is singing of your quest. Let the essence enter the caves of your hearts, for to fill this vessel will give less room for the desires of the other worlds."

She beckons Síonna forth. The future Goddess gazes into her eyes.

"I give you my solas!"

The deity opens her mouth and a great light pours forth, forcing our sages to close their eyes. It surges through Síonna and she feels bubbling in her Heart-Well. When their eyes readjust, they look to find themselves standing back on the sandy cove with the nine-fold bronze shield of the Goddess left on the shoreline. Lightning beings fork through the sky; no trace of the Goddess can be seen.

Síonna walks to the boat and picks up the shield knowing it is destined to protect her. She runs her hand over the beautiful stones and onto the cool bronze oval, feeling the same surge of solas possessed by the Goddess.

"It is destined to shield the merit of your great actions, Síonna," says Grandfather.

She bows her head, sending thanksgiving to the ancient deity for the gift. A great smile peels back her rosy cheeks and she leaps with joy.

"Let us now voyage to the inner shores of our minds. You are but a flower in the ocean outpouring such colours from your wells; they shine like luminous crystals as you share the light of your deepest inwardness."

She bathes in his praise and a voice breaks her trail of thoughts,

"I am Wind-in-his-hair, Mac Corcú Duibne, seed of Duibhne."

They turn to see a mighty warrior gazing from piercing blue eyes and bearing long, fire-red hair that reaches to his waist. A bronze ring is looped through the bridge of his nostrils like a bull, giving him a fierce image. Síonna looks into the pale of his eyes and feels a sense of kindness. More emerge from dwellings hidden within the dunes that are covered by thick tufts of grass.

A tall, silver-haired noble with a young man approaches and stands by Wind-in-his-hair.

"Diarmuid, our noble Taoiseach and his son, the mystical Cian," Wind-in-his-hair introduces the two who stand mysteriously hooded, wearing matching long robes.

"We aspire to solve a task, for the Wells of Eriu are outpouring with the scales of a demon skin that churns the waters with a lunar sorcery," says Grandfather.

"Word has come before you! A great battle is destined to take place. Síonna, you are the beacon of the flame acquiring the solas of a worthy leader that will march with the armies of the Fir Bolg and slay the dark beast."

She arches her eyebrows nervously, hearing the responsibility bestowed upon her within his words. Delivering his stark message, the Taoiseach and his son turn and walk back to the dwellings in the dunes.

The last light of the sun slowly dips behind the horizon. A fire is kindled, and the tribe gathers. Our sages meet the children who give them a display of Bataireacht. Síonna is soon challenged in stick play by their strongest warrior, Eoghan, who flings a furze stick at her. She grabs it, shyly accepting the bout.

Eoghan is a tall, big-boned chieftain feared by many as he and his band of warriors defend the south-westerly lands from raiders who come in from oceans afar.

He swings a huge blackthorn stick with the biggest knobbed-end she has ever seen. The impact of the sticks ring throughout the dunes. She feels his great power but knows it is nothing she hasn't dealt with before. She turns on her skills sensing beyond the movement, deeper to where it is formed with his thoughts. Shifting from another heavy swing, she cracks him on the inner left knee, bringing him down to one leg and sticks the tip into his right shoulder sending him to the sward.

He falls heavily, knocking the back of his head. Dizzy, he scurries slowly onto wobbly legs asking. "Is tú mo chuisle, you are my pulse." Cleary disoriented, his wife Kloda rushes in to save him further embarrassment, pretending that those who were out fishing need a hand at the shoreline to bring in the day's catch. Síonna smiles, thanking the dark-haired wife of the warrior and bows to the applause of the clan.

They gather around the fire witnessing the white horses crested on the incoming waves, racing ashore. Swallows glide in and dive around them and swerve into tiny holes in the dunes. They sit with Wind-in-his-hair prophesying on the quest ahead.

The sage stands and takes a spear with a quartz tip and hurls it skywards. All eyes follow its spin through the dark purple sky whilst it falls to the ocean as though feeding it with a charge of his wish. Horses rise on a great wave and race through the sound towards the sleeping giant, leaving a crystal tail mirrored on the surface.

"Upon the settling of this night, you will acquire a gift, Síonna," says Wind-in-his-hair.

They sit around the fire telling tales and sharing a mead brewed by the elders. The night grows old and gets lost in their great counsel. Wind-in-his-hair takes a horn and blows a mighty breath, releasing a bellowing drone that fills the entire bay. The tribe usher goodnight to our sages and retreat into their dune dwellings.

Síonna watches the hooded Taoiseach and his son walk across the bay beneath the graceful flight of swallows. Diarmuid turns and points at the shoreline and when our sages look around to thank the nobles, there is no trace of them only the flapping dance of the swallows and waves.

Grandfather and Síonna accept the otherworldly goings-on and rest their heads down, soothed by the glow of the remaining embers and drift into an inviting sleep.

Síonna is suddenly woken by a thunderous sound rumbling through the sands. She clambers to her feet to see an army of Darkelve racing towards them on the backs of boars. She shouts at Grandfather to take to the dunes with Ríonach and Zara. She swiftly draws her sword, grabbing the nine-fold bronze shield of Dovinia, excited to test its strength for the first time. She raises it to her breast and faces the onslaught. 'Open eyes, and no thoughts,' she reminds herself to work emotionless.

Seeing the ghoulish eyes of the elves flicker in the moonlight, she fingers the torque of Cúroí on her arm, summoning his protection.

Grandfather casts a light from his golden branch, enclosing her in his magic. She turns the point of her sword into battle and summons up a warp spasm and hurls into the air salmon-leaping into the thick of the elves. Her blade travels in the familiar figure of eight, cutting and slicing through the wretched beasts. She changes levels, rolls on the sward. The boars fall legless toppling the Darkelve onto the ground.

Darting through she rains down her blade and shield, hammering the bronze gift of Dovinia upon them. Spears and bristles rebound off it; impenetrable it is with the otherworldly protection of the ancient Goddess, she cracks heads, limbs roll, bones are left shattered and sticking from the elves. Frothing like a raging wolf, she unleashes fury upon the army of Balor, sending him a clear message that she will not be defeated and is destined for one purpose: to be crowned Goddess of Eriu.

The furious clashing of steel and galloping of hooves suddenly quieten. Grandfather and the tribe emerge seeing Síonna standing amongst the blood-soaked piles of bodies with her blade held skywards, inhaling the essence between earth and sky into her being. Her eyes glisten fire-like. Her mouth is frothing with a desire that burns through her veins showing the will of the warrior that drives her to fulfil this quest. Knowing now the power she embodies; he understands why the shamans and sages trust that she will succeed in such a momentous task. But he also knows this determination may hurt her.

"You so are worthy, but you must play with caution for you possess such a great power," he whispers to himself.

He walks to her as the dawn begins to unfold the first light of the day. She questions Wind-in-his-hair, asking why he didn't come to her aid.

"Great warrior, you have solely acquired a gift last night in knowing that you are the chosen one. Go now into the calling of this tide and quest further until you receive what is truly destined for you."

She gazes into the blue of his eyes. A sparkle of the morning's sun glints off the bronze ring on his nose, knowing now that it was a test he set for her, a challenge that she needed.

They embrace the Corcú Duibne and climb aboard the Sídóg into the wonders of a new stretch of ocean. Síonna inhales the very essence of it, merging her breath and body with the subtle swaying of the tide.

Inhaling and rising with the waves, she exhales and spreads her hands out as though they are the wings of a gracious swan, energetically spread over the white horses that race upon her great bosom. She goes deeper and hears the funnel created that runs beneath the crest of a wave and just before it overlaps, a sound races through the pocket right across the bridge of the wave. And there she captures the magic, that snap of energy. She savours that moment as though her soul flees into the wave before she leaps back into the source of the great ocean.

They row, looking back at the tribe waving from the shoreline and turn, driving their oars into the great expansive belly of the Atlantach.

Chapter 10
The Magic Wells of the Rainbow Isles
The Spirit-Well

"Slanting sun come curving through the sky, higher, sky prayer wanderer. Walkabout in dawns and dusk with swallows gliding in song with the thrush leaping through pockets of the sky with the starlings chirping aho: the quest has begun! So wondrous the gorse and heather meadows as a moon silver bends a golden thread of bumble bees leaving a sun path of magical honey to guide our swift row into her blue hearth. Gallop white horses upon the crest of wishful waves and beach us upon the glittering shorelines of these Magic Wells."

Grandfather summons his wishing verse, looking at the Rainbow Isles looming in the distance, waiting for their eager souls. A swelling tide springs up and the waters quickly deepen. They observe ridges beneath, sinking to unmeasurable depths as the sound begins to churn. Treacherous and testing it soon becomes as they glance back to see the golden dunes grow distant.

The current brings them swiftly into her swelling cauldron and the aroma of kelp hooks their nostrils. Inhaling the freshening scents, they drive forth in a rhythmic row.

After a passage of time, they find themselves well into the mouth of the sea. Grandfather sees the shining black fin of a humpback suddenly breaking the surface. Síonna turns, smiling in wonderment at witnessing the sea giant for the first time. Just when they thought it was alone, another fin rises. The two huge mammals begin to dive into the black abyss in great, wave-like motions and surface again flicking their tails sending streams of water through the air.

As seaspray falls upon them, Síonna holds out her hand. One of the whales swims parallel to the boat allowing her to rub its entire body. She sees her golden lunulae mirrored on the mammal's shiny skin. Grandfather lays down his oars and they watch them make distant, churning circles, the bubbles capture shoals of tiny fish and with huge gulps the whales fill their worthy bellies, before churning a silver path and releasing three mighty breaths from their blowholes. They face the open sea and dive in a final wave gifting a wondrous splashing of their tails before disappearing into the world of wonder beneath.

Grandfather puffs his dúidín allowing the Sídóg to sway, knowing that great magic is about to occur. He quietens his mind adjusting his Wonder-Eye gazing and whispers,

"Still your mind, Síonna, and look across the water. Climb into your consciousness to the Spirit-Well where all the magic can be unravelled. Focus on the shimmering veil of heat glistening on the surface. Now go deeper, seeing that which makes up all living things; see the little fragments of light. Now bring them together like a glowing net and see beyond the veil. Truly open your Wonder-Eye. Do you see it?"

"Not yet, Grandfather."

"Focus, go further, remove the layers of disbelief. Ask this place of power to reveal to you its soul."

With her intention set on the mystical Well above her head, she empties her mind throwing out her request. The mask of disturbance slowly peels from her eyes and the true nakedness of the Isle glimmers through. She takes a breath of excitement.

"Aww, I see it, Grandfather, I see it!"

Her eyes trail the might of the huge black boulders of jagged basalt that rise from the sea, to the three pinnacles with two pillars of quartz that stand either side of a bridge carved of the same quartz, connecting the shoreline to the magical Isle.

A light beams out from the sacred rock and pebble and white sandy beaches slope to meet luscious green meadows. She sees flowering heather trails winding to the summit. Forach, gannett, puifín, storm petrel, fulmar, razorbill, the kittiwake and crósan are busy flying back and forth singing in shrilling chorus. She watches as they dive at great speed, then spear into the abundant waters.

A colony of grey, ghostly seals basks on her shoreline. Birds' nests layer the rugged cliff arches.

"Many species come from afar shores to raise their young here," says Grandfather, familiar with the place of power.

The eddies and currents are stirred by a sudden gale that raises their boat. Grandfather begins to row towards the hidden kingdom. Síonna joins his actions as the swell suddenly lifts and dips to a great depth and she feels the churning motion within her belly.

"Hold on tight," Grandfather calls.

She clings to the beam of the boat as they are suspended on the bosom of waves and dipped suddenly, wishing for the noble wizard to grant them safe passage.

A mysterious sun climbs into the sky and kindles into a blinding glow, forcing them to cover their eyes. When they readjust and regain visibility the seas have suddenly calmed. Sensing a presence, Síonna gazes to the headland seeing The Cosmic Juggler standing on the quartz bridge in mystical attire and holding a staff emanating a wondrous glow like that of Cúroí. A cloak with magical symbols etched upon it reaches to his naked feet. His hair, a luminous silver, falls waist-long and flailing on the winds. A twinned image of his mystique is reflected on the surface of the calmed ocean.

His eyes glint a tone red from the rich sky. Grandfather sends golden words,

"Noble one who-juggles-the-draíocht, and the stars far beyond wondrous man's imaginings, we come with the truth of our glittering hearts as the sun dawns our wish."

"Come forth, sages for you are most welcome within the pulse of this great day foreseen to align as it is already in motion, now coloured by your warming verse, rainbow shaman."

The cosmic one swings his quartz-tipped staff in an arc. A wind rises lifting them upon the crest of a wave. Racing to the shoreline through a glittering sun path pushed by the invisible force, they sway through the rocky arch towards the bridge.

Securing the boat, they climb the luminous steps. Síonna is taken by the shell of violet-white light that encloses him. He warmly greets them,

"Shaman and sage of the Valley of the Stags, tar isteach sa draíocht, come into the magic."

She looks into his glistening eyes and to the violet circle etched on his forehead. His fingers are long and bony, stretching around his staff. She is awed by the beauty of the quartz bridge and the two, huge pillars that rise high above the ocean.

She sees his lightbody trail after his form, leaving sparkling footprints. Crossing the bridge, they follow a green path winding into a steep ascent that leads them to their dwellings. A mighty Cairn sits in the centre surrounded by clochán, oratories and wells. Livestock roams the green pastures, which are blossomed with sea pinks, heather, sea campion, and bearded with circles of gorse and coloured crops that shiver upon the wind.

The dwellings sit like a cluster of silver shells upon this mighty rock in the blue lagoon of the Atlantach. Síonna follows the trace of his violet light as they follow his lead into a cairn, through a huge door carved of quartz.

Corbelled floors and walls sparkle with the same stone. An oak roof stretches above them. Elders are sat circled around a glowing dance of flames.

"Here, we dream and make prophecy at the level of Creator through the Well that connects us to all that is divine."

The elders look alike, wearing white cloaks etched with the same symbols of the Cosmic Juggler. Each emanates the same violet-white light that circles their foreheads. They look as though hundreds of years have passed upon them.

Síonna observes them closing their eyes as they sit cross-legged. Their radiance grows brighter and then dulls into a subtle shimmer as though they are stepping over and back through veils of otherworldly realms. A beautiful fragrance of frankincense suddenly fills the cairn. Each one holds a clay dúidín and the embers light up their faces as they inhale and exhale mouthfuls of the wishful smoke, repeating this ritual over and over while sweeping the smoke over their heads.

Gazing upon their flickering eyelids, she wishes for the haunting in her mind to dissipate, for her weaknesses to grow into strengths, for the whispers of sorcery to turn to words that are powerful and honeyed and for her yearning for Fionn to resolve itself for the greater good of everyone; but strangely she cannot seem to summon any emotions.

The dwelling suddenly lights up, distorting their vision. They peer through the divides of their fingers. A sense of time bending, stretching, weaving into a great spin brings them sweeping through a timeline seeing the otherness of other realms. Like crystals journeying along their clan lines, they witness the entire span of time seeing landscapes and seascapes of strange terrain. They are suddenly whisked back to see a well has appeared, bathed within a circle of white rowan blossoms.

The sky is mirrored upon the surface.

"The first well," Síonna whispers.

And the Cosmic Juggler commences.

"Sages, let us now journey into the magic of the spioradálta Wells. Seven main magical cauldrons spin upon the body carrying the blood and essence around our beings. Two more exist outside the physical structure connecting us to all that is outside of us. These Wells are connected to seven outer shells that extend around us, connecting us with the essences and elementals of nature. The same Wells exist as places of power upon the Earth. These Isles are one of nine places of power."

He pauses allowing Síonna to grasp the importance of the teachings and proceeds further.

"The seven main Wells radiate and match the seven colours of the rainbow. The two divine Wells above us glow golden and white. There are many other smaller Wells on the joints and elsewhere but let us focus for now on the nine main cauldrons. The three lower Wells develop the physical realisations of man where the lower impulses and the sense of survival exist. It gives us a feeling of rooting in a space and time upon this earth. The middle Wells form the ascending mind that rises from the lower impulses of the beast towards the fourth Well, that of the heart, the great emerald that bridges the two worlds of the physical with that of the spioradálta. We must aspire to reach into the Sky Wells to a place devoid of emotions and desires, a golden world."

Síonna listens heartedly trying to take everything in, now understanding the many stories Grandfather told her of acquiring the Rainbow Body. The wizard continues,

"This Isle represents the Spirit-Well that spins outside all physicality, outside limitations, beyond time in a realm that is only visible to the Wonder-Eye. Here, we sense from the level of the Creator, from the soul, receiving as gods, creating life, ideas, thoughts, magic and prophecy. This Well shines of pure white at the top of the ladder."

He lifts his wizardry eyebrows, gazing for a moment at Síonna, allowing his insights to swirl about her mind and sharply returns.

"Síonna, leap into this mystery whilst becoming a Creator outpouring the knowable, for here you are beyond sensation, illusion, delusion and emotion. That is why you could not summon your emotions upon your arrival."

She follows his thoughts which are now beginning to make sense. The Cosmic Juggler takes a big inhale on his dúidín and exhaling, lets out another stream of words.

"You have risen from the entangled thoughts and desires bound at the physical level of the lower Wells, whilst drinking from the consciousness of this source, connecting to the Wells of the Creator. Here, you become the knower no longer searching for all possibilities that already exist. This is the Well of the Guiding Star. Follow the signs it gives you warrior, and step fearlessly into your future. There is an insight that many sages or shamans will never unveil."

Grandfather raises his brow, curious as to what the Juggler will say.

"Béal na huamha, the mouth of the cave, my ancestors discovered it and it has also become known as Crystal Cave. It is the place that occupies our very soul, a cavern at the back of your Wonder-Eye in the centre of your head."

Her eyes light up, having never heard of such wisdom.

"If you truly enter the Crystal Cave without desire or expectation, only then will you come to know and acquire the true éigse of this world, and that of the other worlds."

She thinks of her secret cavern in the Valley of the Boars and of the great inward connections she made there. The Cosmic sage then pauses and beckons them outside.

They emerge, seeing the ocean climbing towards the other Isles that shine like castles of gold, glistening on the edge of the world.

"We have the potential to possess two states at one time. Síonna, bridge yourself with the emerald from the lower to the higher Wells. One can be aware of two lives in one time. One in this time, the other in the unseen realms witnessing from a higher plane. As you do something in this reality, and something in the space of the higher world, you create a unity of body, mind and soul that bridges the movement to your wish. These Isles are the steppingstones, Síonna. Upon each, you must step and embody the experiences while collecting a special solas for your dream, as a unique light rolls from your soul, splashing the world around you in your delightful essence!"

She is humbled beneath his praise and recalls some of the matching teachings of Grandfather, realising he has been gifting her the hidden wisdom all along.

"I see that you behold the great nine-fold shield of Dovinia and the triskele jewel of Cúroí. Síonna, you are maturing quickly and may take what you have learned here and feel that you have become to know everything, but that will only make sense by collecting the insights upon each of the others. You may try to enter the Crystal Cave but many wise men and women before you have failed to go beyond the entrance."

The Cosmic Juggler then taps her Wonder-Eye and blows trails of smoke, allowing her mind to rest.

He shares a smoke with Grandfather, catching up on the many years that have passed since they last met. They rest for a while, lying on the earth, listening to the great churn of the ocean. Síonna closes her eyes, feeling slightly overwhelmed at what has been bestowed upon her and falls into a deep sleep. She wakes to hear their approaching voices and focuses her mind as he soon begins where he left off.

"Warrior, with the mind of a creator you gain the ability to observe the world from above like the eagle and hawk of the East. But make no mistake, for if mankind only developed the higher Wells, he would become a hermit, losing his roots to the earth. Grandfather's gift in reciting riddles is opening your imagination at this level of the Soul, Síonna. The Wells remind us of what is already inherent within like the cycles of the medicine wheel. Mankind has just forgotten. We must return to know the animal wisdom, the mountain wisdom, tree wisdom, that of the elementals, of the earth, of the water, of fire and the wind and spirit and ether and the gods and of all the unseen processes that exist around us. Go now, as the gracious Goddess that you are becoming and walk bridged between this land and the ocean, between your heart and your mind."

Síonna exchanges heartfelt gratitude and compassion by just gazing timelessly into the Juggler's eyes. He then utters his final teaching,

"You will come to two paths. You must choose one and climb the ladder to the Spirit Well and come to know this path by heart."

The man of ocean mystery leaves her within the power of his words and trails back down the corbelled path. They follow his shining form over the quartz bridge. Ríonach comes sprinting, licking her lips no doubt after a feast. Zara is already perched on the bow of the sea-beetle, waiting for the next venture.

After warm embraces with the Juggler, they push the Sídóg to be carried with the same invisible force that brought them to the Isle, taking them out past the guardian pinnacles.

They ease into the rolling waves, arching their backs, allowing a wave movement to propel them forth, raising their chests in a rhythmic row as their breaths merge, leaving a subtle furrow on the abyss of the great ocean.

Síonna looks back at the Cosmic sage standing like a sparkle in the wonder of the ocean. Feeling blessed, honoured and gracious for their time and the wisdom he shared, her mind is etched with images of his magic and the otherness of his people.

Grandfather taps his lip and releases a riddle.

"A wave churns at the core of your being, guiding a tide crested of light, opening your eyes to a wonder that leaps as the knowable to the sky, sparkling the night with a moon and stars luminous as the sun. Like a racing wind, a mystical salmon leaps, colouring silver lore into the tributaries and minds of mankind, the story of a wondrous Goddess of Eriu."

She casts a smile as though all the beauty that ever existed is upon it. She watches the sacred Isle slowly dim as the veil consumes it back into the realm of the invisible.

"Let us now quest to meet with the droopy-eyed dreamy vision of an Fathac-in-a-cholaidh, 'the sleeping giant'." Grandfather suggests.

Chapter 11
An Fearr Marbh
The Root-Well

Swaying in on turbulent tides, they near his huge body submerged and mapped by spires, arches, caves and lagoons and the wondrous green sward that flowers his belly of hills and boughs. The great rock giant lies as though in sleep over the sparkling sea. They float in beneath his towering shadow as waves curve and climb his torso. Síonna searches amongst the spires and arches for his rock eyes.

"Awaken the giant," says Grandfather.

She stands in the swaying boat filling her lungs and presses her fingers onto her lips and leaves out a high-pitched whistle followed by roaring,

"Dúisigh!, Awake," her voice climbs into the dreamy evening like a wishful spear.

The winds rise as though raising her wish to the caves in his ears.

"Dúisigh!" she roars.

Like a flight of birds, her voice swiftly roams to his ears. A thunderous sound grows. The giant lets out a great snore followed by a big inhale. Síonna looks to see his huge eyes opening. He exhales, churning up a wind, sending the currents into a dance that lifts them onto the bosom of a wave. The giant rises from the deep like a great mountain. The swell dips with huge force. On the silver churned crest, they climb as though being thrown to the stars.

#

"Dúisigh be our sharing
With his silver droopy eyes
Fathac
– In-a-cholaidh, in-a-cholaidh, in-a-cholaidh."
Grandfather delivers his usual humour.
"Hold on!" he calls.

Down they fall into the depth of a wave. Swell after swell raises and plunges them into the embrace of the dark waters for several cycles before a calm settles. The giant's voice sweeps across the sound.

"Tar isteach, beautiful people."

A half-moon bends over his rocky torso. His huge eyes gaze in the droopy, dreamy state Grandfather spoke of as though one gazes into two half-eclipsed moons. A deep red light with shades of black emerges behind him as though he holds back a dawning Sun. He casts an enchanting voice like the drone of a thousand bumblebees.

"I am as old as when life began, like that ever-living, unending otherness that sings within our souls. Wisdom grows like the seeds of our great wise oak. Dreams are sown on golden tongues of those who speak the language, that of light; those who endure the long age of cultivating the Aisling. And forget not, those with the forbearance to keep alive the whispers of our ancestors. The great druids, scholáire, Ollamh, wizards and sages, Faery ones and the monks of the most westerly Isles who await your presence. Rest upon me tonight, sages, and we will share a great feast of our honey-mouths."

The sky soon turns from a sunlit sanctuary into a dome of twinkling stars that glitter down as our sages kindle fire and sit warming, in conversation with the giant who rests upright in the ocean. They gaze up into his huge moonlit crystal eyes.

"You have come from the Isle of the Cosmic Juggler and have learned of the Spirit-Wells. You may wander forth beginning at the summit with all that you have learned but let us go back down the ladder and start at the beginning. I share with you the essences of the Root-Well."

The giant takes a breath, pushing out his rock-belly where a well appears adorned with a bush na Fiúsaíos, the most abundant of flowers in Chorca Dhuibhne. The red petals flutter around them like butterflies on the wind.

"Voyage with me into the Well and waters of survival. Once, in our wanderings in the form of spirit, we sought a physical form to which we could express our living light and root our souls within. The Well of the root allows us to stand upon the earth as a human, a rock, or a tree. It glows red like that of the robin's breast or the greatest dusking sun. Our roots spin downward from the meeting of our thighs, reaching into the sod like the oak connecting us to the source of all that is feminine. This is where you will find your grounding, your stamina and sense of smell, your safety and defence, your inner-strength and true love for living."

Images of being a young child flash through Síonna's mind; running through the forests searching for her way within nature, that day when she ran from the hurt and pain of losing her grandmother and parents; and of when she hunted, imitating the animals, how they sensed to know the order of the hunt. The giants rumbling voice brings her back.

"The essence that nurtures the body and organs spins here like a spring well, gifting vitality like the two Spring-Wells at the bottom of your feet that come alive in spring. Síonna, contemplate on the Root to find clear decisiveness; remember, decisiveness to choose the path-of-happiness."

The giant leans down, winking as though knowing the choices she must endure. She smiles and he continues,

"At this Well, you must sense and stand in a balanced state as the strongest trees spread their roots to withstand fierce storms. You must feed the Magic-Wells. The Root Well desires fire. Sit before transforming flames and inhale the red glow through your hands. With your breath send it forth through your spine to finally meet with the spin of your Well between your legs. Repeat this over and over until the charge of the fire accumulates there so that you can unleash the true power of the base Well. And now, let me give you something."

He reaches, touching Síonna on the head with the tip of his rock finger. A sudden stiffness courses through her. She feels as though her blood freezes as she turns stone-like.

"A gift, brave daughter of Sengann. When the shadows of darkness loom, command this stillness. To shed it, just shout dúisigh."

She gazes into the well on his belly and begins to witness the faces of her parents reflected on the surface. Seeing herself sprinting through the forests, screaming, searching for them. Tears fall, sending concentric rings across the surface spreading the red petals.

She calls out,

"Dúisigh!"

She sheds the shape-shifting state and gives him thanksgiving.

"Great giant of these wondrous oceans, you have dutifully gifted me."

A generous smile peels back his rocky lips, revealing his white teeth shining in two rows like pillars of quartz. He returns her heartfelt words,

"Le pléisiúr, with pleasure, red hair, le pléisiúr. Remember the values and qualities of this Well going forth as your survival will depend upon it."

He gulps a big breath of air. The well upon his tummy merges back into his spires and the green sward folds over it. He lets out a huge sneeze, sending waves that climb across the sound. Zara lifts into startled flight and Ríonach scurries behind Grandfather.

"Forgive me, little ones, to sneeze clears the mind. Now let us all wander into a night of rock-dreaming, sages. Go before the first trickle of dawn so that your trail across the ocean will be lit by the first glow of the rising Sun. Contemplate on the values we have shared, Síonna. Ho."

With all he had to give her complete, the giant lies into the belly of the ocean sending a great wave rolling through the sound. The sands around him glimmer like jewels. Drops of moonlight fall upon his droopy eyes. Síonna observes him blinking from the crests of waves that curl around his nose and splash into the huge boughs of his eyes. It appears he breathes in the stars with every inhale and splashes the darkness of the sky with their light when he exhales, as he drifts into Aisling, letting out a big snore,

"Kaww, prrrrrrr, kaww, prrrrr."

Grandfather leaps onto his hands, placing his head on the sod with his legs dangling in the air, beckoning Síonna,

"See from different eyes."

She laughs at his request seeing him upturned, gazing through his bushy brows and sticking out his tongue. She kneels and propels herself up but tumbles over. She tries again and keeps her balance.

"Now, the ocean is as the sky, silken as the wondrous moon gleaming on a gobbly fox's cunning tooth. Observe and see from another perspective."

She laughs at his antics, seeing the great belly of the ocean lifting and dropping, the sky magically taking the role of the ocean, shining where the land should be.

"It is boggling observing like this. It surely dances like mermaids with ivy ears peeling veils from the Underworldly seas, mirroring our Wells upturned, spinning as stars of the sky."

Síonna turns everything upside down as Grandfather now gets to laugh at her riddle. With his head full of blood, he rolls over giggling and she falls after him.

They rest upon the heather sward before the fire as the infinite chorus of the ocean coaxes a welcomed sleep. Within Dreamtime, challenging emotions soon visit Síonna. She becomes distraught recalling the day that Sengann brought the news of the deaths of her parents and grandmother. That sense of loss and pain sears through, recalling how she ran through the woods and valleys screaming and racing from the torment that chased her. The soothing voice of the giant streams through,

"I am so old that such passages of time have passed that I do not remember who my mother and father were, Síonna. You are not alone in this world. They have not abandoned you. They watch over you like your Guiding star, remember this."

She watches a tear fall from the giant's eye in his sleep and trail down his torso like a waterfall. She feels a great comfort as though she is a baby again, been rocked by her mother in the wattle as the giant subtly sways his body in the waters, bringing her mind to a safe place. But he soon delivers the deeper teaching knowing that he has gained her trust.

"Síonna, there can be no future without a present state. It is there you will find the path-of-happiness. You must give thanksgiving to the past and let it go to envisage your future self, wearing the crown as the Goddess of Eriu. There will be a great battle between light and darkness; a Goddess would certainly need to have control over her emotions to lead an army, yes?' he asks.

She stills for a moment on his question.

"The root is a gateway to the feminine, to the Goddess, and when you disconnect from here you lose counsel with the Mother."

Tears spurt in clusters down her cheeks as she pictures herself standing like a bile oak. She feels her roots searching but they only reach the shallows of the earth. She senses the wisdom shimmering like a veil just beyond her grasp. His droning voice returns,

"When lost, and searching for the Mother, the masculine dominates. And you find solace in the hunt, in the desire for more power, for skills. Forgetting relations with all those around you, Motherless!" His roar shakes the ground. "Motherless, do you hear me? Motherless!"

She screams frantically in her dream, startling Grandfather. He leans over and shakes her. Her eyes spring open and she gasps for air with beads of sweat spreading over her brow. She sweeps it with her forearm as Grandfather ritually smudges smoke over her tormented being.

"Shush, little one, shush, you are safe in the hands of the mother owl, coo coo, coo, coo," he whispers, forcing her to smile.

His soothing words bring her racing mind back to when he held her tightly at the edge of the enclosure, that day when the shocking news reached them.

Regaining her composure, they wait for a new sun to push the stars into the light of a new day. Síonna looks up at the huge eyelids of the giant, folded over as he snores. She wishes to thank him again but chooses not to wake him. She leaves with his gift, knowing that she must follow his guidance and gain control over the lower impulses that are driving her desires. Grandfather understands she is revisiting deep wounds that must be bled slowly and quietly.

They gently push into the open sea which is mirroring the twilight sky and then they begin to row quietly from the giant asleep. After a measure of silence, he bestows on her a riddle.

"Lost in a chorus of the ocean, a seed not knowing where the abandoned roots stray like a coiled serpent that sleeps, yearning for a mother to shed the scales of trauma, uncoiling a Goddess snake to climb the Wells to the Spirit and sprout acorns of joy from a wondrous soul that will lead the tribes of Eriu with a bravery ever-boundless, never before seen."

Síonna tries to unravel the true meaning. She chuckles as her challenging thoughts are soon whisked away in the motions of labour. Gazing back, they see the giant has risen and smiles while blowing a gentle breath that gifts speed to their row. Síonna blows a kiss at him before settling into a nice easy rhythm while she quietly ruminates on what she received, recognising the obstacles of the past that she must deal with.

The giant has brought her great clarity to what needs to be shed. She thinks again of the snake that crossed their path at the beginning of the quest and how it shed the old scales of the past.

Wishing for future paths to come easy, they push towards the mystical Isle of An Tiarracht. Síonna takes one last glance back to see the giant's large droopy eyes blinking and his crystal teeth reflecting the light of the moon tinted by the red of the rising dawn. She calls aloud,

"Ho, my rock-wise friend, ho to be merry. In wondrous counsel, we will meet again. The stars will dance in the darkness and the suns of our hearts will light the forests while singing lamenting melodies beneath the wishful light of a gleaming moon."

Grandfather puffs a single stream of smoke, sending it to the sky looking at the wondrous pyramid formation of An Tiarracht beckoning to their roving eyes.

Chapter 12
An Tiarracht
Sacral-Well

"Granddaughter, within us are the processes of the ocean for we were once born with fins and wings and gills to leave crystal furrows through the tides of this life. Our blood runs with the same tributaries of these waters, containing the same light that nurtures us. Spinning our Magic Wells with the glow of the sun, moon and stars, remember whom we share this wondrous glow with is of utmost importance. As we wander to this place of power, into this pinnacle of light, be in constant change."

Ruminating on his suggestions, Síonna gazes at the rocky shape of An Tiarracht, the most northern of the Isles, standing like a pillar pointed towards the gods, submerged in the blue lagoon of the ocean like a giant's tooth. Clouds shroud the summit as though a mighty fire roars within its belly.

The orange glow of the sun crawls down the craggy spired torso to sit luminous upon the ocean wrapping around its base. A sea arch like an eye bridges the two pinnacles reminding Síonna of the quartz bridge on the Isle of the Cosmic Juggler. Grandfather pushes and pulls with great strength towards the eye. He stops rowing upon reaching the entrance allowing the swell to bring them through the passageway. They sway in as though crossing a veil between a mountain and the sea. The roaring sound clatters through the caves on either side of the rock as they dip and rise.

They begin to hear the faint trickle of a sort of enchanting melody. Síonna quietens her mind divining its location.

"The elders say that an old hag walks this rock by day and at night she transforms into the most divine deity, singing a melody of such golden, honeyed sounds that it enchants those who are lucky enough to hear it into an otherworldly state," says Grandfather, breaking her silence.

The melody grows, bouncing in and out, gaining a mystical echo. As though the beautiful sound provokes the opposite in Síonna, a sudden outburst of emotions floods her mind.

Fear and anger sharply rise. It soon surfaces. She begins to direct blame towards her parents for leaving her; towards Sengann and Aibhlin for raising her as one of theirs. A sense of shame elevates, thinking of her secret with Fionn and a certain sense of resentment towards him grows, denying her of his heart. She feels furious at herself and even Grandfather for agreeing to this senseless Quest that is bleeding wounds within her like a sharp blade.

Grandfather senses the shift and seeing the stricken worry etched on her face, uses the opportunity to reveal the values of the Sacral-Well.

"Síonna, beneath the cauldron of the belly button a Well spins majestically orange at the tailbone, said to be 'the dwelling place of the self' a place where we feel lust and desire, anger and fear from the absence of love. From here, seeds of passion can take flight to manifest the true soul-desire. A great Goddess embodying this wandering womb of light will one day take her seat and bring either a son or daughter into this world."

His teaching subtly distracts her and she searches his words trying to calm the racing currents of her thoughts. He reaches with his branch and taps her on the Wonder-Eye bringing her mind further present for his teaching

"Act with passion and contentment and you will find the beast of these fears. The aggression and longing for things that may not serve you will fade. This great pyramid-shaped rock teaches us to form our thoughts like spears and raise them, one-pointed, as it too rises from the ocean to the sky. We too must soar into the upper Wells so that we see clearly, the path of the rainbow warrior."

He winks, twisting his brow, lifting his eyebrows and sticks his tongue out into a point, evoking forced laughter from her scrunched-up face.

"The Sacral glows orange like the great sun. Command it, carry it in your womb as a great light as you wander. Emanate it from your being when darkness falls around you in a spawning ground charged with the eddies of an otherworldly pool while birthing something sacred. Again, like the Root, you feed it with the glow of the fire and that of the sun."

Grandfather pauses, allowing her to reflect as they sway on the breathing swell. To the amazement of her Wonder-Eye appears a mystical well on the surface of the water.

Her rage returns, bubbling wildly. She gazes into the well and observes her lightbody reflected on the surface. She sees her womb suddenly grow with life within it. Her form becomes surrounded by shadows that sweep at her trying to attach their sorcery. She watches her light-double battle with them trying to protect her womb of light. She feels helpless, and her shimmering image quickly fades from the surface. Without thought, she turns and unleashes her torment on Grandfather.

"What is this riddling and diddling of words and mysterious nonsense you spiel? And- and-" she stutters as rage ravages through her and the well suddenly disappears.

"What do you know of me with all your Rainbow so-called knowing?"

Her angry tone fills the archway. Her body trembles. Her face flushes. Goosebumps dot her skin. Hairs stand on her spine. Branched veins bulge on her neck and forehead. She glances back to see the well has also vanished. She realises the hurt she unconsciously cast and bows her head in shame. Tears begin dripping, hearing the voice of Breandán, Sheamuis, Pheaidi Ó Grífín.

"Ask yourself, is there hurt in my words?"

She begins to sob uncontrollably. It grows into a deafening wail.

"I know nothing in the world of knowingness, Granddaughter," his ever-calm voice soothes her hurt. "I am but a mirror of your inwardness, sailing the same ocean that can turn turbulent or calm at any moment. Remember what I said: I am an ordinary man with the ability to think outside the human side of us, that's all. I too have met obstacles, faced death and darkness where love was taken from my grasp many times."

It brings her to think of her grandmother, Grandfather's soul mate who perished that same day with her parents.

"I choose to venture and laugh, though drowned by my tears and pain I knew that I could no longer hold onto anger or resentment, nor onto non-forgiveness, for sometimes the cause of death or illness is outside of this world. This is all I know, Síonna. Death must be starved of grief, of tears, of fear, doubt and regret. But you must find your path in all of this. It is not a mere old man like me carrying a moon-silver head, walking the lit paths as a stag, waving a golden hazel branch, hopping through rivers, fishing dreams of distant scales to unfurl eyebrows wise, whilst spinning the world on a magical rainbow."

Laughter steals the tension of the moment, bringing a sense of lightness. Stretching her cheeks into a subtle smile, her teeth chitter in her frothing mouth. The tide of his humour washes away the surface of her grief, anger, fear and doubt. With a returning belief summoned that she is worthy of this prophecy, she turns whispering,

"Grandfather, please forgive me. I would never wish to hurt you. I love you, my most sacred Rainbow Head in all the worlds that ever-got-lived'd. I will stand in the battlegrounds of my most inwardness where Balor will meet my rooted stance as I create a new time of life for the tribes and lands of Eriu. You are the true embodiment of unconditional love in all its mystical rainbow sage forms."

Grandfather smiles at her attempt at riddling.
'O' you of thousand shining Suns
Granddaughter of the Moon, Sun and Stars
Another seed bestowed
Ever-flowering
Shining
Learning this wondrous light
Where the most beautid'd
Mystique sings
And awaits
For your wishing heart.'

She curls up on the bough of the Sídóg, bathing in his praising riddle that peels the strain of her heightened emotions. A sense of lightness stretches her lips and rosy cheeks and the wrinkles of worry from her forehead. She begins to see the challenges with a sense of humour as worded in his guiding verse.

Grandfather joins the tips of his fingers, forming the pointed shape of An Tiarracht and whispers,

"Join me at the-meeting-place where we bring our desires one-pointed up to the Sky-Wells and carry out a conversation of the gods."

Síonna follows his suggestion, imagining the light running around her body and meeting at the tips of her fingers. She raises her joined hands bridging the light with her mind and directing it into the sky. A great surge of energy pulses through her. She then realises the importance of the visit to the sacred Isle.

"This is the gift, Granddaughter, to bring the lower impulses upwards, climbing into one point like a stone of power such as the Lia Fáil where there is a pristine clarity."

She opens her eyes but cannot form the words she wishes to bestow on Grandfather, so blows a kiss instead, with teary eyes. He returns the gesture by silently pursing his chubby lips into a dance. They catch the pins and spin the Sídóg, guiding it out the archway while hearing the sweet melody of the unseen hag-deity return, beautifully merging with the song of the sea.

They row around the great Isle, seeing her crags and spires and caves running deep into her unknown womb. Two eagles circle her summit singing of something sacred. Sunlight streams down to illuminate the pointed peak in orange like a guiding beacon, reminding Síonna of the embodied light within the Sacral.

She folds her hands over her womb where the Well warms like a magical cauldron. She inhales the charge gathering the lower impulses of her mind and raises them one-pointed into the Wells of the Soul where they dissolve, for she now understands that one must dwell beyond the lower thoughts and desires.

Throwing their wishful eyes south to see Beginnish, the baby of the Rainbow Isles sits flat in the ocean. They look into each other's eyes and make a wish.

Chapter 13
Beginnish
Solar-Well

They row in harmonious union passing several rocks on the way before reaching the flat, flowery meadows of Beginnish. The sun sits vertically over them. Securing their sea-beetle, Grandfather crouches to four limbs and begins slithering up a sandy trail like a lizard, sticking out his tongue leaving a humorous loving light trace on the shoreline.

"Grace the lustrous green sward with a humour tickling the very thoughts of the Earth Goddess!" he shouts.

Ríonach darts by his horizontal form. Zara calls from above alerting them to see a flight of luminous birds in the formation of a V.

The mysterious flock comes forking through the sky in a rhythmic stream and land before our sages, shapeshifting from geese into humans. Brian Mac Daire and his clan greet the Goddess-to-be with a great radiance about them. Grandfather is well acquainted with the powerful wizard, having met him many times with his cousin Cúroí.

Their eyes glint warmly brown in colour. The wizard bears hair like his cousin, silver but spiky with matching eyebrows that thin and rise curling on both ends. His lips gleam a red-blue, bearing skin free of wrinkles, silken white as though ivory. His lean torso is adorned in a white robe that rests above his ankles. His voice carries a beautiful tone,

"Sages of the Fir Bolg, I see you bear the torques of my dear cousin. Come, and join us to feast."

The children meet them, each bearing braided golden hair and the same pale skin of the elders.

"Age is as though it is a ghost that has never reached these people," Síonna whispers.

"Yes, we do not grow old like the tribes of the mainland, for age is but a delusion."

Síonna is amused with him reading her thoughts.

"Because we do not see others growing old, we do not attach that image upon each other, we manifest as we wish. You too would not grow old if you did not see those around you cracking like the burned sod and stooping as though turtles, carrying the weight of the lands upon them. But when you choose to grow old, then you can transform wisely embodying the rainbow body. I will teach you later, warrior, but first, let us feast."

Cauldrons steam, spits flame with an array of fish skewed rotating. Our sages are gifted with a huge array of sea life: bairneach, periwinkles, lobster, crab, mussels and oysters evoking mouth-watering tastes they wash down with a beautiful fish bone broth. The people begin to sing and strange stringed instruments crafted of oak and beech are brought through with rounded bellies and deep holes bridged with strings that stretch and run over narrow straight lengths of wood to the heads where they are attached and wound around copper pins.

"These instruments are weaved of horsehair acquired of another world's realm, created to bring the song and rhythm of the sea to life, sounds of the white horses crashing on the crests of waves, of whales lamenting, of dolphins healing tones, the high call of orca, the shrilling pitch of oyster catchers, the high-pitched yelps of seals; and the ebb and flow of her tides as she raises her voice morning and night, bringing delightful music to all."

The music is charged. vibrant and passionate. Grandfather and Síonna join the clan in a dance around the fires, singing their wishes to the sky until darkness settles upon the youth of night. One by one, the people retreat to their huts. Our sages rest by the embers, taking in the twilight sky and listening to the sacred chorus of the ocean that eases them into sleep after an eventful day. On first light, the wizard comes and beckons Síonna to the shoreline.

"We have much to share, warrior."

She follows the sage down to a deep lagoon that shines turquoise beneath an eyebright tree. An uplifting aroma fills the air. The tree is sprouting an unusual colour of yellow blossoms.

"Usually, the eyebright is purple and white," she whispers.

The surface of the well is without a ripple. He kneels beside the pool, gazing through the surface.

"The waters act as a medium between the man and his soul. It returns the image that is untouched in purity like these yellow blossoms of eyebright. Síonna, you were brought here by the gods to explore the teachings of the third Well, the place of Jewels, where you can transform dreams into living jewels" he says, sitting up and crossing his legs on the ground.

"You have a great fire in this Well, Síonna, but do not become burned by it. This Well spins in the cave beneath your chest bone and holds the important values of courage, fearlessness, strength and the true expression of your being. The opposites are ego, pride, sorrow, shame, temper and a lack of energy to manifest your path and aspire to the greatness of what is destined for you. Remember, looking for perfection never allows perfection. The more perfection you seek in life, the less perfect everything is going to be. If you feed the fire without desire or expectation in this Well, these obstacles will disappear and your true path will be revealed."

She ponders his words, placing both hands upon her third Well. He rises, beckoning her with a silent wave. She trails up the path to where he picks up a staff of white birch and turns, commanding,

"Draw your sword. sage."

He swings it in an arc as she reaches for her blade, hitting her behind the knee of her left leg and sending her tumbling to the sod. She leaps to her feet, smiling, thinking that he is playing a game or got lucky. She glances with slight confusion at Grandfather who observes. With a wide, swift swing that arcs outside her vision, he hits her on the left side of the waist, taking her balance whilst sweeping at her right ankle bringing her to the ground once again. She quickly stands, slowly reddening in the face knowing it is no longer playing.

"Don't you have command of the blade, warrior? And many rovers spoke of your great might, where is it now? Who do you think you are beholding the ancient shield of Dovinia? Our ancestors would laugh; Eriu has no place for a woman bearing this powerful shield and a sword who thinks she can lead an army of warriors. It's an imagined Faery lore, Síonna, time to wake up."

A fire surges through her being like nothing she has ever felt. The veins in her neck and forehead bulge with fury. Never has anyone spoken to her in such a manner.

She summons the power of the earth and grips the hilt of her blade tightly not realising she fills it with the risen rage and tension, weakening her developed skills.

The wizard suddenly attacks with a flurry, she deflects but his staff finds the bough behind her knee, pulling her to crouch on the other and he spins, tapping her on the back of the head and pushes her face into the mud with the stump of the stick. Enraged, she pounces like a beast, swinging without care of the outcome. Grandfather is silent knowing the wizard has captured her at the level of emotion.

Her blade soars in familiar arcs and eights but he dives to the earth avoiding her onslaught, while neatly hitting her upon the knuckles, breaking her grasp; sending her sword into the air he swiftly grabs with his other hand. He flips onto his feet, laughing hysterically, evoking a sense of shame upon her. She glares, summoning a stampede of her anger and races forth to retrieve her blade. He flings it at her.

She quickly lunges to stab him and is taken to the ground again by the same unseen force. She leaps furiously and strikes in an arc, only to be put to the sward yet again by a swift spread of his hands as though he stretches wings before her. She stands looking at him in disbelief with tears dropping onto her blade that run to the tip and sparkle like the fire of her rage within. Just as she gathers her will to advance again, he roars,

"Enough!"

Her eyes are fixed in a silent gaze, her body droops, exhaustion and relief set in, knowing that she lost all control of her emotions.

"A Goddess would certainly have control over her emotions to lead an army," the words of the wise Ollamh come flooding back.

"Ego, pride, shame, anger and temper are just that, Síonna, emotions. But remember emotions have power," he says reading her thoughts. "You must seek victory over these lower instincts and desires and unfurl them like unwanted symbols from your mind. When you achieve this, you will become a true inheritor of that inner strength you truly behold. You must accumulate boundless energy by gifting this Well each day a source of light. Thank you for sharing and do not be hard on yourself for we have all endured challenges such as these. You are brave, daughter of the Fir Bolg, brave like nothing I have seen before. When you truly silence the emotions like the running waters, emotional intelligence and control will gift and guide you far!"

She sits upon the sod, shaking and tired from the anger and frustration. The wizard brings her waters from the well. She drinks of the essence and rests, gathering her strength. Overwhelmed, she says,

"All I saw were the furrows left by his stick and his wings darting by. And I could not summon my inner skills."

"Our consciousness receives impressions, Síonna. Shame, fear and anger arose from a place you never knew existed. All your life you received praise from your clan. I brought your energy down by casting curses upon you and finding a wound to enter at the level of the emotions. And to enrage you further you could not understand how you fell to be dominated by an old wizard with a stick. She-who's-masterly-of-the-blade made to look like a mere beginner. Anger veiled your true sight like an otherworldly skin preventing you from carrying out your skills. You already know this, but I went deeper unravelling hidden emotions held in your lower Wells."

She lies upon the sod drawing a quick succession of breaths.

The wizard unfurls a handful of goose quills that are sharpened like arrows and hands them to her. With a swift swing of his arm, he hurls the shell of a periwinkle through the air, followed by a spinning quill that pierces a hole through the back of the shell and falls sticking into the sod with the feather left standing skywards.

"Take these and practise with the swift wings of your hands, warrior of Fir Bolg, for they will serve you when needed."

She thanks the wizard repeatedly. Grandfather taps his lip and gives the people a riddle.

"Mac Daire, thank you. A memory of youth glitters in lagoons of the soul - snow-feathered dreams golden the twinkle of the eye that whisper beneath a slanting sky, formed of the ocean and spun by a silver whale's tail telling of a goose clan casting ivory-bodied spears that soar swiftly on a wind from another world's luminous egg."

His riddle peels the tiredness from her mind. Their laughter lifts the veil of tension. She stands sheathing her blade, casting an eye of thanksgiving upon the wise wizard and puts the quills into the scabbard of her sword. He places a kiss upon her forehead, whispering,

"Command the values of this the Well, the Jewels of the Sun, of fire, of the east where you will rise with clarity of emotion as a Goddess with courage. With fearlessness and a sense of self-satisfaction, stand before the fires of Balor and he will fall before your true might. May the flight of these quills be swift when called upon."

He winks and wraps her in a warm embrace. One of the elders approaches and whispers into Síonna's ear,

"Our humble wizard came from a long lineage of 'samildánach', widely known throughout the land for his fiannaíocht, service with an ancient warrior band, skills. There was an ancient magic used there, Síonna," the woman smiles.

Síonna thanks the elder, not feeling so defeated.

Grandfather comes and grasps her hand and begins joyfully skipping towards the shoreline, stopping halfway there to turn upside down on the sand and walk down backwards like two upturned beetles, much to the amusement of the tribe. They reach the Sídóg and tumble over and stand with great honour to hear Mac Daire's parting words,

"Síonna, as you journey on, carry two values forth, that of an emotionless state and courage. Be prepared for you soon enter the realm of the heart."

To part with the same humour instead of handshakes or embraces, they leap and spin mid-air and butt their bums together. The clan bend over with laughter bestowing blessings on their onward journey. They push from shore and turn into the rising mist with new gifts, venturing towards the largest of the Isles to encounter the true emerald of the ocean.

Chapter 14
Blascaod Mór
The Heart-Well

A path like the silken trail of a snail is left following the sea beetle as they make great pace. A pod of dolphins appears, looping through the water, spinning and churning crystal eddies. Ríonach stands with her two paws rested on the side, observing their play. Crashing down, they send spray over the boat before lifting out of the water and propelling themselves backwards as though tiptoeing on their tails, casting beautiful song.

Síonna looks into their eyes divining the consciousness, finding a great stillness as though they beam this unseen glow to her heart, opening the flowers within her, to give and receive.

"To do any of this work successfully, you must find forgiveness. Non-forgiveness is a limitation to be thrown away at whatever cost. Do not waste your energy on the unforgiveness of yourself or others, and do not spend time trying to get out of things that didn't exist until you created them." Grandfather's words sing to her as she bridges eyes with the mammal who spins three times in the air before diving into the depths. A voice roars from the summit of her thoughts,

"Síonna, take a leap of consciousness!"

The pod swim before them until they near the Isle where they turn towards the southern sound, leaving out a succession of high-pitched tones and disappear beneath.

White horses climb up the sides of the rocks, high mounds that are coated in several shades of green shrouded with a great blossom of flowers. Rows of stone walls bearded with lichen divide grassy meadows that slope to the headland. The land is dotted with grazing livestock and the midday sun falls on the glittering sands of the shoreline of Trá Bán.

The Isle gives home to a large colony of seals that beach on the warm sands like a tribe of gatekeepers. Some dart through the waters to meet our sages' approach. They pop their heads above the surface, gazing through curious, human-like glinting eyes before racing with great speed through the clear waters.

Grandfather steers the Sídóg through a góilín to be met by a group of oileánaigh.

"Tar isteach an oileán draíochtúil," come into the magical Island, an elder woman says. "Our scholáire have been waiting and have much to teach you. Words will flutter on this sacred rock like cotton spindles, swivelling on a summer's wind and when you leave, your mouths will spin a new silken tongue."

Síonna admires the elder's similar red hair, her blue eyes luminous like the clear bay. The women and young girls' long tunics are woven with great patterns, their locks and braids and buns like golden nests upon their heads. She looks to the boys donned in furs of wolf and rabbit and hides with torques and knives fixed on their arms and waists that glitter beneath the warming sun.

Our sages follow the tribe up an ascending trail emerging from a bough to see a cluster of dwellings spread upon the green pasture in a circle within a hollow of rolling hills.

Stone roundhouses with thatched roofs are surrounded by an outer circle of clochán. They see Scholáire writing, painting and reciting from scriptures. Others are teaching children how to craft 'Súgán' a rope made from golden straw put through a twisting implement that binds it tightly into beautiful strands used for chairs, bedding and other purposes. Children run about chasing dogs and cats and more puck balls with sticks of furze.

Women are making butter, salting fish, smoking meat and weaving clothes amongst other chores. Druids are going about their daily routines, bringing water from the wells, fish from the shoreline, tending crops, sprinkling bluestone on potato stalks and seeding newly-ploughed earth for another harvest with the help of seaweeds laid over the sod. More are gathered in pins, harvesting and cutting the sheeps' woollen coats.

Tall and strong, the men bear sinewy necks with hands almost the width of pikes, gaining such strength from daily rowing, pitting their limbs against the strong currents of the Blascaod sound, ploughing and digging the lands, sowing crops, harvesting and drawing hay and turf.

The elder brings our sages to a clochán in the centre enclosed by a grove of trees, whilst announcing the name of each one.

"Yew, birch, rowan, alder, willow, ash, hawthorn, black thorn, elder, pine, gorse, heather and aspen."

They look in the window of a half-door to see a blazing fire stretching its glow over the corbelled walls and floor, revealing a scholáire sitting at a table with scriptures laid out around him. He gets up and opens the bottom half and ushers hens, dogs and two lambs out before welcoming them.

"Ag bothántaíocht, tar isteach," visiting, come in, he invites them in with the ancient tongue.

Long silver hair falls over his shoulders, blending into a bushy beard that hangs to his waist. His eyes are as green as the land, looking as though he has at least a hundred years endured on his head. His skin is brown and cracked, beaten from the life of the oileánach, Islander, who endure hot summers and long cold wind-beaten winters.

His eyes glisten from the embers of his dúidín; he puffs several times sending smoke around his jolly face.

"Sit with me and warm the hearth, sages. I am Ogmu, Rí na tOileán mór, King of the big Island, an Rí na Rí, the King of Kings."

The wind howls down the chimney. A smell of damp peat hooks their nostrils as he gathers scriptures and piles them into a heap whilst turning with an eager quickness, gazing owl-eyed at Síonna and whispers,

"Warrior with the hair of the gods, allow me to take you into the magic of the emerald Well, the spioradálta bridge of all the Wells. These spheres spin telling us of the position in our lives where and how we stand upon the earth, balanced or unbalanced just like our medicine wheels of stone. Through these, we can read the cycles of the sun and moon, the winds, the ocean, the earth, the mountains and the stars. A great Guiding Star is leading you, Síonna."

He puffs, spreading a scroll upon the table revealing a map.

"An Léarscáil de na úscraí, the map of Essences. Upon it, you see the drawing of our wise ancestor, Ogma, who first revealed the Magic of the Wells to us. He began to see with the Wonder-Eye the colours and how they spin. He studied them until he could unveil their values and teachings."

The elder places his finger at the Root-Well on the picture and runs it up the image, calling out each colour.

"Red, orange, yellow, green, azure, blue and indigo; as you know these same colours make up the magical bands of the rainbow and above the sage's head, you see the two spheres, golden and white. Now follow the seven layers stretching outside his form that look like the coloured shell of an egg around him. Our ancestors unravelled the great mysteries through embodying the values of these spheres we now know as magic. The shamans have handed this scripture down through time teaching us of the findings of this wise sage. My dear Goddess-to-be, know that there is always one Well that leads the others. For you, I believe it is that of the heart. The very emerald that this Isle represents."

A tint of red floods her cheeks.

"To truly open this Well you must first love yourself and then your enemy and by doing so, you will destroy the enemy within him."

His powerful words echo within her mind as she sweeps her gaze up and down the spheres painted on the map. He continues,

"Before movement, there is thought and then shape! Know these Wells at the most inwardly level and you will come to know your true self. Like the stars that glitter in the sky, the sod holds crystals of light left by the ancient trod of our ancestors keeping their movements, memories, wishes, tasks and aligned actions embedded in the places of power scattered across Eriu."

He takes a big puff and points to the map, sweeping up from the Root up to the Well of the Heart where he explains,

"Climb this ancient ladder, Síonna, and bridge here through the emerald of the heart, the physical to the spioradálta. To see the signs, enter your heart, wish deeply and divine and all will be revealed. A mysterious quest has brought you over these trails trod by the sages of old. You too will leave footprints for those that will follow your way. On this voyage, most importantly, you must seek a position from where you will not stray from the-path-of-happiness, staying on the-path-of-the-heart."

The elder holds out his palm revealing a sparkling rose quartz. He swings the half door back and walks outside, kneeling to the sod where he sweeps the crystal over a cluster of Bliúcán and with his other hand, he draws the subtle light trace from the white umbels of the flowers into the crystal, saying,

"Use this crystal to collect the essence of nádúr, nature. Set your intention and form a wish, then feel where the crystal leads you to the light that you need, whatever that may be, a rock, a plant, an animal, a human, a ruin or a place of power. And in the same manner that you feed the other Wells, stand and pour this 'special light of the dream' into the crystal. Through this light, understand your unique being and when the moment comes, you will know what to do with all the light that you have collected."

Síonna gazes into his green eyes to witness a quartz-tipped spear soaring through the air. He blinks, stopping the image and leans over, whispering to her ear,

"Do well with this secret! There are three steps of collecting light, Síonna. Receive and process it for your wish and it will accelerate the fulfilment of that wish. Secondly, receive and process it for others, gifting healing. And the final step, receive and process it for the light for the greater good of all living beings."

He winks giving his silent signal that his work is done. He takes a quick succession of puffs on his dúidín, allowing the smoke to curl around him and closes his eyes. The elder who welcomed them to the Isle comes and ushers them to follow. Síonna bestows blessings upon his silent form and leaves, carrying the wonderment of his teachings.

"Fill the bottom of the Well where the sun reaches, shining!" he calls out from his ruminating state.

Síonna acknowledges with a gracious smile and raises her sword skyward, so the sun spears forth from the mirror of her blade.

The children and their dogs come to accompany our sages around the circular paths. Little lambs leap about the meadows and the ocean swell rises and falls like their working breaths. Calmed and silent in a placement of loving footprints, they gift a trail of prayer around this sacred land. Druids are out tending the crops, piking seaweed into furrows, spread and cut with sickles and then layered upon potatoes and vegetables. Great rows of yellow silken corn colour the sod.

Cows and bulls graze on the grassy sward. Donkeys are being worked, bringing seaweeds and baskets of fish back and forth from the shoreline. Rabbits sprint the sloping hills disappearing into burrows. They reach Sliabh an Dúna where another cluster of beehive dwellings sits over green, south-slanting fields. Women and men are salting porpoise and other fish. others are bringing turf from the headland and stacking it into cnuchairí, heap of footed turf.

To the most westerly point of Ceann Dubh, they ramble and come to the narrow sound separating an Blascaod Mór from the Isle of the Na Sí. They continue and reach the shoreline of shingle at Trá Bán where the seals are beached beneath the midday sun. They gaze across to Cuas Buí, yellow inlet, in Cloighear seeing the white horses leaping through the air, crashing off huge basalt rocks; how the waves climb her sloping shoreline only to be sucked beneath her golden sands before meeting the next gushing onslaught. Further west, they see the sloping hills of Dún Chaoin being bathed in spray.

They follow the distant edge of the horizon southwest to see the mysterious twinned Isles of Scealga. A pungent sharp smell hooks their nostrils bringing them back to observe the seals; some are resting, more are propelling their blubber bodies with wave movements where a fight for dominance begins.

Bulls snarl at each other and face off, barking before meeting and wrestling and biting, until one surrenders. A mating ritual unfolds as male and female wrestle and roll, subtly biting until they bow and merge into a silent act of love. White pups bond with their mothers, rolling over each other on the soft sands. What joy our sages receive witnessing the play of the colony, hearing their ghostly calls shrilling like baby lambs or women keening over a mortally wounded warrior.

Our sages complete the circle and return to the Oileánaigh, Islanders, in the bough of the humble hills where a great fest is been prepared. A lamenting sound of happiness pours forth. Butterflies and dragonflies flutter by. The children are leaping around, the older ones are playing bataireacht. More are playing hurling, hitting the ball with sticks of ash. Others are singing, reciting poetry or helping the women bring fish, crab, limpets and winkles ashore. A smell of roasting rabbit trails the air. Fish of all sorts are boiling with vegetable broths on roaring fires. Crabs are laid upon hot ashes sizzling slowly.

Animals roam in and out of the houses. Each roundhouse sleeps cows, sheep, pigs, dogs, hens and whatever comes in through the bottom of the half-doors at night. Síonna admires the craftsmanship of the thick stone walls bound with clay, how the thatched rushes and reeds are tightly woven, seeing cnuchairí stacked against the eastern gables.

She is amused watching the young boys climbing the roofs and slowly reaching their hands into the thatch searching for the warm or cold touch of an eggshell where the hens lay. A few young lads beckon her down to the shoreline where men are hammering working rhythms, making boats from hollowed tree trunks. Women are weaving hazel for baskets they call 'ciseán' used for lobster and crab.

The boys whisk their hides off and dive into the deep crystal waters of the inlet. Síonna watches the white of their skin trailing deep shimmering as the water bends their forms before they disappear into the depth and re-emerge, darting to the surface holding crabs.

"Come, Síonna, try it!"

With excitement, she flings her yellow brat on the rocks and leaps into the cool turquoise waters and swims beneath to see, with slightly blurred vision at first, until her sight adapts and she sees caves on either side of the rocks.

She enters one, searching in the dark with her hands and finds the hard shell of a crab. She kicks her feet floating to the surface, displaying her first catch with pride.

"O' you have it, it is a 'Collach', a female crab, Síonna. The male is called a 'fuaisceán'. Go down again and try to get a male," says Seáinín.

A sharp inhale and she dives further, reaching a bigger cave. Her eyes adjust more, seeing clearer. With two hands clutching crabs, one female and one male, she returns leaping from the water, trembling from the cold and navigating her hands to a position upon the crabs where they can't latch onto her fingers.

"A Fuaisceán, boys, I hav' it, ho!" she calls, holding up her proud display with a gracious smile.

An hoileánaigh seem to hold no sense of cold as they make several dives, waving their feet propelling them through the deep swell like the dolphin. pitting their wills against the freezing waters. A daily routine as much as the ocean allows them.

"You have done well, Síonna. Wisha, it is of ease to you. Great fun, isn't it?"

"It is most joyful, lads, thank you for sharing with me," she sputters, in a trembling voice, her body shaking from the cool waters.

She pulls her brat on with speed and looks at the boys, at the innocent delight spread over their youthful faces and learns a great teaching: to look at the world through eyes so afresh!

"And now for a trick of hunting, Síonna," says one of the boys.

He pulls a ferret from inside his jacket and they approach rabbit burrows in the slopes. He puts the ferret into a hole and stands silent, waiting. An unsuspecting rabbit leaps from a connecting hole into the grasping hands of one of the boys.

"Amhain eile, another one, for the fest lads. Yerra, sure it's no task to find them upon laethanta breátha, fine days."

"I am impressed at your skill, or should I say the skill of the ferret," she answers, smiling whilst winking.

Seáinín whispers into her ear,

"Next time you visit, we will bring you to the secret scairt. Only a few dare to venture to the dark cave but we will take you, Síonna."

"Seáinín, one day I will return here and bring you back the trails we wandered to see the Valley of the Stags."

A swirling wind brings with it mouth-watering smells of the fest. They arrive at the bough alive with movement. Elders and children are sitting around Grandfather, listening to the lore of his many teachings as a Leigheasóir.

A great fest is had beneath a red, mackerel-clouded sky. Grandfather brings their minds sweeping over his colourful ventures. Fish broths juice their mouths fused with an array of vegetables and herbs. Water made from Limpets and soft Carrageen boiled in freshly squeezed milk from their cows, wash down their salty thirst. The crab meat melts on their tongues, sweet and soft from the roasting ash. Song and music follow; melodies and beautiful voices fill the bough. The tribe honour the earth with a dance.

Síonna and Grandfather join heartily, stepping with prayer upon the hearth of the Isle. They send the pulse and light of their souls before them while feeling the joy of past hoileánaigh and hearing the whispers of their ghostly tongue. Síonna feels a sudden heaviness within her chest. Her mind wanders back to the Valley of the Stags seeing Fionn. The yearning returns before a huge wave crashes on the rocks below bringing her back.

"Sa cruthaitheach damhsa, agus ag canadh sa teanga dhúcais, creative dancing and singing in the mother tongue" says one of the young lads as they leap around her yelping and singing.

She sees an elder with high, rounded cheekbones, emerge from a beehive bearing a slanted hat with side-locks of black hair. His earthy face arrests her. Like all the elders, he puffs on a dúidín carved of clay. Smoke trails each side of his smiley face as he approaches.

"I am Tomás, an oileánach."

Síonna gazes into the glint of his eyes. The left one is misted with a growing of a hazy-like skin. The right one sparkles with clarity. He sweeps a swirl of smoke over her head and beckons her to follow him.

He takes her to a well. Ivy curls around the stone wall that is bearded with a heavy coat of moss.

"Sage, you stand on the Oileán of the Heart-Well. Within the pulse is where you will find your freedom and power. The heart is the most wondrous," he says and places his hand upon her chest. "When you climb the inner ladder of your spine, sit within this Well and find all love. It holds the wind that drives your lungs, that circulates your blood giving you a sense of the pulse of others. Heal the wound in the cuisle do croidhe and emerge unbound. Here, seek out an answer for your indecision and command your responsibility. Lastly, attain emotional control and learn to understand what it is you truly desire."

Silence hangs as she gazes into the deep of the well, wondering how he knew about the wound in her hand. She begins to sense a sudden burning sensation in her chest. Fionn's eyes appear on the surface. The yearning, lonesomeness and secrecy arise as she contemplates how she is withholding her secret from the clan. The sense of not being worthy tares at her spirit. Her tears drop to the surface.

She lifts her gaze to see the elder's eyelids lit orange by the sun as the wind subtly shifts his hair. He stretches his arms skywards and yawns, opening his eyes wide upon her.

"You carry wounds, daughter of Sengann, that only the opening of the heart can heal."

He takes her two hands, placing his fingertips on the inner side of her wrists where the pulse sings.

"Close your eyes."

She senses his pulse trickling from his fingertips, merging with her bodily beats. It travels throughout her to all places of the pulse until a thunderous pulsation rises heavily extending beyond her body.

"You are now in true rhythm with the heart of this Isle, Síonna. When you journey onwards bridging the Wells by way of this inner emerald, awaken the sleeping serpent, shedding the lower desires and rise pulsing to the sky like a winged Goddess."

Gratitude-filled tears light up her eyes.

"With great passion, I will practise this ancient teaching of the emerald bridge," she says, wiping her tears with her sleeve.

They share a wondrous smile. She gazes into his hazy eye as he lays his hand upon her head saying:

"With the truth of the heart - siúl ar an tír dhúchais, walk the mother country."

With the task complete, he walks with Síonna back to the hearth of the Isle.

Grandfather stands before the Oileánaigh giving a farewell wisdom.

"Make a wish, sacred people. Let us bend the world to where we wish it to be."

They follow his suggestion.

"Now, witness," Grandfather says taking a stick of hazel and bending it into a loop and thrusts it into flight.

Zara follows it, circling the dwellings like a magical bee summoning new events for their tasks. He walks to the centre and raises his hand catching it.

"As your wishes. What goes out will truly come back blessed, ho."

Awed, they shower him with praise and then walk in silent contemplation to the shoreline. The women sprinkle waters of the wells onto their sea beetle, blessing the future path. To the four directions, earth and sky, everyone turns, completing the ritual. Our sages leave knowing that they have encountered a people that they may never see the likes of again. Tears well up as they feel they have truly touched the sacred.

The same elder who welcomed them sends them into the mouth of the ocean with a blessing in the ancient tongue.

"Na titfedh an t'anam asat - that you may not lose your soul."

Grandfather rings his bell three times, honouring the hoileánaigh.'Ogmu and Tomás stand puffing, blowing loops of smoke to the wind-whisperers. Each sweeping the wish with their pipe-hand and with the other held upon their hearts.

Síonna smiles and whispers,

"I will pray through the emerald of my heart a great healing."

Tears of happiness run the crest of her cheekbone. They look upon the far-sighted people and drive into the open embrace of the sea.

"Granddaughter, not many nobles get the honour to experience this kind. We who bravely walk the passage of the sage, shaman, and warrior are granted such privilege."

Síonna, too, honours the encounter with a dán.
'As the sun reclines
And night curls into day
A new dawn beckons
To bathe the senses
Of all whom we encounter
With an emerald tongue.'

Grandfather claps his hand, rotating his eyebrows in quick succession.

"Bravo, bravo, such a wondrous, honeyed tongue unfurling landscapes that leap like the butterfly scaling a serpent who rises, uncoiling, climbing otherworldly stairs rising deep within a luminous belly to face a danger path."

She wanders the words of his riddle, trying to unravel the meaning behind "the danger path". The string of words keeps her fully engaged as they turn their sea-beetle towards the Isle of the Na Sí.

Chapter 15
Port Na B-Pucai
Cauldron of Impressions
Wonder-Eye

Their heads are bowed rowing into the rumbling tide. An undercurrent tests their strength and will. Enduring a long passage, they finally near the mystical rock and Ríonach throws her nose to the sky sniffing, whilst Zara takes flight for a heightened view. Grandfather whispers,

"Éist, hidden riddles swirl to the ears of elves in worldly listening realms who churn a melodious sea thrashing of waves to curl her tidal fingers upon a golden shoreline."

Grandfather guides them in puffing out his mysterious words. Ríonach darts from the boat, always first to tread a new land. She races up a meadow path. The faint echo of a distant fox bark rings out.

"Curious little belly, keep safe," he whispers.

Zara spears after the vixen. Fastening their beetle to a boulder, our sages follow up the earthen path.

Meadows of great beauty stretch before them, rabbits, birds and bees and with butterflies fluttering through the sky. No sooner have their feet touched the earth, when a rainbow arcs to the ground. From the magical bands steps the Faery King with a band of his Na Sí. Accompanying and towering above the Faery is a pack of yellow-eyed wolfhounds. Síonna feels a huge shift of presence. Despite their size, the little ones emanate powerful energy.

"Masters of the veils at your command. I am Fawnóg and you are most welcome as the Sun God moves over this Isle into the second cycle of this sacred day," says the little King, stepping forth enclosed in a blue glow and holding a staff dotted with shining emeralds.

A great bushy hair, fire red like Síonna's, adorns his head. He gazes from bright blue eyes crowned with curling red eyebrows.

Síonna admires his tiny hands and little fingers that curl around the staff, his thick forearms wrapped with two leather armlets, his rose-red puffy cheeks that sit over his twisty beard that swirls into a point bound with nine golden torques that hang to his chest. A weasel skin, dyed with the colours of the rainbow adorns his torso. She chuckles at the cuteness of his little shoes of hide tied with golden strings.

She looks closer into his eyes, seeing one is blue and the other green.

"Sages, we the ancient Faery are older than the inner rings of the biggest oaks in these lands. Your feet are no longer a mystery to our sweet meadows. Welcome and enter this dreamy kingdom."

The mysterious King throws bells of foxglove and petals of na Fiúsaíos into the winds, reciting a diaga dán, divine offering.

'Veils of the faery
Rainbow aglow
The ancient winds I know
Swirly whirly, wonder flower-earth
Wandering we go
To burrows beyond
Where golden meadows
Shroud the jewel of the soul.'

The most magical bridge made up of the bands of the rainbow appears.

"Enter, sages, for those noble can cross this ancient Bridge. Those who attempt and are not worthy will sink into the muds of the Underworld and never be seen again."

Walking through the rings, their senses are bathed in colour watching Zara disappear before them. Ríonach trails behind wary of the huge wolfhounds.

They emerge to golden meadows that stretch to distant horizons. Roaming valleys are dappled with flowers, sun-yellow with furze that sprinkle forth meeting the blue of a magnificent ocean. Birds sing a wondrous chorus. Sweet scents sweep to their nostrils.

Faery ones are pushing little barrows of flower petals and churning golden honey of huge cauldrons that steam over fires while they cast herbs and potions singing incantations. Elves roam, clad in coloured skins bearing pointy ears and large eyes. Spiral symbols painted with pollen decorate their tiny foreheads. Each is going about chores, sowing the land, furrowing the rich black earth. Donkeys and horses ease their labour, bringing heaps of seaweed and shellfish from the ocean.

Young faery and elves eyes are lit with such a living thing as they learn from scriptures, casting words of power to the winds to acquire the three sacred branches of the Bard, Ovate and Ollamh.

While ushering hens and ducks aside, our sages admire the snugness of their dwellings hidden in boughs of oak.

"A busy colourful world of little gobbly ones," says Grandfather, puffing on his dúidín which he shares with the little King.

It doesn't take him long before he has Faery bent over in laughter. A clucking cock chases Ríonach around the enclosure. Zara soon darts through the skies with the winged species of the land.

"Come and taste this," Fawnóg beckons them to a steaming cauldron full to the brim with a dark brown syrup.

He dips a wooden spoon in and hands it to Síonna. Knowing it will most likely be sweet, she gobbles it. Her mouth comes alive. Her eyes open owl-eyed. It swirls around her tongue enlivening her taste buds with a strong honey-flowered fusion and swivels down her throat to sit warming her breast like the potent Poitín of Toose.

The Faery King takes a sup. He licks his lips and lets out a big, jolly sigh with sparkling eyes. Síonna laughs, seeing it dripping from the torques on his beard. Grandfather follows with a scoop.

"Ahhhhhh, gulp, gobbly, uhhhh," he lets out a big burp to the laughter of all while licking drops of the syrup off the sides of his moustache.

"The nectars and flowers of this world and other worlds are churned here for our Faery love potions, courting spells and for whatever desires we want to manifest. We can use the same nectar for a task applied in battle by infusing it with a poisonous flower and singing a Faery Áer. Síonna, now let us delve into all that is spioradálta."

Fawnóg sits on the green sward crossing his legs, ushering our sages to take the sacred position on the earth beside him. They follow, folding their legs. The wolfhounds form a protective circle around them. The little King takes out his clay dúidín and puffs wildly before revealing more magic.

"Let us venture into the two Wells that command the sense of taste, sound and sight, those of the Throat and Wonder-Eye. You have just experienced all that is wondrous of taste in the Well known as the Cauldron of Magical Powers, also known as purity. Keep that honeyed tongue pure and sweet, Síonna. And now to sound. The throat Well controls the temperature of the body. Adorned with such fiery red hair and rising emotions, control is something you will need to practise daughter of Sengann," he says, twirling his hand around the nine torques of his beard taking several puffs, to continue,

"Here we manifest our dreams and creativity and gain control over our fears of speaking out the truth."

His jolly look soon turns sour as he throws a glare, darting at her like a spear with his eyes. She feels uncomfortable trying to hold his gaze knowing he is referring to her love secret she withholds and she lowers her eyes breaking contact.

"Do not let your fantasies spill into other worlds, you know nothing about. Take control of your sleep for this is where you build your power," he pauses, glancing around the meadows at the work of his clan.

She knows he is reading her every inner working, the secrets, her nightmares over the loss of her loved ones, her yearnings and desires and knows that it is just for this that she is here and must offer up these lower impulses if she is to truly embody the values of the Wells.

"Sit in this luminous Well and you can summon the skill of invisibility and speak without words, acquiring mastery in whatever path you choose. And most importantly, this Well gifts voice to all the values of the heart to where you honour the insights with sound and give your unique voice to the world around you."

The King throws another fistful of petals into the air and waves his staff. In the blink of a Faery eye, a cauldron sits before them steaming of another golden syrup but lighter in colour.

"Now we will enter the Sky-Well of the Wonder-Eye, the cauldron of the eyes," he says, scooping a spoonful of the syrup and handing it to Síonna.

She drinks of the brew. It's just as sweet and potent as the first potion. A lightness falls over her brow. A flashing of lights, like lightning beings, grow within her Wonder-Eye, darting back and forth through her mind. Grandfather too drinks of the brew and closes his eyes, enjoying the induced state. The little King smiles and words more wisdom-sharing.

"Síonna, now see the divine. The Sky-Wells are supported by the Earth-Wells just as the trees are supported by their roots. You have seen the map of your ancestor. The Wonder-Eye is the cauldron of unlimited power. Síonna, the power of the lightning beings you now see within is also outside. Through this Well, you must learn to shed everything that is bodily. Gain control over your doubts and fears to know you will one day acquire the éigse."

He curls his lips, scrunching his face, lifting the dúidín in his mouth while peering at her, knowing what is enchanting her. Her stomach churns. Her fears intensify. Anger surfaces. She wants to hit out at the Faery as she did at Grandfather beneath An Tiarracht as the King is unveiling the same desires and emotions, but she grips the urge with a sharp inhale and exhales, releasing the tension. As though he senses her intention, he cuts the moment with a commanding tone,

"You must shed the robes of the past and grow feathers to fly into the shamanic realms where you can manifest your true soul desires."

She is enthralled with the teaching, understanding the obstacles she must overcome and promises to put into practise the suggestions of the Faery King.

"My final honeyed words on this matter, red hair warrior. As you go forth discovering the true insights, remember if you truly embody the values of each Well you too will become a master of mighty magic."

Síonna swears blessings upon the King. He returns her gesture by showering her in the golden petals of gorse he manifests with a swipe of his hand. He swings his manifesting staff in an arc and our sages suddenly find themselves rolling at great speed through a rabbit's burrow to emerge into a cavern-like hollow underground.

The cavern is lit with the flames of a roaring fire. A band of warrior-looking Faery and elves are standing in a green ráth, earthen ring-fort. They part for their King and guests. Síonna admires their large eyes sparkling like solar gods of the skies. Each of them bears the same rainbow hide as the King with similar leather armlets and pointy ears with white eyebrows. Speckles of golden pollen adorn their Wonder-Eyes. They peer mystically through long flickering eyelashes. Long strands of white braided hair rest on their silken shiny skin.

"Such pretty little beings," she whispers.

They stand with bows and swords in their hands and bags of arrows strung upon their backs. Tiny torques glitter on their arms. Great smiles peel back their little bubble cheeks.

"Meet the Nángod, skilled samildánach of the elve," says Fawnóg.

A boyish-looking skinny elve steps forward pushing out his chest, trying to enlarge his presence and utters in a high-pitched voice,

"Gandal at your elvish service."

"It means 'gander' in the ancient tongue. He acquired the name from chuckling like a funny bird when playing his trickery pranks on others. Be aware when Gandal is near," says the King, throwing a jolly eye at his comrade.

The stringy-looking elve quickly tries to redeem his status.

"Take out your rose quartz, warrior."

Síonna is surprised that he knows she beholds the jewel and takes it from her brat and holds it in her palm. The elve pours a golden nectar upon it and beckons her to stoop. With his tiny finger, he paints a spiral with the same nectar syrup upon her Wonder-Eye saying,

"Golden be your spearful eyes in a magical flight that soar on winds to meet the roaming eye of the Underworld."

Feeling blessed, she looks down to see the crystal mysteriously gone from her hand. He smiles displaying it sitting upon his head. He flips backwards and catches it mid-air and lands on his feet while placing it on his shoulder. He rolls it down his long bony arm into his palm where he flips it back into Síonna's hand, winking. Then with his tiny fingers, he reaches into each of her Wells circling his hand, spinning each of her inner cauldrons.

"Wells aglow will now flow of elvish magic as you carry your secret through many worldly veils," Gandal says with a big smile parting his bubbly cheeks.

"Our pointy-eared one does have magic, I will give him that, but always the joker. And as though he wasn't enough to handle in this elvish wonder world, you have yet to meet the other gander of the elves, Uaisle. Also known as 'nobbly'," says Fawnóg.

The mighty one comes pacing, bearing two sticks on his back. Wrapped in a brown hide with matching armlets on both wrists and arms that bulge with muscle like the rest of his little torso, he comes bearing his famous little potbelly.

Uaisle is much taller and fiercer looking than the rest, hence the tales of his mighty battle skills, a master of wrestling, always eager to test his might. A sun-orange, bushy beard rests over a stumpy chest with matching hair that is wrapped and braided in leather strings that hang each side of his thick neck. He bears a big nose and wide lips with chunky white teeth and a large tongue that hisses when he speaks and struggles with words beginning with the letter 'S'.

Uaisle fastens his little hands around Síonna's finger and lays three kisses on her knuckles before turning and grasping Grandfather's hand with great strength and says,

"S, s, s, s-ages, welcome. A mighty task we will s, s, share to fell the armies of the Underworld."

He winks at Síonna and squats down in the centre of the ráth opening his hands calling a test of her skills.

"Yes, wrestling is his joy, warrior of Sengann. Show your worth," says Fawnóg.

"Cheeky one, isn't he?" replies Uaisle.

Síonna lunges deep. His eyes are fixed seeking the first motion of her play. He licks his big lips and curls his tongue, making the hissing sound. It is said he uses the sound as a tracking sense he sends out around him.

She waits, giving nothing away, remaining still. Eventually, her patience works having heard that Uaisle is known for his quick temper. He lunges forward interlocking his arms around her arm and bends his knees to lift her from the sod. Síonna, knowing the process relaxes leaving all her weight returning the tension into his hands while rooting into the earth. The more he lifts, the heavier she gets. His frustration grows; veins bulge on either side of his forehead.

Gandal and the others giggle. It annoys Uaisle further. He puts everything into the last effort, hissing wildly. Síonna rises, giving him a false sense that he is lifting her and invokes the gift of the jolly giant, turning as heavy as stone as he tries to throw her. She falls upon him as he crashes to the ground calling out,

"Duisigh."

He shakes his dizzy head knowing no warrior in any kingdom has defeated him in wrestling. He rises dumbfounded.

"Uaisle, know that emptiness is the state that will gain you victory." She wraps her hands around his torso, squeezing with all her might. "Feel this tension. As I exert more, empty your body with your breath and accept it on the inhale. Allow it to pour into you like liquid and down into the earth, and now as you exhale bend your knees and summon this power back up from the earth through your body and give it back to me in a wave."

Sionna grips him wildly. He sharply inhales accepting and allows her power to flow through him, and then exhales dropping more relaxed than he has ever been, and pours the power like water back into her, sending her to the ground.

"It works, it works. I will defeat every being in every land known, with this skill added to my almighty strength." He twirls in joyful leaps. "It works. The Goddess has great magic."

He takes her hand and kisses it three times.

"Nobbly, nobbly, nobbly," Gandal mischievously shouts, provoking him.

Reddening in the face, Uaisle chases him hissing wildly and grabs him and flings him into the air in a temper. Gandal flips and lands on his feet sticking out his tongue and then turns pushing his bum out calling again.

"Nobbly, nobbly can't catch s-s-s-super Gandal."

Síonna and Grandfather are in hysterics watching the antics of the trickster.

"Never a serious moment when the great Gandal is about," says the little King.

Our sages enjoy the games. Other elves step into the ráth to test the new skill of Uaisle. He demonstrates Síonna's gift with great ease taking victory after victory.

"Sages, let us now return," the King says, swinging his staff and they swirl up the rabbit burrow back into the golden meadows of the Na Sí. The sun soon warms their skin.

"Allow me to give my final gift. Sages, the veils are growing thin. The Darkelve are burrowing through the earth in armies. The lunar light of the sorcerer will blaze across Eriu. Síonna, you must find your strength through forgiveness. Both the throat and the Wonder-Eye contain the values of compassion and the flowers of the heart. With 'the Cauldrons of Impressions' you will hear your inner voice gifting you to see the sign so that you can choose to walk different paths, the correct path; those of a leader not open to others."

He cups a little forked branch of holly with three red berries from a tree he makes manifest and whispers,

"The sorcerers will provoke you at the level of emotion just as Brian Mac Daire did. You must take heed and gather control over the running waters of the mind."

He hands Síonna the holly which she pins to her brat and gives more teachings.

"Cast forth your spear and sword with destiny carrying your force for the will of your men will be duly tested by a darkness so strong they have never felt. Look not at his substance but feel the essence within you, no matter what form stands before you. Remember, the soul teaches the body to feel, to see and to know it by heart."

The Faery then sweeps his staff in an arc and our sages find themselves beyond the golden meadows at the edge of the ocean where a river pours into its mouth. There to greet them is Uaisle and Gandal.

"We assemble at the meeting place of the waters where the river gives its body back to the ocean. I chose this location just for that purpose for the passing of this final teaching," says the little King.

The others wait for his signal. Gandal being the trickster that he is pulls Uaisle from behind at the right shoulder and left of his hip sending him backwards into the water. He springs to his feet, his hide wet like an otter about to grapple with his elve brother only to be halted by Fawnóg.

"Enough, little ones. We have an important task to complete here."

Síonna ruminates on what is to occur. The King ushers everyone into the water where he follows, giving the structure and order of his teaching. He conjures up another voice that is husky and warm in tone,

"Cross your legs, Síonna. You may have wondered why we didn't reveal the lands well to you like the rest. The ocean is our well, the very source of all wells where you will learn of your gift."

Everyone takes a position supporting her in the water. They gather around Síonna who eases herself into the spioradálta position bathing her being in the water. Grandfather and Uaisle stand at her back as Fawnóg and Gandal take the front.

"Now all together, lift."

They raise her so that she is suspended on the surface crosslegged.

"Now close your eyes, Síonna, and follow my count to nine, going deeper with each command. One, feel the sense of lightness enter your feet as though two suns grow within your Well-Springs. Pull them up through your legs into your torso to the red glow of the Root where they become one. Two, with your breath, pull the sun into the Dwelling Place of the Self. Three, swirl it around your Sacral feeling it climb towards the emerald. Four, see the green glow expand out as you exhale enclosing your floating form. Five, direct the glow up into your throat spinning the Well of Magical Powers. Six, command this blessed light into your Wonder-Eye and enter the entrance of the Crystal Cave of your mind. Seven, see the white light of this cavern outpour, flooding every crevasse of your being, merging with the light of the ocean and glowing upon your Crown. Eight, the sun has grown into a great golden bright light. Nine, see it expanding outwards filling the ocean as you reach higher like a sunrise up the magical ladder into the luminous white of the Spirit-Well connecting to the creator. You are now bathed in a bath of bliss. With every inhale, you suck the ocean through your being and let it out on the exhale ebbing and flowing with the source."

The others fall into sleepy states following the King's trail of words. Síonna enters a sublime space feeling as though the entire light of the universe shines from within her being. They lift her out of the water so that her folded legs float on the surface and submerge her again, repeating this over and over.

The deep drone of his voice fades back in,

"Síonna, remember this state. What you smell, what you hear and feel and sense. How your balance is, what colours you see, what emotion you attach to it. Embody this lightness through all senses and as you go forth when you enter Crystal Cave, you will summit to this sensation and manifest your wildest dreams. You have a Guiding Star. If you truly gain command over this teaching and the light within the Crystal Cave you will walk amongst the Guiding Stars."

They lift using only the tips of their fingers, giving her the weightless sensation as though she is levitating of her own accord. She frees her body and mind of all attachments allowing the properties of the salt water to help elevate her further. A sense of freedom like nothing she has ever experienced surges through her being. Such lightness she feels something shifting within her mind connecting her to the very breath of the ocean. They continue with the ritual until the Faery King is satisfied that she has truly captured the sensation and halts their actions.

She opens her eyes to be bathed by the light and colours of their Wells and the layers surrounding them. The lapping waves emit a blue light. Everything has heightened to her Wonder-Eye. As they walk ashore, she feels as though she is floating from the sands. Fawnóg turns, supporting her sensations.

"You have now felt the lightness and true freedom from bodily weight and emotions. You must embody this Deasghnáth with unbreakable belief, Síonna. Climb into the upper Wells and secure that inner belief as you command this magic. Free yourself of everything that is bodily as we see this river offering its body back to the source of the ocean. You have now come to feel the same source within."

The Faery beckons her to stoop where he taps her on the Wonder-Eye with his staff. A shooting star suddenly spears through the sky of her mind. Her eyes spring open with surprise. He then flicks his two fingers to the sky and with great wonderment the same shooting star blazes through the dome of the cloudless sky. She looks owl-eyed at the little Faery shaman who explains his trick,

"Goddess to be, I put the image within your mind and it was you who manifested it. You already know this. It is enough to believe. Now go onwards beyond our kingdoms to the clan who embody another special essence, that of the sun, moon, and the stars."

Her head feels shrouded with a lightness and overcome with the magic she has felt and witnessed. She smiles, offering her gratitude by forming the shape of a heart with her hands, feeling as though she is still sitting on the surface of the water with her legs crossed. With a swift swing of his Faery staff, our sages find themselves back on the rainbow bridge.

"Everything occurs at a speed of the blink of an eye when you enter the realm of the shaman, Granddaughter."

She is almost oblivious to the events that just occurred. She silently smiles at Grandfather not able to word her feelings and whistles for Ríonach who comes sprinting down the hill followed by a fox she befriended and with Zara fast on their trail. They cross through the bands of the rainbow and all is as it was when they stepped afoot on the enchanting sod. Grandfather rings his bell three times, wishing blessings to their sacred encounter shared.

They are soon swaying and dipping on the western swell embodying the new magic of the little ones. Síonna looks at the rose crystal still glittering of the golden syrup, thinking of the elves and wishing that she could spend more time with them recalling their funny antics and then ruminates upon everything that she has acquired so far on the voyage.

As if she wasn't carrying enough praise and magic, Grandfather shrouds her with more.

"Within the darkened boughs of the mind, the beast grows silent, as you enter Crystal Cave releasing your bent bow. Your Goddess voice soars spear-tipped with magic nectar into the hearth of the stalking darkness."

She quietly winds his words together sensing a certain shedding of her old skins to unleash her true voice and see her soul desire manifest.

They continue churning through the waters west, striving to reach the Isle of the people of the sun before the magical sphere retires from the sky.

Chapter 16
Inish Mhic Aoibhleáin
Well-of-the-Cosmic

"Shape-shift wanderer, walk the luminous threads of a spider's dream to merge into one sparkle of the knowable! It is time to ascend, Granddaughter, ascend to realms never trod. The people of the sun are like nothing of this worldly realm. They arrived at Eriu from a land afar across the oceans somewhere beyond the great Atlantach, a land whose people bear a dark-brown skin, tall and beautiful from a lineage of mystical kings who lived in pyramid-shaped dwellings. A star people that unfurl a light from their souls like that emanating from the sun and moon."

'Sunpath
Moonpath
Embers of thy heart
Guide our gaze
On the-sage-way.'

The sun hangs luminously over the Isle. Grandfather guides the boat into a bay with a swift sweeping of his blades. Síonna looks to the red-clouded sky, seeing the people standing erect against the horizon. With hands raised they chant, gazing into the settling ball.

As they ramble up the trail, Síonna sweeps the light of flowers into the quartz jewel, hearing the drone of their incantation grow louder. They reach the enclosure seeing the tribe with their backs to them and lie down to observe their ritual. A heart-raising sight, Síonna admires the pyramid-shaped stone huts rising against the red horizon. Quartz caps each dwelling.

She looks at the towering warriors holding yellow quartz-tipped spears. Golden torques sparkle around their necks and arms. Leaders bear headdresses of stag and boar with furs draped over huge, muscled torsos. They are gathered in a circle. Spirit symbols are drawn upon their faces. Drums thunder through as they draw the light of the sun to each Well, feeding them as the jolly giant suggested. Síonna rolls onto her belly gazing through two shining blades of grass allowing them to complete their ceremony.

The sun slowly dips behind the horizon. The dancing, voices and drums fall silent as the luminous tip of the sphere falls into the sleep of the night, drawing forth her glow across the bosom of the ocean. The clan douse their beings in the last shaft of light to complete the ritual. Grandfather and Síonna rise to greet them.

Síonna is captured by the glow of their eyes and the beauty of their dark, silken skin. Their hair is thick and black; some wear it spiked and others bear long braids with feathers attached to the ends. They move with incredible beauty, swaying over the green earth. Each has a spiral of red earthen-dye painted upon their Wonder-Eyes with dots and star symbols trailing their foreheads resembling the circling cycles of the solar.

Towering over our sages, they part in the middle. The women wail with excitement as a mighty Taoiseach steps through. He comes bearing three golden symbols, one upon his eye of wonder and two that circle each side of his forehead. Strong, tall and lean with long limbs like those of Sláine, he walks with thighs like tree trunks bearing a torso adorned with sinewy, muscled shoulders and arms. Veins bulge in his turtle-throat neck that is wrapped with a golden torque. His skin is youthful. A thick tuft of spiked hair adorns his head. Two braids fall on either side of his huge, rounded chest.

His eyes glint amber-like. He holds a huge spear with the same yellow quartz tip. Síonna can't help but notice how well-proportioned he is in every sense of his physicality which may explain why so many of the women are entranced by his presence, clearly wishing to bear his seed. She feels the same charm. She admires the muscle that ripples from his belly, winding around his ribs, handsomely wrapped in a heavy coat of curly body hair.

He pulls the two of our sages together into one warm hug. Síonna sees one of his eyes are blue, the other brown like the Faery King.

"It brings great joy to our hearts to have you sages, welcome," says the Taoiseach and beckons them to follow him to a pyramid-shaped dwelling.

He pushes aside a door revealing a roof of the same yellow quartz that caps their spears. She admires the great quartz pillars that reach to a corbelled floor where a great dolmen stands with a well carved out of the centre stone emanating a violet-white light.

"Here, we dream, sages, and spin the worlds as we do in Aisling. Let us dive into the sacred and share the essence of the Magical Wells. This Isle represents the Well-of-the-Cosmic sitting on the crown that glows a violet-white. We feed this with the light of the sun, the moon and the stars. This is where you will make a prophecy."

The mighty Taoiseach raises his voice in a ceremonial tone,

"First, make a connection through the root and begin ascending the ladder, bridging through the emerald heart, bringing with you the light of the lower Wells with the Star-Wells."

The Taoiseach then quietens his mind. A stillness sits in the dwelling. Síonna senses that something powerful is approaching and through the door comes a Goddess of remarkable beauty.

She walks to take her place beside Sléa Grianmhar. Smoke circles their forms. They grasp hands and close their eyes. The murmuring of an incantation grows. Their bodies begin to sway. Darkness suddenly falls across the roof. Grandfather and Síonna find themselves unconsciously matching the rhythm and start to sway.

The Taoiseach raises his staff. A glimmering moon emerges lighting the sky. Surrounded by twinkling stars it looms over the enclosure sending luminous light falling in arcs around them lighting the surface of the well. Waves of energy surge through the dwelling. The Taoiseach summons the lunar being from the sky. They witness his magic unfold. The moon descends through the roof filling it with such luminosity they feel as though they are bathed in another world's light. A chilling sensation floods over the room. Adjusting their eyes to faintly see, Síonna observes how silver shafts dart out as the sphere enters the Goddess through the Well-of-the-Cosmic and sits there before pouring down her body to rest at her belly.

"Sages, inhale this lunar power and feed the Wells," the Taoiseach commands.

The drums quicken. Their voices gather into a sharp chant. Hands are raised. A great power floods the room. The Taoiseach leaves out another thunderous voice and through the clouds, a glorious sun descends. A sweltering heat swarms the room forcing them to shut their eyes, illuminating their eyelids a bright yellow.

Beneath the intensity of the Sun God, sweat streams through the pores of their skin. Síonna peers through the orange-lit skin between her fingers to subtly make out the Taoiseach seeing the Sun God descending through the shaft of his spear and then enters his body through the Well-of-the-Cosmic where it stops for a moment and descends to his belly to join with that of the Moon glowing from the Goddesses womb where both merge into one luminous glow.

Our sages have never felt such illumination of their beings. Síonna takes her crystal, collecting the powerful essence observing the mighty power of two solar beings in great union. Words of Sláine come to her mind,

"Unleash a feminine that has never been seen nor understood before!"

"Remember your body is the bridge once you will the mind to rise from the level of the beast. Ascend and when you stand alone on a dark path, summon the light of the sun, moon and the stars to shine on the surface of your Crown and say to yourself: I am in the light of my life."

The revered leader stoops to one knee and whispers into Síonna's ear,

"Do well with this secret, Síonna."

The Taoiseach and Goddess leave the room. As they follow Síonna's eyes are drawn to the well where she sees the same two solar spheres encircling each other on the surface before quickly vanishing. All emerge as though carrying a special solar light born within their bellies. They are beckoned to follow to the summit. They reach a high-standing rock to see a fire burning over the ocean.

Síonna feels the soul of the sod pulsing on her naked feet. She draws it with her breath into her heart and gathers her pulses until the heartbeat of the Isle sings in unison with her being. Feeling the great charge of the solar within she salmon-leaps from the sod.

The Taoiseach looks at her hair that is lit fire-orange, wearing the light of the flames. Three women approach their leader carrying a golden cauldron with a symbol-decorated, rounded neck, steaming of some potion. The Taoiseach cups a horn full of it and takes three sups and turns, offering it to Síonna, saying,

"Drink and see through our eyes."

She follows his example taking three sups. A pungent taste swirls around her mouth. She quickly swallows it. The taste crawls about her mouth, overwhelming her senses.

Síonna passes the horn to the Goddess, Om Rela, who then gifts it to Grandfather and onwards until the entire tribe have drunk from it.

Dizziness grows over them, legs wobble, their sight suddenly alters. The veils lift. Síonna looks to Grandfather to see his eyes wildly lit like those of the tribe. She feels a sudden rumbling in her belly and crouches to four limbs, throwing up all her stomach's belongings. It splashes from her mouth like a river, fluid and food. She burps and throws up again as her whole body jerks, getting rid of everything as though emptying old, not-needed energies to enter this new state.

After several cycles of spitting and coughing, she sinks into the sod surrendering to this new otherness. Emotions churn in her mind like stars rotating around the moon. A sense of yearning roars hauntingly. The forbidden well suddenly appears gleaming in all its delusional brightness. The golden husks warm her eyes. Divine music sweetens her ears. She feels enchanted to reach out and grasp the silken hazels and acquire the otherworldly éigse. She reaches into the night sky as though grasping the nuts from the stars, but anger and frustration quickly seep in, realising they are out of reach from this world.

The white owl appears and sweeps the image from the dark of the night casting an otherworldly whisper,

"Seek the hazels, Síonna, and the éigse will be yours."

She leaves out a shrilling call like a distraught warrior keening over the death of a loved one. Circling above, the bird flaps its wings in time with the racing pulse of her heart. The whispers grow louder, deafening to her ears. She screams like a beast, covering her ears, grunting and frothing at the mouth. The owl suddenly vanishes.

She is shaken but slowly comes around to the sounds of the people moving about her. To try and distract her mind she summons the fox state she acquired from observing Ríonach and crawls on all fours, sniffing, barking and trotting upon the sod. She runs and leaps, tracking footprints and markings of animals. With ears cocked attuned to all subtle movements, she races to a nearby oak on the bough of a hill and leaps, spiralling down through a burrow. She emerges back into the delightful golden meadows of the Na Sí.

Joy pours over her being. She hops over the fields of flowers and runs like a racing wind through the forest trails. Within its dreamy boughs, she wanders trailing rivers to waterfalls and bathes in their sparkling crystals. She chases hares and rabbits who spring over rushes and observes the swans and geese and all sorts of winged flutter through the air.

She sees the Faery and Elves in the distance going about their daily chores and thinks about the levitation ritual they carried out that day at the edge of the ocean. She wishes blessings upon them and leaps into another burrow and spins at great speed emerging back to the Isle gazing to the sky to see her Guiding Star appear. A furrow of light reaches down connecting to her crown sending a glow of indigo emanating around her red hair. She senses an empowered alignment and hears his sudden approach.

She turns. Their eyes meet. Desire rises. A yearning sensation grows over her breast. He swirls around her like a mysterious light. Her eyes trace the after-furrow of his lightbody. His endowed form arouses a sense of desire within her. The ceremony around them heightens. Women cast shrilling yelps as they spin faster. Her heart races as their eyes connect. The towering Taoiseach reaches and grasps her hands. He begins twirling them in ritual step. She is drawn to his brown and blue pupils and to the three spirals on his Wonder-Eye and forehead that begin to spin mysteriously as they quicken.

She feels a hot sensation pour through her being and looks down to see his luminous belly merged within hers, glowing as one sphere like in the ritual he played out with the Goddess. A huge surge of energy courses through her veins, arousing her. Surrendering to it she groans. He squeezes her hands in successive bursts as though casting his light like a river warming her veins. A tidal pulse erupts to purr through her.

Groaning like beasts entangled, waves of pleasure flood through them as the light of the sun and moon bind in a blissful union. Their chests rise. Necks arch. Lustful sounds outpour like they are two howling wolves courting beneath a blood-red moon. Their breaths climb. Síonna feels the pulse of his manhood and looks down to see a ball of great light surging back and forth between them as though the stars of the night sky enter the darkness of her womb.

She then realizes he has brought her to a state of sublime without physical contact.

"Ag gnéasnasctha, sex-linked," he whispers.

"Síonna, know your leadership as a worthy carrier of this light. Go forth and spin it so wisely on your Goddess head."

The Taoiseach releases his grasp. They slowly part, each holding that luminous glow. She moves in a state of rapture feeling more beautiful than all the Isles of the ocean, more beautiful than the most luminous flowers or jewels of the land. Like a walking peril, she skips across the sward to join Grandfather who acknowledges her heightened state with a great smile.

Sleá Grianmhar ushers the drummers to stop.

"Let us smoke!"

All gather around the fire. He takes out a sandstone dúidín, lights it with an ember and puffs three times and passes it to the next warrior. Circling sunwise until each member smokes. Síonna takes three puffs and sweeps the smoke over her Wells.

A lightness falls over her brow. Her sight starts to alter. She closes her eyes and is suddenly running down a dark tunnel hearing beautiful music. A light appears at the end. she fearlessly leaps through entering a valley to witness there in the most beautiful bough the glittering hazel tree at the forbidden well, the golden husks so enchanting. She outstretches her hand but is woken by the sharp beat of a drum.

Sleá Grianmhar gazes through the smoke of the fire.

"Choose wisely."

She receives his message through the silent interaction of their eyes.

Animal fat from spits and cauldrons burned in the enclosure is brought to the summit and thrown into a huge fire pit. A warrior dips his foot, testing the temperature and gives the sign to Sleá Grianmhar who raises his staff and starts howling madly like a wolf. The entire tribe howl with him arching their necks to the sky. The pool of fat bubbles.

"Istigh ag gnéasnasctha. Our ritual begins," The Taoiseach shouts.

Our sages watch in awe as the entire clan crawl into the pit and begin fornicating wildly within the warm juices. Men take women and even other men. Our sages are awed. The entire tribe explore in a surge of passionate lust. Sliding and slithering like snakes engaged in beastly like actions, Síonna is curious, observing the cluster of naked bodies writhing around each other. Eyes are fire-like as they wade through the steaming fat grunting and moaning, feeding beastly desires.

Necks arch. Waves of pleasure sear through them. Some grunt and chant incantations. Others cast spells and enchantments upon others. She thinks of Fionn and her charged experience with Sleá Grianmhar. A beastly desire suddenly climbs upon her to engage in the wild ritual.

Grandfather leans over whispering,

"It is a test of the lower impulses."

She searches her thoughts thinking of the values and challenging aspects of the lower Wells, screaming within to surrender to the beastly urge but she climbs the ladder into the emerald of her heart to rest her mind and settles on a decision to abstain.

Sleá Grianmhar is entangled with several, whilst lustfully glancing at Síonna, teasing and trying to draw her in like a cunning snake. Om Rela slithers through masses of warriors, serpent-like throwing her capturing eyes of lust. All yearn for her endowed erect breasts that shine to their entranced eyes like those of an erotic deity. Beneath her charm they bury their heads sucking as though the nectar of the gods is born of her breasts. She has her fill of pleasure with each and wades through the fat elegantly until she eventually engages with the Taoiseach in the centre.

They interlock. The light of the sun and moon pours out of their bellies. A great intensity grows. Síonna feels a certain envy. The tribe pant and groan encircling them. They bring the energy to a height grunting wildly. A ceremonial leader arrives at the pit carrying several quartz-tipped spears. He hands them to the warriors who raise them howling wildly. Our sages observe the moonlight glittering on their fat-soaked skin. Heads are raised in pleasure. Ecstatic groans grow sharper as the energy builds. Pushing their breaths into fast rhythmic beats they draw the final surge through their bodies with sharp inhales and exhale sending it into the quartz tips.

Emerging from the pit, owl-eyed and charged the Taoiseach gives the command to bring those who need healing before the fires where a laying-of-the-spears is carried out just as the Fir Bolg do with their swords.

Those receiving lie on the earth with the spears placed along the centre of their Wells. They begin to shake and moan and cry releasing and healing. Those not engaged in the ritual begin to dance around them drumming and chanting that continues into the early hours of the night until Sleá Grianmhár suddenly roars at the top of his voice,

"To the waters!"

The tribe follow the Taoiseach to the shoreline where they dive beneath the moonlit waters. Síonna and Grandfather are given spears. Taking a sharp inhale, they trail after them into the silvery world beneath. Shoals of mackerel swirl around them as spears leave bubbling yellow furrows like lightning beings beneath. They surface with bundles of fish skewed on the spears. Grandfather and Síonna each acquire a worthy catch. The sea bounty is brought back to the enclosure to fire pits where a roast and fest steams into a night fest.

Great wisdom is shared beneath a luminous gathering of stars before sleep sweeps over the Isle like a silent ghost collecting the warriors one by one. They settle upon the earth with their bellies full. Their lust and desires quenched. The fires reduce to glowing embers as sleep lowers them into Dreamtime. A night of prophesying is had.

Dawn sends shafts and spears of light awakening another day. The clan gather around our sages at the shoreline, praying healing to a reddening sun casting a copper shawl over the ocean. Síonna follows the actions of the Taoiseach who draws the light into each Well feeding the source that nurtures the body and mind. He joins his hands giving thanksgiving to the new sun and faces our sages preparing for parting words.

Síonna gazes into his enchanting eyes as he whispers,

"Within your beautiful Wells, you carry the light of the entire solar. Síonna, you are ready for the Motherwell of Scealga. The source that feeds all other Wells. You are one-that-is-chosen, Goddess of Eriu."

Blessed beneath his praise, she places her hand upon his heart and with the draíocht-of-the-fingertips exchanges a heightened sensation.

Our sages cast blessings to the tribe and wander back to the shoreline, carrying with them a string of magical moments.

Zazie and Ríonach are already waiting, eager to discover another land. Síonna rows from the shoreline as Grandfather rings his bell three times, looking back at the sacred tribe. She begins to ruminate on the mystery that is before them as the Motherwell awaits.

Chapter 17
Scealga
Soul-Well

'Motherwell
Soul-Well
Where source, and Soul
Whisper of the solar and of the Earth
Calling the Ollamh, Ovate, Bard and Druid
Monks and sages, and the far-seeing
Offering a ladder outside of time
To souls who know: the soul-way.'

"Heavenly stairs reach a wondrous realm beyond the steps of man's mind uncoiling a rainbow snake so that we climb the spioradálta ladder outside of time, Ancestral time."

Grandfather releases a ritual smoke. Síonna inhales his weaving of words as though she can taste the ancient place in the smoke that circles her face. They still for a moment observing the mystical Isles on the distant horizon. She swishes his verse around her mouth peeling magic from the words looking at the twin spires of the Motherwell.

Determination to reach the place of power sets in. The click of their tholes soon merges into a steady rhythm. Their pace builds with their excitement. The sea-beetle sways and rocks, rises and falls as the sound grows choppy. Gainéad sing in shrilling pitch and plummet like spears into the vast blue of the ocean.

The crags and spires of Scealga soon disappear as they dip behind huge swells. A great passage of their time is spent in silence. Síonna bounces back through the experiences of the quest. Seeing the Cosmic Juggler, Cúroí, Crom Dubh and the mystical sages and wizards, faery, elves and all the wise tribes of the Rainbow Isles to the great jolly giant. She ruminates on what position she may be on the medicine wheel.

A storm begins to brew in the cauldron of the sea. A sudden

current churns. The winds grow. Dark clouds suddenly sweep across the sky. They are attentive to their row to make distance on the Isle. A sudden mist falls, veiling their visibility.

Spray begins to slap their faces making it difficult to keep direction. The waves are growing unmeasurable in size. Grandfather turns to see the spires of Scealga, calculating their distance. A sudden fear tickles Síonna as she senses something otherworldly approaching. The swell grows angry. Ríonach curls into a ball beneath Síonna's legs. Zara is perched behind Grandfather with her wings folded, her beak lowered.

The scar on Síonna's forearm begins to throb as though the poison of the demon has awakened. The sound sings of another presence. Mountainous swells keep rising, crashing down filling the bow and stern. They fight to empty her, trying to keep her afloat.

"The Shadows of the Underworld are trying to halt me from summiting the ladder," she whispers, thinking that she may be still in the position of south on the wheel and needing to shed more as the sorcerer still finds a wound to enter.

They pull and push with all their might, but the ocean is merciless. Making little advancement, Grandfather shouts over the growl of the ocean.

"Ná ligimís ár maidí le sruth, let us not lose our oars to the current." He says in the mother tongue, and follows it painting the two languages together. "Glac É Go Réidh, steady on there, hold on tight, Síonna, we must sit it out!"

And out of the deep comes the haunting whisper raining to her ears,

"Seek the hazels, Síonna, and the éigse…"

She halts it pushing her fingers into her ears looking in disbelief to see the wretched bird stretched high in the sky luminous against the dark clouds. Something drags her gaze down into the infinite belly of the ocean to see the wondrous image of the hazel tree bending in the flapping of the waves.

A power floods her being before Grandfather's voice rattles her ears,

"Síonna!"

She leaps from the seat nervously smiling trying to refocus her mind. Torrent rain whips the surface of the ocean into a frenzy of swirling currents.

Fearful, knowing they are deep within her mercy they lift and drop into a mass of waves that spin them in uncontrollable circles. The wind-whisperers suddenly plunge the laughing tones of the witches to her ears followed by an image and voice of the haggard face of the-crone-that-holds-the-light and darkness.

"All will not be lost; a warrior is already inherent in your bloodline."

Just as she begins to regain a sense of clarity the eye of Balor appears on the waters glaring, stirring the Well of her heart.

Churning up an ocean of desire within her she struggles with the inner battle. Grandfather grips his oars commanding her to drive into the storm while giving a riddle.

"Otherness rainforest trees sing branched songs colouring a blue pigeon's dawn, plucking a silver bush-plum shaved by a golden ray of the sun curled around a Cockatoo's claw sweeping a Dreamtime magic with a wand from a Faery sky, and from a serpent land she paints a sweet honey on the lips of mankind, to unfurl a tongue of otherworldly sorts from the mythical Shaman."

She chuckles and brings her mind back to the task at hand as they work in rhythmic assembly upon the treacherous waters rising and falling into the huge depths.

Suddenly the whirlpool of an otherworldly realm churns up either side of their boat spinning it within the centre of this sorcerer's cauldron. Síonna is thrown overboard to be saved by Grandfather's swift blade as he pulls her from the twirling tide. Shaken and shivering, she grabs her oars and without thought, they drive forth.

Ríonach clutches on with her claws. Zaza is tucked beneath Grandfather.

"Síonna, climb the ladder and calm the storm of the emotions, it is within this is manifesting as the Faery King created the shooting star within the window of your mind. Gain control."

Recalling the magical event, she enters the upper Wells searching the crevasses of her mind to see the inner storm blazing about the same window where the Faery formed his image of the star. She wipes it with her vision from her mind as though sweeping it with the sleeve of her tunic.

A sense of calm floods her body. She opens her eyes to see the magical, the winds have calmed. She looks at Grandfather in disbelief and the mist suddenly lifts unveiling the most beautiful sight she has ever seen, the twin spires of Scealga. Every sense imaginable she has is bathed. The sheer mystery of the place of power pours over her. He smiles seeing the unveiling of her power honouring it with a riddle.

"Yellow pearls sing from the mermaids of your emerald eyes manifesting what you truly desire. Only that which makes your heart sing. Now dream the crystal of your soul to the Isle, Granddaughter. You have already tasted its golden apple."

She returns a great smile.

They merge into a charged row and gain pace on Scealga Beag. A sunpath falls on the surface reaching to the otherworldly rocks as though gifting them a felling-of-the-way. Shafts of light fall upon the green meadows, ever-changing in shade. In her contemplation of the final stepping-stones Síonna whispers,

"Truly a place for the spirit to be revealed. I bestow you with the name of 'The Fruitful Breasts of the Mother,' dear beacons of light in all my imaginings I had of rock-dreaming, you are truly worthy."

Seeing the twin pinnacles rise with spires, arches and sea-crags and the spiral steps weaving around the body of the rock ascending to her breasts in the summit, she knows that she has arrived at a mountainous sanctuary like nothing she has ever seen. Scealga Beag is covered with colonies of birds. She draws with her fingers the essence into her rose crystal.

As they near, Grandfather halts their row and closes his eyes and sits for a while listening to the sweet chorus of the Gainead, feeling blessed on the edge of the world before this mystical being that sings to their souls.

Síonna directs her attention, climbing the spioradálta ladder hearing Grandfather's suggestion again,

"Take the leap, Granddaughter. It's time to jump from the herd and become the leader you are destined to be."

Looking skywards she sees a glorious flight of swans and glances down seeing their luminous forms ocean-mirrored. She follows their flight until they disappear behind the summit and recalls a story Sengann once told her of how a group of pilgrims came to Scealga at the beginning of time and were met by sorcerers who tried to capture them. Upon escaping, the pilgrims asked the gods for guidance and they granted the holy men the guise of the swan so they could travel between the Isles unnoticed by the sorcerers. To this day, it is said that the mysterious flock can be sighted here.

"Now we have great work to do snooting from our golden, silver-billed beaks that churn the waters with a flickering of green eyelashes spinning yellow crystals upon a mermaid's brow who winks from half-moonlit eyes telling the world it is time to leap!"

She giggles at his riddling humour. He reaches over, tickling her while puffing away on his dúidín. He blows trails of blessings before their arrival, whispering,

"Síonna, you will never witness the likes of this again, like the eyes of a bumble bee perched on a purple knapweed blossom, eyeing a nectarous harvest of truth. Now make your wish."

She forms a wish feeling she has emerged through south to engage with the direction of destiny and journey inwardly into the west. Grandfather rows the last stretch gliding in through the sparkle of the sunpath. He takes a bodhrán placed in the boat most likely by the mysterious Diarmuid and his son and begins rubbing the skin with the palm of his hand. Warming and holding it above the water he strikes, singing,

'Water, holding the feeling of time
We gather your solas
Water, that is before us
We honour your solas
Water, that will come after us
We honour your solas.'

"Granddaughter, as we drum, remember, these waters are the same tides that ebbed and flowed before the eyes of our ancestors and will be the same tides that will glitter before those of our descendants. Cast our wishes beneath and see them held forever within her crystals that sear through the tides of time, carrying our impressions and imaginings to the past, manifesting them in the present and prophesying them into the future."

She closes her eyes sending her wish into the clear waters before they finally touch the shoreline of the sacred Isle. The dúidín has grown cold in Grandfather's mouth. Síonna still shivers from her untimely dip in the ocean. They greet the mystical place of power, receiving the sense of shedding the skins of an old story while emerging into a new, wondrous time. Shedding all from whom they came as, opening to the opportunity as to whom they may leave as.

Grandfather kneels to the sod, guiding Síonna with spioradálta suggestions.

"Open the stairs to where there are events, to where all realities exist. Every placement of your feet is a motion for new desires. Your vibration creates the outcome. Trust the-feeling-of-the-way and be aware of the signs."

He ties his bell to his big toe and shakes his leg, hopping on the other while whistling like a bird, matching the melody of the bell. Síonna grows weak in her legs from laughing. Ríonach and Zara tear up the southern path before them.

The High King of Consciousness places his foot on the first step with his arms outstretched and fingers pinched, he sweeps back his imaginary kilt from his waist and hops up and down the step a few times, singing,

"I pray for healing upon our stony voyage as we roam a sight so gobbly wondrous you forget to breathe."

He then begins to lead the way with a slow trot. Each step becomes a prayer.

Síonna sweeps the crystal, collecting the living trace left by those ancient tribes and sages who trod the steps before them, feeling for their tasks that they may wish to share with her.

Rabbit burrows trail both edges of the path. The climb breaks a sweat upon them. Síonna feels a sudden dizziness. The winds circle bringing the ghostly voice returning to her ears,

"Seek the hazels, Síonna, and the éigse will be yours."

Grandfather, feeling the shift within her quickly announces,

"Remember what the Cosmic Juggler said: 'You will come to two paths, only one you must choose. Pay attention to the unseen. There is more than one path."

Mist hides the summit. Grandfather breaks into the wandering air of Port Na B-Pucai and no sooner he begins, a rainbow bends over the steps. From it emerges the glorious Faery King with his rose chubby cheeks peeled back by a gracious smile. Fawnóg opens his multi-coloured eyes wide, fiddling with the nine torques in his red beard.

"To who gathers upon these steps and to who may pass them that come with great ideas, tasks, wishes and desires but may go with none or with a soulful knowing that you have reached closer to that, that which shines within. Síonna, when you climb the ladder, a jewel will meet your wondrous eye."

He delivers the message and lets out a roaring laugh and vanishes into the mist leaving a tone of his chuckling voice. Grandfather smirks at his swift visit.

A melody suddenly pours through the mist. They hear someone approaching, whistling. A shadow suddenly pushes through, followed by the white beard and face of a monk hooded in a cloak of sheep's wool. Ríonach appears sniffing by his feet followed by Zara who cuts through the mist like a spear. The monk gazes from glinting brown eyes, capped with bushy red eyebrows, holding a great smile.

"Grandfather, my heart leaps with joy to see your humble face amongst us again."

"Fionán-of-the-white-beards, meet my wise granddaughter, Síonna, the future Goddess of Eriu."

"So elevated is my heart to meet you. I have heard many stories from rovers speaking of your rise into the great warrior of Eriu that you are. This Isle is now a sanctuary for your worthy presence, Síonna."

She blushes beneath his praise as he wraps them both in a tight embrace.

Grandfather offers his dúidín in prayer.

"Meet us in counsel for all who cast wishful spears and lilting tongues prophesying to unfurl for all the people of this world. Peace. Love. Joy."

Fionán smiles, remembering Grandfathers great riddling and leads them on the steps of prayer.

After a measure of silence and a steep climb that winds and winds they come to cross cove, hearing of its position on the great sanctuary that leads to the path of ascension.

The mist that hid the steps dissipates unveiling the huge stairs. Steps reach into the cloud-covered, shale sandstone summit. In awe, they imagine the ladder leading into an otherworldly wonderment as six hundred or so steps of the hermitage path have brought them this far. Songs of kittiwake, guillemots, razorbills and puffins fill the air. Grandfather responds, whistling a melody and rotating his eyebrows, his hands outstretched evoking great laughter as they gaze over the grassy banks adorned in flowers of sea pink, white clover, spear thistle, and pennywort.

Huge slabs trail skywards in a straight line. Pinnacles loom on each side guarding the final ladder into the monastery.

"My sages, the kingdom that awaits you is something that you will not have seen before. You have acquired the sight of the Wonder-Eye to witness such beauty and mystery and so, now be endowed by this otherworldly grace. Leave compassion and thanksgiving in your footprints walking the final ladder while holding the deepest love in your hearts. Go now to your most inwardness and the spring Wells of your centres will shine."

Gazing into each other's eyes, Grandfather rings his bell sending the tinkle before them like music carrying their wish upon the path. Sensing the essence that awaits, they turn, each in their own silence and begin stepping upon the otherworldly stairs.

A slight mist follows them up the spine of the saddle. Síonna directs her attention to her heart, feeling a rising surge of love. It sings, stinging her desires. Her yearning for her lover grows. Her mind suddenly bounces to different events in her life while hearing the words of the oileánach, Tomás,

"Ascend the stairs like climbing your spine, step over the bridge to sky. Summit at the level of spirit. You carry wounds, daughter of Fir

Bolg, only the love of the heart can heal these. Summit the stairs bridging the Wells, awakening the sleeping serpent."

"Awakening the sleeping serpent," she repeats, before continuing.

Her pace begins to slow. Her sight grows blurry. Her legs tire and begin to wobble. She stops and stoops to one knee, inhaling, expanding her chest to revive the heaviness. Grandfather and Fionán make distance up the ladder. With every step, her legs grow heavier. Her pulse thickens. She looks up to see two paths suddenly appear, shimmering like a cloud beneath the midday sun. She wipes her eyes with her forearm, but the image remains.

"Is this another test, a warning? What did he mean by another path?"

She hears the churning of waves thundering below and out of the moment comes the mysterious whisper hitting her like a falling star. Like the poison of the boar's bristle, it drains her of strength. She looks to see the Owl soaring like a dot spread over the summit. Sweat sprouts from her brow and a weakness rises to surge through her. She struggles to regain her footing. The whispers dart through as though the winds are casting them in and out of her ears.

Like a rising dawn, she summons the light recalling the teachings of the people of the sun,

"Ascend the stairs like climbing your spine and step over the bridge to sky."

She collects her pulses. One by one they merge until her body attunes with that of the sod drumming upon the soles of her feet. The essence pours through like a warp spasm. She gives movement to the task repeating his words,

"Step over the bridge to sky ascending the stairs like climbing your spine."

The whispers soon fade. The path becomes clear. A glitter of raindrops sparkles on the luminous moss bearding the steppingstones. Grandfather shuffles his feet in the distance, turning, smiling and tapping his lower lip knowing she is being tested. Zara soars over her as though praising her bravery. She waves to Grandfather with a sense of lightness returning, whispering,

"I, Síonna, future Goddess of these lands, hold within my spirit all the imaginings of my forefathers to reign the lands of the Fir Bolg. O' Fruitful Breasts of the Mother, embrace me into your tender grasp."

She envisages the ladder as steppingstones leading to her royal seat at the Hill of Tara. Seeing the tribes waiting. With each step, the chanting and pounding of their drums grow. She senses the delight. Seeing the sparkle in Grandfather's eyes as he waits to take her hand in ceremony before the clans. The hill is in rapturous chorus. Just when she thought the feeling-of-the-way was lit, a sudden storm grows.

Clouds blacken and race down, swooping upon her. Heather and grass twirl in circles around her feet. She struggles to stay on the path with torrent winds sweeping in from both sides. She leans into the force with all her might.

Grandfather and Fionán are veiled by the mist. Teachings return.

"There is another path, the path-of-danger. The shaman lives between two worlds, with one foot in the physical and one in the unseen. Bridging two worlds, the lower ones spin towards the sod and beyond the bridge of the heart, they spin to the sky, the unseen."

"Now I understand, my wondrous Rainbow One."

The storm worsens. She fixes her eyes forth in disbelief to see the red fiery eye of Balor appear glaring from the middle of the path. Mirrored upon his eye is the otherworldly hazel tree. The enchantment returns. The otherworldly power surges through her veins. Balor stirs her Wells with his lunar light churning her inner desires. Sealing his image and shadows within her, his barking laugh curls into her ears. Shadows dance around her.

Fawnóg's wisdom arises.

"Tread the steppingstones, for one shines into another that will guide your feet away from underfoot of shadow that climbs aside your every step."

She hears the distant chuckle of the Faery King and shakes herself. She summons her roots to sink into the dark earth as Balor tries to enter her wounded heart. And climbs the inner ladder calming the wounds of her emotions speaking to them like a loving mother calms a crying baby,

"Shush, shush now, everything is fine. Shush."

"Síonna," Grandfather's voice startles her reaching through the storm.

She looks to see his warm eyes spilling his beautiful light forth. The green band of a rainbow reaches through as though bringing his joy forth to close the wound in her heart. The beast's eye suddenly disappears. Wispy blue clouds reappear. The winds drop.

She looks ahead and out of the sky soar three bumblebees leaving a trail to follow the blessed way. Charged, she bounces up the final steps after the little Goddess beings, summoning the lightness she felt in the ocean of the Na Sí. She follows the bees as though her feet don't touch the steps and comes to the step of ascension watching them continue into the hermitage. And there on the top step sits the most beautiful emerald stone sparkling to her eyes as Fawnóg promised.

Captured by the glow of the jewel, a huge sense of relief floods her mind knowing she has reached the special place of power.

Grandfather opens his arms and she eases into his loving embrace.

"Remember that you behold a mountainous strength. You have climbed the ladder showing great determination but unbeknown to most when the time comes 'determination' will be something you must cast from your mind."

She is puzzled.

"How can I rid the very thing that will help me to conquer the hounds and demons of Balor?" she asks herself.

The monk approaches with a great smile parting his rosy cheeks.

"Take this powerful jewel to the Valley of the Stags where it will be inserted into a sword that will guide you to lead the armies of the Fir Bolg against the sorcery that haunts your lands."

Her eyes well up, humbled with the sacred task he bestows upon her. She stoops and picks up the emerald, caresses the jewel feeling the quartz-like, cold sensation of its structure. A surge of energy floods her being as though several lifetimes of wishes are assembling into that one moment.

Images of a huge battle appear in her Wonder-Eye. She sees herself raising this great sword with the emerald eye on the hilt casting a green glow before the clans of Eriu. Fionán brings her back, handing her a white cloth saying,

"Wrap this sacred relic and carry it close to your heart, protecting it until you reach the Valley of the Stags."

She does so with utter honour. He looks to the green glint in her eyes, smiling as she places it into her tunic, close to her heart. A tingling sensation spreads throughout her breast and up her forehead into the eye of wonder filling it with a glow of green heightening her vision to see the subtle worlds expanding around them.

The monk winks.

"The emerald will open a sight within that you could only have imagined, Síonna. Now we are about to enter a hermitage beyond the veils. That beyond temptations and desires where we embrace what hardships surface and forge our wills to see through the delusion. We aspire to ourselves so that others will be inspired by our actions. Let the belongings of the physical follow after you as you cross the bridge to the sky, stepping from one ladder of time into another."

She looks across the sound recalling words of the Goddess Dovinia,

"Let its light enter the cave of your hearts."

She vows to take a leap of consciousness as they enter the mysterious summit.

She steps up seeing the high stronghold of the monks that arrests her eyes. Her gaze scans the dwelling place of the gods seeing earthen banks form the outer circle that enclose six rectangular roundhouses. Layer upon layer of stone is wedged to build this sacred place of dwelling. Flowers dapple the green sward. Zara sweeps between the beehives, past the two boat-shaped Oratories and a ceremonial building. Ríonach leaps after her, sprinting most probably hearing four-legged rustling in the undergrowth. Something ancient beyond time whispers to Síonna. She senses something that has lived here for a very long time seeing shimmering forms float about the place.

Awed at the craftsmanship, it seems as though a race of people descended from the stars built this great kingdom of sandstone and gifted it to the monks of Eriu. Grandfather contemplates,

"Bridging two worlds of earth and sky into a magical hive where seagulls glide through wondrous veils, singing of star-beings afar that unfurl a temple for the sages of mankind to ruminate on, within the majestic swell of the sea."

The rumble of the Atlantach sends her ocean music to sit on the summit. They catch the drone of a distant voice. Fionán brings them to one of the Oratories. He pushes a thick wooden door aside to meet with the voice of another monk, reciting from scriptures spread before him on a table. A sweet scent of Frankincense swirls to their nostrils. The monk does not move nor glance but remains deeply engrossed in prayer. Rays of the sun beam through a small west-side window casting his shadow upon the beautiful stonework.

Carvings of Ogham decorate heavy slabs wedged upon each other forming the shape of an overturned boat. A sundial stands in the centre for an aligned Suncatcher shaft to pour through, dawn and dusk. Fionán closes the door. The roar of the ocean is silenced by the thick walls. They observe their shadows ghost-like stretched upon the stone, waiting until he completes the last incantation. The final drone stretches until the silence of the room consumes it.

"Etgal, guests from the Valley of the Stags."

His face lights up seeing the familiar face of Grandfather. He draws back his hood and grasps both his shoulders, gazing into the cornflower eyes of the Ollamh and then pulls him into a warm embrace. Frankincense smoke swirls around them. He turns to Síonna. His glinting green eyes arrest her with such clarity she feels as though she is looking through two pieces of clear emerald.

"My dear, sages, humbled is my heart to share with you our Isle that is now your dwelling for as long as you wish, and for your future quests whenever you return. You had the bravery to endure the crossing and climb the ladder. Let us now prepare your time here with a fast. Nature has dutifully given," he says while bestowing with his fingers a blessing of the four directions over our sages.

He leads them out into the hermitage to where a well sits, the clearest sky-mirroring well. He stoops and cups a handful of the water casting blessings. He then dips his two fingers and rubs it upon our sages' Wonder-Eyes again drawing the sign of the four directions.

"You will begin to see whilst drinking from the source of the Motherwell."

Síonna and Grandfather each drink of the water. He then leads them to the second Oratory, revealing a long wooden table with chairs carved of bog-oak. Similar stone walls are chiselled, rounded. Arches curve under the windows. A hearth glows with pots hanging from a crane releasing warming aromas.

The monk's long orange beard turns a sunset red along with his hair. His green eyes glitter with delight beneath his bushy orange eyebrows that curl into spirals. His smile revealing his most beautiful ghost-white teeth. Síonna admires his silken skin and notices the bottom half of his left ear is severed. He addresses them in a warming tone,

"Let us now fast and enter the dreaming of this sanctuary and we will feast on the eve of your return to Eriu."

Ríonach comes back licking her lips. Zara is most probably gliding the summer airstreams. The sun slowly rolls down in the evening sky giving way for the hearth to glow brighter. They warm around its glow. Etgal lights a dúidín and passes amongst them. He then takes a flute of oak, purses his lips and releases a breath. A beauty pours to their ears as they offer thanksgiving to the place of power with wish-filled puffs. Síonna closes her eyes, allowing the melody to seep into her and draws it to her crystal. It soothes her travelled, weary body and mind.

The melody shifts through every key imaginable. She feels it provoking emotions and tensions within, unravelling knots in places she never knew existed as though a river of light is coursing through her veins and slowly climbing her spine coaxing her mind to follow.

As the last tone fades, the monk draws a four-directional cross in the air and offers wisdom.

"Music is a language of the soul, humming like the earth beneath our feet. When I carved this flute, I tuned each key to the tone of each Well for healing sounds like the ocean, the sun, the moon and stars. A curling wind or the pulse of the mountain or the droning murmur of the thunder gods. If we listen deeply, we will hear, and these sounds will heal us at levels unknown, at the bog level, at mountain level, at river level and so on. Now, my friends, it is time for you to lay your minds to rest from this day that has travelled well upon you. Show our dear sages to their dwellings."

Blessings are passed on the night and Fionán leads our sages each to their own beehive. Zara follows Grandfather and Ríonach trails Síonna.

Síonna watches Grandfather retreat into the stone hive backwards, bowing several times while ringing his bell. The tone follows him until he shuts the heavy door. Síonna enters her ancient dwelling, laughing at his antics and lies upon her wattle with the wonder of the day's experiences running through her mind. She revisits Ergal's words,

"Music is a language of the soul."

She begins to hum, imitating the tones she heard from his magical flute. Each key she voices, she feels the sensation throughout her body and she goes deeper each time until she can feel it within climbing the ladder of her Wells. She goes deeper still until she hears the Isle singing to her, merging with the drone of her voice like the pulse merging with the pulse of the earth.

A great síochán settles upon her. She feels awed, summoning this new teaching. And the day's events soon weigh heavy on her mind but heavy in a relaxed, sleepy way.

She feels as though she lies into the night sky itself, sprinkling her thoughts like stars as sleep sweeps through like a calming mother's voice. Dreams come fast.

She is woken in the middle of the night by a ghostly sound, hearing a fluttering of wings around the hive. Smelling a beautiful scent of frankincense, she looks out of the door to see shadows of winged ones soaring back and forth around the summit.

Darting at great speed between the huts, the last embers of the fire give her sight of the birds she identifies as an Chánóg Dhubh, a winged species native to the Isle.

Ríonach listens to the otherworldly-like visitors with one ear cocked. Síonna steps out and stands beneath the stars gazing over the swell lit by moonlight, feeling connected to the Rainbow Isles. Enveloped by the magical glitter, she takes the emerald jewel from her brat and imagining stretching her lightbody over the ocean she sees the beautiful green glow of the emerald reaching with her across An Atlantach, bestowing blessings upon the Rainbow Isles. She casts her mind further, journeying over the trails of the quest they have walked to soar down into the Valley of the Stags and sprinkle blessings upon her sleeping clan.

In a timeless state, listening to the lapping of the waves curling the base of the Isle, she returns and merges her breath with its tone, rising and falling, imagining the cleansing tide sweeping through her body charging the cauldrons and lakes of her inner being, filling her Wells like a golden sun reaching to the bottom of a deep earthly well. The luminous spectacle brings her back to when she was a young girl sitting beneath the trees, merging with their pulse, seeing the living glow of the forests come alive. Or when she would journey in the dark of night venturing into caves seeing with the Wonder-Eye as though in daylight, unveiling the power of the elementals.

Empowered, she retrieves bringing the essence with her and sweeps the precious emerald over her body, bathing her being in its solas, whispering,

"I am receiving and perceiving a higher godly light, with a consciousness of síochán to share with all sentient beings, thank you, ho."

She sweeps her hands over each Well making a wish, spinning them like magical cauldrons and returns to her beehive to crouch into a ball beside Ríonach with the emerald jewel held to her heart.

A droning sound soon wakes her. She opens the door to the light of the rising sun. She walks out to see a yellow mist combing the bosom of the ocean. Grandfather is on the edge of the summit, puffing his duidín, casting prayer. She hears the incantations of the monks. She sits imagining their voices as though beacons of light that rise from the oratory upon a wisp of frankincense smoke and magically sweep across the sound like a veil of great healing, sprinkling blessings over the tribes and lands of Eriu.

She contemplates her humanness and how small she is, sitting upon the huge Isle, sitting in the vast stretch of the Atlantach. She observes the silver-belly swell and fall, changing from turquoise to a deep blue, green, black and many subtle shades of orange, and finally to a bright red as the sun takes a stronger position in the sky.

Each day they wake with the monks blessing the dawn. They sit at night in ritual silence looking into the star-mapped skies, casting wishes and forming dreams. They roam her trails by day learning about the herbs, about the rhythms of the ocean. About solitude. Sometimes spending several days and nights in complete darkness in their hives, journeying the landscapes of their minds, embodying the inner teachings of the Wells.

Silence becomes their music, the ocean a voice, the stars their guiding light. The yearning for food, a sign to rid and conquer the impulses of the lower Wells.

Story warms the night while assembled around ceremonial fires. Síonna and Grandfather learn the honeyed tongues of the wise monks. Several cycles of the full moon pass. They rise one morning with that sense of knowing, as a small disc of the moon sits faintly within a cluster of clouds sweeping through the pale blue sky. Síonna catches the unusual light and knows something is to occur.

Fionán softly approaches.

"Etgal will gift you today while Grandfather and I will fish the sound and we will honour this special evening with a great fest."

She feels a sudden knotting just below her chest hearing of the fest, knowing they have come to the final day of their time upon the sacred Isle. A sense of happiness soon overcomes the lonesomeness as he suggests further,

"It will be an important day in your Quest, Síonna. Remember, have strength and control your emotions. Read from your inner stars to gain a feeling-of-your-way! Remember the gifts and everything that you have gathered from your silence and fasting, have clarity within your thoughts."

The monk then taps the brown beauty dimple upon her cheek and whispers,

"A symbol of the gods gifted to a true leader, fulfilling a great destiny."

She is all silent, excited and empty at the same time learning that it is to be their final night on the sacred Isle.

Grandfather and Fionán soon set off. Zara accompanies them while Ríonach stays with Síonna. She walks with them to the top of the ladder. Grandfather winks and proceeds down Spirits Saddle. She stands with Ríonach hearing his words spear through the mist,

"Granddaughter, nothing, nor can anybody hurt you unless you give them the power to do so; unless you give them the power to do so. Your way is lit! Remember, from your soul splash the worlds around you in your delightful light."

She smiles, grasping his guidance.

Etgal approaches asking,

"Where are your weapons, Síonna? You will need them."

She is surprised at the request. She walks to get them, ruminating,

"What can a monk teach me about battle skills?"

Emerging with her blade, shield and dagger, she follows him into a tunnel leading into the ground. They walk through to the second Oratory. Light pours through the eastern window revealing a water font in the centre.

"I see your desires, Síonna, they are written like stories within your eyes, within the creases of your face and upon the joints of your body as you move. The body is like a map mirroring our stories. Some bear backs bent like turtles carrying heavy burdens and fears. You must connect with the soul of your body and learn to release the tensions and knots held within."

She listens deeply.

"You are a warrior and already understand the workings of the mind. Your breath is your weapon, use it. When you set a task, a desire or a wish, ask yourself: is it a personal desire or a true soul-desire that will also benefit your people? Gather yourself from different points in time and emerge where your wish already exists. Remember, if your soul is singing whilst manifesting the desire, then it is what is destined for you. Look for signs that will lead you there. Fulfilling your wish is the only way that you can take reign at the centre of your own life."

Her eyes fall to his bushy brows and into his dreamy glinting eyes.

"Coordinate a time that creates an image, that contains both expressions of you. You that is standing before me and you that exists in another point of time. Enter the higher Wells to see where your task is already realised."

He leans against the wall, revealing a hidden door which he pushes aside. The light pours in, merging with the daylight. Another well sits on the earth mirroring the blue of the sky.

"Enter the Soul-Well spinning golden above your head where the untarnished spark of the soul never quells. It is timeless. The place of source: 'dúrún', the quiet space that all sages seek. Dwell here to acquire the importance of being unaffected by the death of the body and disengaged from the mind. If you truly connect here, you will hear the very laughter of the universe."

She recalls the teachings of the Cosmic Juggler while gazing into the Well.

"If you truly enter the Crystal Cave without desire or expectation only then will you come to know and acquire the éigse, and the wisdom of this world and that of the other worlds."

A sense of clarity opens in her mind, that of a knowing she has long yearned for.

She turns to see the monk holding a magnificent spear.

"The Sleagh Solais," he whispers. "This weapon was left within this chamber by a mysterious warrior many moons in the past who sought sanctuary here and lived out his days, knowing the importance this spear would play for a future event. Some say he was the King of the world 'Daire Domhan'. Others say he was just a warrior of the Milesians from a land over the oceans. One thing we know is that it is destined for your cast, Síonna. Gazing through its quartz eye, it will seem as though time will slow but it will quicken for your foe as it speeds to the target."

He hands the quartz-tipped relic into Síonna's hands and leaves her to reflect by the well. No emotions or desire seem to come to her mind, just a silent murmuring of music that she has never heard. A charge surges from the spear like that of the emerald jewel, evoking a warp spasm of strength within her. After a long passage of silence visiting the values of the Soul-Well, she emerges into the midday sun and lies upon the warmed sod laying the spear over her body, connecting the ladder of the Wells.

A state of mind soon rises where she feels beyond. Her roots release to soar into distant landscapes. She recalls the floating sensation in the ocean of the Faery and wills her mind to truly release the physical. Peaceful and beginning to wander, the voice of Cúroí breaks her summoned state,

"When there is a disturbance, you will sense it."

She feels a sudden presence and takes heed, fleeing the ascended state, taking the spear from her body and flips to her feet. She tracks the hermitage for a presence, seeing the same shimmering forms she saw on her first day and arches her neck, roaring,

"Hear me, ancient ones. Stand with me and let us protect this sod from the footprints of lurking shadows!"

With her heart energy summoned, she draws her sword and places that intent upon the edge.

The clouds suddenly race over the face of the sun. The moon brightens, turning yellow. She glances up to see the eye of Balor occupying the surface of the lunar sphere. The wind rises. A veil suddenly appears in the centre of the summit. Boars and hounds burst through, swooping into an advancing gallop. With mouths and eyes streaming fire, they rage forth like a wave ravaging for her blood. She summons a warp spasm and leaps from the earth like a wild beast unleashing her sword with her shield held low.

A charge of sorcery soars over the hermitage. Ríonach runs to the safety of the roundhouse.

"When darkness falls over you, you must step into the light."

Recalling the guidance, she runs into hand-to-hand distance, swinging her blade with precision. The hounds soon fall to her brutal speed. Emotionless and fearless, she swings her weapons, meeting their oncoming gallop, sending a scattering of blood soaking the sod red.

Boars and hounds soon squeal to her carnage-making. She cracks skulls beneath her crashing shield. Weaving through them, she unleashes her skills with proficiency, swirling in a figure of eight, accepting their tension, changing levels, squatting and leaping whilst sending their tension back to them, and using impressions from her eyes, tricking them, drawn them into her trap. She purrs through them like a hunting wild cat until she reaches the centre. There she stands rooted on the sward of Scealga. Standing at the centre of herself, seeing the shimmering forms of her ancestors around her, she roars,

"Come beasts and drink from the source!"

They race forth in clusters. With each breath, her warp spasm grows in strength. The boars of the poisonous bristles thunder forth with Darkelve on their backs, thrusting arrows she deflects on the shield before beheading the creatures with her blade. Diving and rolling amongst them, she rotates both sword and dagger dismembering the legs of the beasts when the Eye of Balor suddenly arrests her. She feels his sorcery trailing her spine like running waters. She turns hearing whispers billow through,

"Princess-of-the-red-hair, bound you will be, ha, ha, ha."

She scans the field for the wretched hags to finally give them their demise for what they did to her in the forest and screams over the sounds of the battle.

"Show yourselves, haggard creatures, for I will cut the flickering witches tongues from your mouths, you toad-eyed beasts, come to my solas."

But they dare not appear to face the might of the Goddess. The whispers grow louder, distracting her and a spear gets through her defence, impacting directly on the emerald held within her brat.

Bouncing off the sacred stone, it sends a discharge of green light empowering her even more as Grandfather's voice echoes,

"Let the turbulent waters calm, Síonna, splash the worlds around you in your delightful light."

She recognises her anger building and with a sharp exhale expels the emotion into the tip of the Sleagh Solais, calming her breath by way of the pulse of her heart. She quietens her mind, waiting in silence between the beats and suddenly leaps, hurling the sacred spear, envisaging it splashing everything in its path with the charge of light. Casting her mind to the future as the monk suggested, she enters a time that already holds her victory.

The spear travels its warpath as though in slow motion but surpasses the ability of the eye of the foe to track it and bursts through demons and hounds, leaving an afterglow like the sweet taste of her wish. With her breath and intention held upon the tip, she wills it to find the sorcerer, envisaging it as a golden arrow shot by a mystical wizard as Grandfather often riddled. With rapid speed it plunges through the shimmering form of Balor, sending him fleeing to the depths of the Underworld.

A great light returns to the summit. The beasts and hounds quickly vanish through the veils that brought them. Balor's lunar soul-stealing moon retreats in the sky. A glorious sun bursts forth casting an orange shawl upon the green mountain-like sward. The Sleagh Solais stands vertically embedded in a rock. Ríonach runs towards her cowering, with her tail between her legs.

"Oh, little beans, come, my red belly one and raise that tracking tool of great power and fast as you blink those long lashes that wash your beautiful hazel eyes."

She pulls the spear out to see the tip intact and sends a stark message to the shadow ones.

"With the living thing fed by the presence of our ancestors, I will fell every demon of yours, Balor. We will meet again Dark Lord, and dance between the edge of my glittering blade that will gift your freedom from this darkness you are bound to, ho."

Sensing another presence, she turns to see the hooded form of the monk approaching.

"How did they get to enter this world?"

"Síonna, that is not important. What is important is that you carry the heart of your people and tested that will be. There is a lot at stake depending on your actions and will. Never doubt the power of the darkness. The veils between shadow and light always coexist. Your ancestors have chosen a worthy warrior in you, showing such bravery as you did today. When you return to your lands, know that you are prepared."

They walk to the well of the Rowan replenishing. She drinks and shares with the monk who gives further,

"Look into the waters, casting your gaze through the clan lines of time. See the start and ending points of your journey, connect them. See Balor falling before you. Exist in this expression of energy and as before, sense it, feel it, hear it, smell it, feel balanced within it and now drink from it and know it by heart!"

She imagines through all her senses and gazes upon the stillness of the water to soften and clear her mind of the day's enduring events.

A great joy arises on hearing Grandfather's chuckling laugh in the distance. She runs out to see Zara leading them from the final step, carrying two loads of fish and rabbits skewed on sticks. She runs to greet them with news of her victory and leaps into Grandfather's embrace. Gazing into his arresting humble eyes, she blurts her words so fast they are strung together like one sound,

"Grandfather, I met the beast's lunar eye. As light penetrates darkness, I surged like a wind hurling this sacred spear. It swept the beasts from the summit. I- then I- I-," she stutters with excitement.

"Slow down, Granddaughter, and calm the belongings of your mind and the sun and the moon will shine on your being. Like the tension of a warrior's bow stretched, release it to hear the bowstring ringing like sweet music. Now take a deep breath."

She inhales and exhales, falling deeper into his embrace.

"I conquered him but I am not fooled, Grandfather. He will return this, I know."

"Just accept what is for now for we have much to face when we reach the Valley of the leaping Stags. Always trust the feeling-of-the-way and you will find joy in the journey. Now rest and let us feast with these gracious men as we come to realize that everything can be found within the simple ordinariness of nature, such as the flight of a wizard's golden arrow."

He subtly pushes her from his chest and winks beneath a dance of his eyebrows.

They assemble around the fire. Etgal dutifully praises Síonna,

"Daughter of Fir Bolg, you upheld a great bravery today. You are truly insightful. Allow nothing to tarnish your spark. Remember this when you face the hounds of Balor again."

"Wise brother, you have gifted me abundantly and that I will treasure."

After many moons of fasting, the fish and herb broth stew strengthens their bodies with nourishment like seeds starved of light. Enlivening tastes circle their mouths as though their tongues reach into the very essence of the sea, connecting deeply with the life given. They chew with great thanksgiving, and for being blessed with presence amongst these great nobles. After a passage of munching and licking of lips, burping and yawns, counsel opens.

Grandfather revisits their day.

"Out in the wilds of Atlantach, we rowed, Síonna. Into the singing sea alive with crystal jewels. Reefs of gold, red weed and rose coral emanating glorious colour. Watching all manner of finned and winged creatures dart back and forth. And after a long day courting her silver-belly, to then gaze at this mountainous sanctuary, with meadows green as the frog spreads her skin sleeping on a dry sward, snoring beneath a scorching sun, is a sight for blessed eyes that I will never forget."

They laugh at his jolly ways of expressing, looking at his head tilted, his forehead wearing the wondrous light of the evening sun. A laugh purrs from his lips straight from the solas of his warm heart. Words of gratitude are shared while they watch the sunset bending gloriously over the belly of the ocean. The swell rises and falls coaxed by the approaching moon, giving way for the stars to slowly twinkle.

Listening to the thundering waves beating against the rock they watch the night slowly spatter the sky as though painting the freckled forehead of a great deity to watch over them.

Grandfather and Etgal begin to compare their discoveries of star formations and encounters with solar beings beyond. Etgal tells of his observations from Scealga. Grandfather shares stories of his strange visits in the lands and mountain summits of Eriu. Both draw constellations upon the sod of images of small-bodied beings bearing large heads and luminous eyes. Grandfather using a dotting painting technique his Mother taught him, displays his encounters.

By the evening's expansion, they have most of the sky's wonders etched upon the sod with figures of these mysterious star people, life-sized as though they stand amongst them. Night falls completing a day of worthy rituals. Grandfather gifts graciously.

"Allow me. Close your eyes and recall the most joyous experience of your youth. Feel and sense it. Capture this state and bring it with you before the fire and let it merge with that of one another's. Do the same now with the future, bringing all that is already aligned. Everything you need is there. Bring this joyous feeling back. Now see our dreams merging. Feel it. Ho. And it is so, people of the soul."

They silence their minds. Only the crackling of sticks and the ebb and flow of the tide can be heard. After a long measure of time, they open them feeling a great merging of joy creating the wish between them to serve all. After the eventful day, sleep creeps slowly over them.

They wish blessings on their shared ritual and each walks quietly in contemplation to their individual beehives to enter the vast space of Dreamtime, honouring the last night.

Birdsong soon peels back the dawn. Our sages walk around the summit inhaling the very essence of the great rock, remembering each experience. They lay their hands upon her green sward casting beatitude, casting a memory of their light into the sod. Síonna kneels and kisses the earth, grasps a piece between her thumb and forefinger as she did on Blascaod Mór and tastes it. She then rubs it in circles around her Wonder-Eye announcing,

"I will return when my voyage is complete and place the walk of a noble Goddess upon you, le iontasaí nua gach lá, with new surprises every day."

The monk's approach Síonna carrying a cloth. Grandfather strolls over to meet them. Fionán unfolds it unveiling the magical Golden-Relic-of-Scealga. The jewel sparkles as she recalls the many tales of its mystique. Her eyes circle sunwise around the spiral etched into the oval stone of gold. She thinks of the third Well of Jewels seeing her dreams manifest.

"Goddess to be, you who has endured the Quest of the Magic Wells, take this and voyage to your lands and gift it with the emerald into the hands of a skilled Gabha Dubh, blacksmith, who waits to forge a blade of magical strength. Alongside the stone of emerald, this relic will be placed into the hilt as a symbol of power and protection that will help seal the fulfilment of the prophecy. You are worthy, Síonna, you are worthy, so worthy. Remember this, if you lose your path, use this sword to connect to your Guiding Star. And one final teaching I will now dutifully bestow upon your worthy soul."

Her eyes light up with tears.

"The teachings of the Wells that you have gathered are missing a piece. The secrets held within these Wells can be unveiled by a few things, spinning them and the fields surrounding you as though a great wind churns the spheres into an abundant dance. Do this each day and when you accumulate enough light by feeding them with fire and the essences and elementals of nature, take this accumulated light and enter the Crystal Cave and the true secrets will become known to you. Such is this truth."

He leans over, whispering like the others into her ear;

"Do well with the secret, Síonna," and hands her the Golden Relic.

Her tears drip from her chin, such joy floods her mind. She wraps both monks tightly into a gratitude-filled embrace. Grandfather wipes his bottom lip, wet from his tears of happiness. She searches for words to fit the sacred moment but the emotions of happiness prevent their formation.

Her joyful tears are enough to thank the monks. She rises with a sense of lightness, casting her gaze over the summit, inhaling the charge of this ancient place of power for the last time. Grandfather rings his bell spinning in a dance sunwise. Ríonach tears around them, sensing the heightened sharing as Zara swerves back and forth between the beehives.

Fionán gifts Síonna his final guidance.

"Síonna, sense the danger, hunt, rest and move through the trails along the path-of-least-resistance and let the energy uncoil and slither up the spine, as you journey through the Wells to emerge dreaming as a great Creator."

And the moment that must be passed lingers, stalking to break that moment of pure peaceful presence. Within a shared glinting of their tearful eyes, they embrace again and leave the monks cocooned back into the silent realm of Scealga.

Grandfather carries out the same ritual as he did before ascending. He pinches his fingers, pulling out his imaginary kilt while stepping down and up the first step much to the amusement of the monks. They wave one last time and begin the journey from the summit.

A mist comes down that soon swallows them into its mysterious grasp. Fionán whistles the same air he gifted on their ascent. Ríonach scurries forth like a wind with the yellow beak of Zara darting forth soon after. The monks lamenting whistle slowly fades as the billowing sound of the ocean climbs to meet their march. They step further from one world approaching the lagoons of another.

All the wisdom shared comes flooding back. The great mystery accompanies Síonna upon each step as she ruminates on the journeys that she has taken through each Well.

Descending the stairs in three levels, she ventures through the inner ladder of the lower Wells and into the bridging emerald of her heart to finally rise into the great light of the Sky-Wells. She tries spinning the cauldrons one by one at first and then all together. A certain power courses through but she knows that a great kingdom is not built in a day and like every skill it will require a daily practice. She summons up the image of the Crystal Cave within her head trying to enter but doesn't pursue it further, knowing she would need to sit and truly quieten her mind.

She knows the greatest task going forth will be to embody the levels and values of the Wells all at once, knowing that acting through one sense will lead to the same cycle of mistakes but to merge all into one will give a clarity to unveil new secrets and truly enter the-Path-of-Happiness.

Each in their own deep wandering, our sages climb the mountains of their minds, summiting their thoughts while descending back into the realm of mankind. They reach the final steps delighted to see their worthy sea-beetle lying on the golden shoreline with Ríonach and Zara racing up and down nearby.

They cast a final blessing on the Isle and push into the waiting swell. Easing into a row, they crest a wave that takes them out again into the swirling mass of the ocean. Grandfather gazes back upon the fruitful blossoming of one of the great wonders of the world, tapping his lip.

"Into a dark resting pulse of hibernation, our light will fall into winter's grasp to wait for the return of the fluttering swallow, and for the sweet shrilling Corncrake singing summer's lament, hovering over fawn meadows. Equinox come, open the west of renewal and give darkness her fill as the time of light within the seeds of Imbolc spear their Suncatcher rays, awakening the magical salmon to leap forth, birthing the wish."

Contemplating on his dreamy verse, Síonna looks at the towering Isles as they gain distance with every churn of their oars, knowing that one part of her journey is complete after acquiring the rose quartz, the Sleagh Solais, the Shield of Dovinia, the Emerald Eye, the Golden-Relic-of-Scealga and the gifts and teachings of each Well!

Knowing that Samhraigh, Summer, will soon give way to the darkening cycles of Lughnasadh, Cross Quarter Day, Síonna somehow feels that her Quest will continue even after she acquires the throne of the Goddess. They row for long measures of time in silence, trailing slowly through the Blascoad sound. She glances back to see the sanctuary of Scealga veiled once again from the scavenging eyes of mankind.

"In time, all will seek your light, the suffering and the noble. I cast my prayer earthward for my wish to grow within you so that the children of the Fir Bolg will sense my footprints left upon your sod and my wish held within the glitter of your ocean. And in their wanderings, in their deepest instinctive state, may they find you and know you as I do. I see my enraptured soul fleeing, entering again your great presence, tasting the sweet golden apple of your orchard and sing I will of this Aisling, for a sacred assembly."

Grandfather shares that deep loving gaze, knowing that she is acquiring the tone of a great leader.

"Your gifts are growing like the silken, silver hairs of a leaf of silverweed, gathering into a gracious yellow flourishing flower, shaking a pollen of merit like the fluttering tail of a yellow wagtail. Agla na hagla, to be sure, a whirly swirly magic-beaked one plucks seeds of a golden apple to harvest an orchard of such unknown beauty, the trees will bear a Goddess fruit. Such is this truth, warrior daughter of Eriu."

Her laughter spills out, her heart misses a beat. After a long day's rowing and contemplating on all that has unfolded, they see the wondrous sight of the Rainbow Isles sitting on the outer edge of the ocean. The swell suddenly climbs. They look Northwest to see the jolly giant standing with water gushing off his knees. Grandfather casts a voice,

"Noble giant, when this great destiny is sealed and the reign of our sacred lands is in the gatekeeping hands of our people, we will return."

He then turns to Síonna.

"Granddaughter, the greatest emotion we can experience is the mystical. Our past, present and future are strung together by a thread of the wish. We must meet this sacred union each day."

He chases his teaching with a riddle.

"Otherworldly gobblies danced on the sea and land into realms and witches' hands. Potions, notions and the motions of the beast cast spells beneath a veiled well. Horridly frog-tongued hags seek the mysteries of the sun-flowered Faery who burrow beneath the fox's tail, carrying wandering wombs of joy to the foothills and mountains high. On walkabout beneath the sun, star and the moon, through the crystal seas sits a hermitage where a Golden Relic sparkles beneath the glint of a Suncatchers monk's eye who foresaw a mighty Goddess taking her noble seat as a brave leader of Eriu."

Chapter 18
Lughnasa
Valley of the Stags

Our sages are reunited with their beloved horses and with the wise Ollamh, Breandán. They share a ceremonial smoke followed by a welcomed broth and tell of the draíochtúil experiences and events that they encountered throughout their voyage. Graciously thanking the wise Ollamh for his gifts and care of their animals they waste no time and set off swiftly galloping through the evening and night beneath the stars, holding the task to reach the Valley of the Stags before sunrise.

"Owls shrieking hoot stirs the scent of the beast on curling winds deaf of whispers warning, unravelling a snake's tongue that spits the truth whilst hurling rainbows trotting the same path twice – stuck in one sense," Grandfather gives the stark riddle as they stop to rest before entering the trails of their homely valley. Síonna ponders on his lingering words.

They see again the great sight of Mother Mountain looming over the valley. Dawn begins to dapple the hills in light and crawls down, lighting their dwellings cuddled in the familiar figure of eight within the glistening waters of Abhna na t-Sionainne. The sight warms their hearts.

Scents soon trail forth beckoning their hungered bellies. They offer up a ritual to the gods thanking them for the safe passage home. Grandfather taps his lower lip and curls the hairs on his moustache before spinning and bowing to the Valley while peering beneath his dance of eyebrows with his tongue stuck out, wriggling it wildly, shaking his head side to side evoking great laughter in Síonna.

The valley wears a slight mist. The tribe are up carrying a blessing of the wells through the stronghold, as word of our sages' approach travelled before them on the tongues of rovers out hunting.

A band of warriors gallop at full tilt towards them with their swords held skywards, yelping. They thunder past, casting gazes of honour upon Síonna before turning to accompany them into the valley. Silent Galloper and Toirneach Bán are let loose and race through the meadows to the advancing screams of the children who run like young wolves with glistening eyes. Ríonach races down the green trail; Zara is already perched upon the old oak at the centre of the enclosure.

Tears drip from Síonna's eyes, seeing the children's heads bob up and down as they race over a field of rushes. She opens her arms, embracing as many as she can when they leap into her wide grasp before falling to the ground. Tumbling around her as though hungry cubs feeding on a mother returning with a kill, their joyful cries fill the air,

"What did you see? Where did you travel to? What of the wizards and the magic of the Rainbow Isles, Síonna?"

In one sweep they are up leaping towards Grandfather, dancing around him, hanging onto his arms, legs, back and head as he gifts a returned humour.

"My brave children, what a sight to see your smiling hearts and gleeful frog cheeks of joy parted again. Little innocent beauties emanating the sun, moon and stars that grow within those little bellies, ho. My glowing gobbly gobs, I missed each one of your joyful souls. We have brought many gifts from the mountains and oceans, lightning within our bellies that roar thunderous, wobbly tongues and dragon eyes that have seen wretched witches and ghouls and frog-eyed hounds. We ventured into valleys where wondrous wizards roam, speaking the lore of other worlds' folk. And from the pulsing breasts of the Motherwell, the ancient sanctuary of mystical monks, we bring the glow of her ancient lore within our hearts."

Giggling at his humorous tongue-twisting, they ask,

"Can we learn the magic of the wizards, Grandfather, please?"

"Little Éanna, you have much training still wrapped in mystery to unveil. When you unravel your own gifts then we begin the teachings of the Magic Wells. One steppingstone at a time, my wise friend, ho."

The children run through the meadow, shouting,

"They're home! Grandfather and Síonna are home, o wibbly-wobbly ho, they're home."

A drone of horns rises. Fionn stands at the centre blowing a breath of great welcoming through the instrument to his secret lover. It stops Síonna in her tracks as they walk the final green path leading down into the enclosure. Her heightened emotions trail before her. An enlivening smell of gorse and roasting game curls to their nostrils. Warriors from afar, out gathering crops hear the calling drone. Women by the river and the wells let down their tools. All stop and go forth to the meeting place at the centre, as though a hive of bees returning to honour their noble queen mother.

Smiles emanate from hearts. Embraces are tight and emotional. Doused in kisses and petals of flowers they are sprinkled with the sacred waters of the wells.

Grandfather gathers the children. They form a large circle and sit as he gifts stories. He raises his thick eyebrows, scrunching his face when mentioning the witches, stretching his arms with his fingers mightily spread like claws, pronouncing some of the enduring challenges of the journey. The children listen with eyes wide reacting to his every gesture and movement.

"They lurked above us, frog-eyed with fire spilling from their tongues. Spells and claws and blades were cast that speared towards us. Down they swooped, grabbing us!" he roars, making a leap for them.

They scramble. The clan are in hysterics at his antics as he chases them around the fire pits before calling them back into assembly and gifts a teaching of the Well of the heart.

"My little fluttering's of light, Éist le mo ghuí for it is with pure delight of my honeyed tongue to return and share with you. You are the wells of the Earth, my children, shining, blossoming like orchards while carrying the fruit of your souls like stars of the night spinning gloriously. Let us now speak of the magic of the Heart-Well."

He takes a deep breath before their eager eyes.

"Our Wells glow, red, orange, yellow, green, azure, blue, violet, gold and pure white. The heart shines of a wondrous green like the most beautiful emerald found in the mountains that can only be seen through an owl-eyed princess who lives where all rainbows are created."

He takes them wandering with a magical riddle, puffing on his dúidín much to the amusement of the elders.

"The Well of the heart swells like an ocean full of love singing of laughter, joy, happiness and compassion that is fit for the gods. Trust the emeralds of your hearts, little ones for these are the beacons that will lead you to the-paths-of-happiness!"

They listen with their heads tilted, grasping each of his words.

"Find forgiveness for yourselves, for your wrong thoughts, actions and deeds and gift compassion to everyone you cross in this world. Non-forgiveness is a trait that must be cast like a dark shadow, eclipsing the blazing suns of your singing hearts. From your eager flapping tongues speak a tongue with a nectar honeyed of joy in all your words. Most importantly, recognize the impact of thought, intention and action while asking yourself: is there hurt in my words? Feel your words as they go out to the world and know the intentions as your rose lips clip and clap, casting words that can never be retrieved, once released. So, gift thought to what you say before it is too late. Remember, by hurting others, you only hurt yourselves."

He pauses, allowing them to bathe in his words before completing the teaching.

"Now let us celebrate and put the wonder of these little pulsing hearts and genius minds into practice."

Síonna catches Fionn's glance. A warmth floods her heart as though a river springs from the centre of her being outpouring her lust and desires.

Sengann calls to his son,

"Gather the warriors, Fionn, and prepare for ceremony."

She lowers her eyes in a sense of shame and turns towards the company of the women, trying to control her trembling legs and churning stomach. They walk to the Máthair, mother, Turtle Roundhouse and assemble in ceremony, drumming and singing sacred chant. Sweet song fills the dwelling.

Síonna steps forward summoning her words.

"Máthair, Seanmháthair, Mother, Grandmother, within my heart lies a great honour as I face you. With strength and energy, I will lead you as a warrior and take to the battlegrounds with your men and face the shadows that have haunted our lands throughout time. As huntress, I will raise the Emerald Eye and shine its gleaming edge into the deceiving eye of Balor before the High Kings of Eriu. The beast will fall beneath this blade and the blades of our tribes. The hills and boughs of Tara and Uisneach will clatter with the song of our reign. The ancient sod will rumble beneath the stamping feet of our clans. As Goddess, I will fulfil this destiny, I promise you this! Let us gift this wish with the dance of the turtle."

Their voices rise as they move into a Turtle dance, swaying slowly as though carrying the world upon their backs. Crouched, they move around the fire switching from one leg to another, sensing the pulse of the earth on their naked feet. Shells on the hems of their brats rattle to the drummer's swift beat. They soon quicken into spontaneous fits of leaping, spinning, squatting and twirling whilst summoning states of various animals and deities, raising a charge to take to the elders.

Roundhouse of the Athair Sun

The women emerge to cauldrons steaming on great fire pits. Síonna walks to the roundhouse to be met with a sweet scent of sage from the ceremonial fire, encircled by a band of her elders. She kneels before them speaking of the quest.

"My elders, the great Atlantach unfurled a depth and height in me that I had not realised. A great light uncoiled within as the serpent climbed the spine, outstretching the wings of my mind. I seared into the realm of the soul to see an emerald and golden spiral glowing like the Creator's eye. Upon Scealga, in the ancient dwelling of the monks, I was gifted the sacred relic and emerald jewel, and the final insights to the magic of the Wells. I give you now from my heart and from the Fruitful Breasts of the Mother, these relics."

She lays the relics into the receiving hands of Sengann. A measure of tears well in his eyes. One falls and lands in the centre of the golden spiral.

"Daughter, with a great strength you come wearing the torque of the wizard, embodying a bravery enduring that which no one has done before you. You will now become the beholder of a great sword and lead the armies of the Fir Bolg as foreseen by our shaman, for it is your destiny as a true leader, ho. It is now spoken and witnessed before the order of druids, ovate and bards. And such will be this truth, Síonna."

She bows gracefully before the council and leaves the roundhouse as it fills with heightened voices. Sengann summons Fionn forth. He stoops to one knee.

"Future King of Eriu, carry these jewels to the Gabha where a great work will be carried through the night."

He receives the relics with honour and leaves to the sound of incantations. His mind soon wanders to her hazel eyes, imagining the pulse of her heart beating within the light stroking of his hands. He quietens the emotion and delivers the relics into the hands of the blacksmith.

Fires blaze. cauldrons steam with soups and broths, spits of roasting game fill the air with belly-drawn scents. Music sounds, drums pulse, pipes are played. A great night of feasting begins. The deities and gods are invoked and celebration billows. Our people leap and dance and shape-shift, journeying the landscapes and seascapes of their minds, courting and prophesying. Enacting battle games, the sound of their laughter can be heard ruffling into the twilight sky.

While the fest is in full strength, the Gabha hammers a ritual rhythm upon the makings of a sacred blade. Clouds of steam seep out of the gap in the door. The sound of shaping and banging echoes around the stronghold as he works on his creation inside the forge long into the night. The first shafts of sunlight fall. The strong-limbed craftsman steps outside with sparkles of sweat speckled upon his neck and brow that drop into the cooling pool where he plunges the fine blade.

Carrying out this action repeatedly, the children gather, observing his ritual. How the blade goes from a red ember-like state into that of a cooled silver-masterwork that would impress the gods. To follow, he spends the first half of the day sliding the blade up and down a whetstone before carrying out the final intricate placement of the Emerald Eye and the Golden Relic upon the finely crafted hilt, made for the subtle grasp of a worthy Goddess. On completing his task, he steps out and raises the sword to admire his godly creation and the deities answer sending two Suncatchers, one spears through the Emerald Eye, the other hits the centre of the Golden Relic sending shafts of sunlight around him. The children are owl-eyed looking at the beauty of his masterwork.

Chapter 19
The Hill of Tara
Autumn Equinox

Concealed in a sacred bind, covered with leaves of laurel the Gabha brings the sword of the Emerald Eye to the roundhouse of the elders and hands the precious piece of his skilled labour into the hands of Sengann. The High King gives the command to the clan to prepare to journey into the heart of Eriu, to the hills of Tara and Uisneach where a handing-over-of-the-blade will be carried out.

The horns are sounded, taking his command. The tribe go about the duties, gathering the horses and dressing in noble attire for the sacred task ahead.

Sengann fastens the mighty sword to his horse as only a High King can gift it to another who is taking the ancient noble seat. Fires are lit. Horns and trumpets call them to assemble.

Síonna is showered with blessed waters of the wells as she walks to the centre of the enclosure before a rapturous roar of the tribe. Donned in her yellow brat with the sprig of holly pinned upon it, the rainbow críos fastened around her waist. Her sword and shield rest each side of her thighs and her torques and lunulae glitter beneath the sun. Her hair is braided, bearing the familiar string of buttercups. The Sleagh Solais adorns her back. She stands erect in spine, holding her gaze fixed on the horizon.

The swords and shields of the clan glimmer. The noblest of dress is worn. Some bear tribal tartan pinned with elegant brooches to one side with skulled harnesses fixed around their waists, bearing horns sticking from them. Bronze and wooden helmets crown their heads. Chainmail is worn. Iron and bronze shields hang from their waists. Horses are groomed with symbols painted on their hair. Torques glitter around their muscled arms and necks. Hair is either spiked or braided and dyed with limewater.

To a billowing drone of horns and trumpets, the clans mount their horses and ride out from the enclosure to the applause and casting of blessed waters.

Word was sent to the four corners of Eriu for the four High Kings of the Mac Dela to assemble at the sacred hill. After many days of journeying, Teamhair na Riogh, Tara of the Kings, appears before them ghosted by a mystical mist. Síonna wonders on the mighty Goddess who sits beneath the earth within the array of these earthworks that stands over five hundred feet above sea level, spread out across the green valley of the Boyne.

The clans are in awe of the ancient sight. Dúidín are smoked honouring the meeting place of power. A glorious but cooling sunrise marks the approach of Autumn Equinox. Trails of warriors can be seen coming over the rolling green hills from all sides. The valley is alive with the incoming trod of hooves and march of feet.

Sengann rides, leading his Fir Bolg band cantering north through the sloping trenches to meet the four High Kings who already wait at the entrance to Tech Midchúarta, the Banqueting Hall. He leaps from his horse. By the neighing of his animal and the neighs of the others, the people know that a special time has aligned.

The five brothers embrace, sealing the gathering of the Cúig Ard Ríthe, the five High Kings, of the Fir Bolg. The clans of five Provinces stand gathered as foreseen by the noble seers and shamans. United, looking ferocious and mighty with swords, battle-axes and skulls hanging from their waists. Bodies are painted with the symbols of the gods. Hair is worn long or spiked representing one's spioradálta connections, the red-haired said to bear magic, beauty and luck. The silver, the connection to the Earth Mother and the other worlds; and the blonde are said to be closer to the spioradálta powers.

Síonna feels the eyes of the people fall upon her. Whispers and stories circle of her mystique and mastery of the sword, of the quest she endured to reach the kingdoms of Light and acquire the insights and magic of the Rainbow Isles.

The red glow of the sun seeps through the clouds. She gazes into Grandfather's eyes. Tears begin to stream from the gratitude she feels towards him having guided her to this time in her life. The noble ones begin to lead the High Kings and Síonna through Tech Midchúarta, trailing amongst the crests of earthen banks towards the Ráth of the

Synods.

There, Sengann passes the sword of initiation to Sláine. The King of the east takes the honour and leads them through Tara to the linear passageway to the Fort of the Kings and mound where the initiation will take place. Síonna and the kings dismount their horses and walk the rest of the path behind a procession of elders and noble druids, ovate and bards led by horn bearers.

A bellowing of horns rings out. Druidic chants rise, invoking the forefathers. The procession stops outside the grass-covered mound of the Synods before continuing north to Dumha na NGiall, Mound of Hostages, for the solar alignment. Autumn Equinox is one of two times in the cycle of the year that the Sun God sends his Suncatchers and lights all chambers of the places of power across Eriu. The mysterious mound of Dumha na NGiall stands nine feet high and seventy feet wide, bearing a core of stone that forms a cairn under a mantle of clay a few feet thick.

The inner tomb is roofed by two huge slabs that rest on dry-stone walling, built above the side stones of the chamber. Ancient solar drawings carved upon the back stone are only visible by the casting light of the Sun God on these two sacred days.

The clouds dissipate. The first reddened flame beams down. The gods send a bolt of lightning acknowledging the gathering of the kings and clans who assemble around the tomb. Silence ensues. Before their eyes, the shafts of light spread out upon the portal at the entrance. Síonna holds her rose crystal collecting the essence as the orange glow crawls over the stone, lighting up the chambers, imagining it lighting the chambers of their hearts.

Their eyes follow the Suncatcher arc of light through the passageway, reaching through three successive caverns, entering deeper into the tomb. Síonna feels an inner warmth growing, doused in the light of the Sun God. They wait for the full strength of the sun to manifest and the light races into the womb, like a final breath. They observe it penetrate and exhale with a sense of awe as the beam reaches the back stone, lighting up the drawings of their ancestors.

Síonna places her hands upon her womb as though divining a future life to take birth that would bring her and Fionn together. Reaching deeper in her imagining, she inhales seeing the ancient stone tombs of their forefathers revealed. She feels her body roar as the Suncatcher illuminates the darkness. She gazes in, past the portals to see bones, food vessels, bronze knives, coins, jewellery and a battle-axe lying amongst the untouched dust.

"A grave for the ashes of those noble of this land or maybe a race from the stars that peer within the embrace of daylight waiting for the voice of night to welcome them in through a veil of the sky with a luminous, gazing eye," Grandfather whispers in her ear, evoking a smile with his riddle.

"Yes," she replies. "Those maybe killed in battle or ritually sacrificed, or possibly a Taoiseach buried with his ceremonial belongings."

She looks deeper to see a bronze awl, some golden torques and a necklace sitting attached to a skull that has amber, quartz, faience and stone of jet unmarked and preserved within the chamber of death. She ruminates on the people and the rituals that may have taken place there.

Drawings of the Solar and spirals cover the face of the rock, telling of the traces of those of past tribes, such as the Cessair, Partholón, Nemid and Formorian whose bones and presence are scattered over many of the places of power in Eriu.

She closes her eyes asking for the help of those who have walked before them as the clans stand in silent reflection, witnessing equinox aligning the light of the sun with the darkness of the womb.

The earthly tomb, fertilised by the tool of the Sun God, reminds the people of the light and shadow processes within their own Wells, of the balance they must embody within these spheres upon their gifted time on the Earth.

A noble elder blows a horn three times. The warriors unsheathe their swords and spears and are led by an order of hooded druids. With wands of hazel, chewing acorns and summoning vision, they point their blades skywards bursting into a druidic chant. Each mantra rises as they stamp their feet. The mighty force of the thousands who have gathered sends tremors through the earth. Síonna closes her eyes gathering the charge into her crystal.

The charge floods her veins before a sudden silence falls as the Sun

God pulls his Suncatcher tool of love from the passage. All watch the beam of recreation retreating through the caverns gifting darkness back to the womb.

They journey onwards to Ráth Na Ríogh, Fortress of the Kings. A ring of fire pits surrounds the outer Ráth.

"An Lia Fáil, the Stone of the Gods, I have truly arrived," Síonna whispers, sensing its enchanting power.

A butterfly crosses her path. She watches it lift into the sky, spreading its colour against the blue window of the world reminding her of the bumblebees on Scealga and Cathair Conroí.

A muttering of voices grows. She sees the clans pointing and looks to a flutter of butterflies trailing above with the procession. She thinks of how the caterpillar climbs the ladder of transformation to emerge as the most magnificent butterfly.

The noble ones enter Ráth Na Ríogh. Síonna looks to the hilltops, to the plains that stretch to the distant provinces. Sunrays shave the surface of the sod. Thousands of warriors stand gazing. Circling barrows, mounds, stones, wells and roundhouses are spread throughout Tara. Great earthworks built by the druids, seers, and shamans of old Eriu adorn this place of power.

She senses the memory of a great people and looks at Ráth Na Ríogh with the two inner circles resembling two souls entwined for eternity where two lovers are united by one heartbeat. An Lia Fáil stands in the inner circles. The rivers of the Boyne and Blackwater curl nearby and sparkle onwards through the valleys.

A chorus of drums rises accompanied by a drone of carnyx horns and pipes lifting clusters of birds from the surrounding trees. Sengann reads the signs of their flight before beckoning Síonna to enter.

"Bhanríon Síonna, Bhanríon Síonna," they chant of her fortcoming initiation where she will acquire the title of a Queen, timed with the pulse of drums.

A band of druids and the Gabha dubh walk around the outer ráth three times accompanying Sláine, carrying the mighty sword in his grasp before entering the royal enclosure. Grandfather follows.

She watches his slow, erect gait across the sward bearing the Stag-horned headdress, the antlers representing branches of light emanating his Rainbow wisdom. The sun disk of Cúroí glitters on his breast shaved by a ray of sun. His Ollamh branch is held parallel to his body pointed skywards. He bows three times sweeping his imaginary kilt before the assembly and begins tapping his lower lip. A tear runs the course of his rosy cheek and glitters through his moustache circling his fingertip and glistens upon his nail as he walks to stand by Síonna and gives a verse of empowering words.

“A hawk sings of a dawning song, telling of a great vision most worthy for Eriu. A female Goddess never seen before peers through an Emerald Eye spreading her blades like the wings of a great swan gifting darkness the seeds of light that were sown within the orchard minds of wise shamans, who kiss the heart of the soul of Eriu with their prophecy. Upon the navel, she will marry, and a great light will take birth. Upon the navel, a young woman will be sworn to the Earth by the actions of her great merit. I give to you great clans of Eriu, Síonna, She-who-leaps-as-the-mighty-salmon.”

He rouses up the clans who acknowledge his status with a huge cheer. He grabs his looped hazel and thrusts it into the air, spinning it around the enclosure as though raising their applauding voices. All eyes follow the flight until he leaps, outstretching his arms catching it and shuffles his feet in circles to see the thousands, as his injured spine won’t allow him to twist and look behind. He taps his lip pulling that warm boyish, humble face and utters a teaching that he has practised all his life.

“For what you put out will return with great abundance.”

The sound of hammering blades on shields fills the enclosure. Sengann walks to Síonna, holding the great crown which is woven with green ivy and adorned with a white feather, the crown that she will be bestowed with. Then he raises his kingly voice,

“Take your noble seat, my warrior daughter.”

Síonna sits before the clans on the royal seat.

“Take this noble crown and your rightful place amongst the High Kings of the five provinces before the tribes of ancient Eriu, before the brehon, ovate, druid and bard, I bestow this crown upon you and worthy you have become to receive it, warrior.”

Síonna lowers her head with great honour. The mighty King places the feathered crown upon her, announcing,

"Rise, Goddess of Eriu, rise and stand as you were imagined and foreseen; as you dreamed yourself; as you envisaged with a great vision. Remember the words of my dear, wise brother Sláine: 'Unleash a feminine that has never been seen before.'"

A mighty drone of horns rings through the rolling hills followed by the warriors clashing their swords and shields and stamping their feet. Upon each summit across Eriu fires are lit announcing the initiation of the new Goddess. The message travels afar until a warrior waiting on the summit of Mother Mountain sees it and kindles a fire in the Valley of the Stags sealing the ritual. Celebrations sweep across the provinces.

Síonna gazes into Grandfather's eyes sharing that loving look before rising from the throne to meet the eyes of Sláine, seeing the wolf-spirit mirrored. A howling voice fills the hills. Packs of wolves appear encircling the mound. Goosebumps race down her spine as she stands receiving images of the Goddess Éire, of her Mother and Father, of a future life taking birth within her swelling womb.

She connects to everything feminine and vows to be bound to the Earth. A noble elder woman comes bringing ribbons laid out on a bronze plate representing each colour of the Magic Wells for a fastening of the hands, and some salt, a dagger and a little cauldron and hands them to Grandfather.

Grandfather grasps a handful of the salt and with it draws on the earth three circles sunwise, sealing the ceremonial space. Antlered like a horned deity he waves his golden branch beckoning Síonna into the circles that represent the White Moon Goddess, denoting innocence, purity and newness, springtime, dawn, eternal youth, the vigour of her Mother energy and the ripeness of womanhood.

A rainbow arcs down upon the three circles, colouring the ritual ground. A druidess wearing a white robe enters. She takes a red ribbon representing blood, the life force and the first Well connecting to the earth and wraps it around Síonna's wrist on the cuisle do croidhe, connecting her to the pulse of the earth.

She takes ribbons representing each colour of the Wells and announces their properties.

"Clans of Eriu, ascend the spioradálta ladder with me. Through the lower Wells collect the lower impulses and desires while rooting into the earth. Rise and bridge these desires with the heart and cross the barony into the Sky-Wells to arrive at the well of wondrous gold where the sun merges with that of the Creator and the all-dreaming gods. And from this magical cauldron go further into the Well of Spirit, existing as the source of all the most sacred. Here we receive and connect with the Guiding Star."

The tribes follow her trail of suggestions. Síonna revisits the teachings and experiences that she received on the Isles. The ritual voice of the druidess brings her back.

"We begin travelling the colours of the sacred rainbow, bringing with us the wishes and tasks as we further initiate the Goddess."

The ceremonial leader then wraps the coloured ribbons around each of Síonna's fingers upon her left hand, that of receiving. She takes the dagger and slices a cut upon her wrist, raises Síonna's bleeding hand and allows her blood to drip into a cauldron. She follows by dipping a red ribbon into the cauldron and then wraps it around Sionna's little finger where the cuisle do croidhe connects to the heart.

"Goddess to be, now drink to your marriage, merged with the heart of the Mother upon the mound of the High Kings."

The clans raise their voices as Síonna raises the cauldron of blood before them.

"Within the innermost space of power of this circle where all life springs forth, bind your love with the Earth Goddess."

Síonna drains the cauldron of her blood before the tribes.

The Druidess continues,

"Let us triumph over darkness and step into the next circle, banishing all shadows that haunt you."

Grandfather accompanies them; each circle representing the triple unity within darkness, light and shadow.

"Now, to the final circle, that of infinity. The dwelling place of creation."

A thunderous yelping rises. The clans look upon their Goddess, her brat luminous beneath the glow of the ever-present rainbow, her cheeks reddened with roan, bearing the erect stance of a great leader, just as Sengann and the Bull-Dreamers foresaw her.

Grandfather raises the Emerald sword above her. She opens her arms and gazes into his eyes. Their two spirits merge upholding the privilege of their birth and union.

The High King of Consciousness hands the highly crafted sword into her hands. The five Kings draw their blades. Síonna unleashes the shining steel from the sheath with a sharp inhale to the awe of the tribes. They look upon its thick, mirroring edge to the words inscribed upon it: Eriu, grá mo chroí, Ireland, love of my heart. The Emerald stone glistens like an otherworldly eye. Spears of light glitter out from the golden spiralling Relic-of-Scealga.

A sudden surge floods her being. She roots herself like an old oak allowing the energy up her spine to pour into the double-edged point of the sword. Arcs of light spear over the clans who witness the balanced state in which she raises it to the sky. With both hands, she grips the mighty hilt, sensing the source and balance within her belly. It shakes within her grasp. She sinks, embodying the surge and stretches erect with the blade balanced, exhaling and sending her breath through the weapon standing within the trinity of circles.

Grandfather's voice sweeps over the tribes,

"Clans of Eriu, behold your Goddess and feel the same power that surges through her veins from Eriu beneath. Sense her courageous dúlra, nature, and the charged will that forges her determination. Wizened, she will walk and lead us. Eriu is truly singing!"

Gaining his usual respect with a thunderous cheer they step from the trinity of circles with the Druidess and join the Kings forming a sacred circle around the Lia Fáil. Ritually raising their swords around the place of power, the tips meet one-pointed around The Stone of Destiny just as Grandfather foresaw in Aisling. Síonna grasps the essence of the meeting-of-the-blades with a sharp inhale and pulls it down through her sword to flood her body.

Silence ensues. The winds rise and race through the valley. The thunder gods rumble through the sky. Lighting-beings answer the assembly and arc down hitting the tips of their swords sending a great light surging into the sod. They hold the circle unharmed, standing as the axis of light between the earth and sky. A humming sound erupts. The stone sings as it has done for every initiation in the past.

"The Deasghnáth is complete!" roars Sengann.

A force of solas sears through them as the Stone of Destiny sings,

"The ancestors are in acknowledgement of our newly crowned Goddess. Our new leader has taken her marriage with the earth."

Veils between the worlds dissipate. The ancestors emerge in their droves and dance ghostly around the enclosure. Swords are raised. Sengann continues,

"The gods are singing. The Stone of Destiny has roared with approval. Síonna, Goddess who bears the crown of the White Wolf. She-who Leaps-as-Salmon will tread wisely upon this earth. Behold, for the gifts and values of our forefathers, are truly alive within her. Behold, for she walks carrying the solas of the Magic-Wells within her actions, ho."

Lightning-beings continue to arc through the sky. Sunlight spreads over the hills and meadows. Síonna steps up and taps her throat with her fingertips three times, clearing the Well to unleash a mighty voice,

"High Kings, Grandfather and all my relations, beneath this blade I will reign and pray for healing. Its edge will end the suffering of the armies of the Underworld. I promise you this. When darkness falls this Emerald will light a path-of-happiness through the battlegrounds. Action, I promise. Victory I know. We will soon walk our lands freed from this darkness for the truth of mankind rests with our upcoming actions. Eriu is lit!"

The newly crowned Goddess takes the crystal from her brat and places it upon the Lia Fáil. With one touch of the edge of her blade, she opens a cut on her hand and raises it before the High Kings and clans. Her blood drips onto the crystal as she sends a prayer,

"I cast my soul-desire upon this crystal so that my blood will be charged with the dreaming that is present here today. I have opened the wish. Let us now walk, gifting light and action to our task whilst paying attention to the signs that will guide us."

The valleys fill with a roar of voices, followed by a sharp clashing of their swords and shields. The clans know that the moment will stay etched within their minds and will become a story told forever more around the ritual fires of the land.

Grandfather rings his bell three times acknowledging the

completion of the initiation. The High Kings lead the way, walking from Ráth Na Ríogh with the druids and druidesses, circling the outer ráth three times. They march from there up the northern slope to Teach Miodhchuarta. Stags, boars, elk, fish and beef are roasting on spits. Stews and broths, wine and honey-fused mead steam from cauldrons. Mouth-watering scents trickle from the open court that is lit by the light of many fires.

Huge wooden posts stand upright in rows forming long aisles. The five brothers of Mac Dela and Grandfather are directed to a round table at the top. There they wait for their newly crowned Goddess to take her seat amongst them.

She enters the hall to a rapture of applause and walks with an elegant gait, showered in their cheers. Her red hair glows fire-like beneath the most beautiful crown of flowers. The one strand of buttercups luminous-like. They are in awe of her queenly form adorned with the golden torque, the Emerald Eye, the Relic of Scealga and the crystal-tipped Sleagh Solais, all glistening like the great sparkle in her eyes.

She takes her rightful place joining the High Kings of Mac Dela at the top of the table. A mighty fill of game, mead and wine is had. Cauldrons are emptied and filled again. Horns of Poitín and leighis are drained. Music pours through the banquet hall. The energy rises. Druidic potions induce journeying minds. Harps are plucked. Pipes are played and dancers begin to whirl and leap to the climbing rhythms.

Drones and melodies swirl about them on the winds opening their consciousness into new states. Ollamh recite ancient verses. Maidens sing in beautiful tones. Tricksters are dancing and fire-throwing giving great displays of samildánach.

Children mimic the elders enacting battle wrestling and sword playing. Warriors sit around and rage about their battlefield prowess, telling of invasions, of sorcerers and armies they defended; of courting the most beautiful maidens of the land and taking them as wives. How many heads and scalps they cleaved! They display skulls, filling them to the brim and drinking from them, claiming they are of both man and demon.

Longbow archery challenges soon begin with prizes of livestock and weapons to be had but some seek more rewards, such as new wives whilst others who overindulged in Poitín, overstand the boundaries of agreements. A great chorus of laughter echoes throughout the hill. Heated conversations over land and battles soon surface over unsettled differences. Warriors boast of spioradálta attainments, of acts of their strength, of the noble lineage of their blood. Tech Midchúarta becomes the meeting place where some clans have not met for many moons.

Dreamtime potions are passed, opening their minds and inducing Aislingach, Visionary, states. With fierce passion some begin to shift-shape taking on the role of their power animals, crouching, leaping, crawling and stalking, displaying traits of each four-legged they summon.

A young woman with a crown of flowers steps up announcing,

"Áine damhsa stoirm anseo, Ann, the dancing storm here, follow me in step, gracious people of the soul, and pour your spirit into your step. Hup!" she shouts, leaping into a fury of movement, tip-tapping her feet across the sod, adorned with a white tunic that ripples behind her as silver bells, sewn on the fringed ends, ring in unison with her lively steps.

A brooch of golden filigree sits on one side of her breast with a pin decorated with animal deities on the other. Her hair is nestled into a circle upon her head pierced with a golden needle. She moves swiftly, chuckling most jolly.

Grandfather joins and grasps her hands. They twirl wildly in figures of eight across the hall. Twirling erect is the one motion he loves that doesn't affect the restricted movement of his spine. In full antlered headdress, he spins chuckling in his humorous manner. Others join in, throwing similar whirly movements. Rectangular cloaks pinned to their right shoulders spin around their dancing feet. Sláine stamps his tree-trunk legs and crouches, stalking like a wolf before leaping into a spinning charge, sending vibrations of his prowess through the sod. He unleashes his battle-axe and twirls it in great arcs around his body at great speed. The others scatter from his wild antics.

Others sit around the fires howling to the Moon. Áine leads a surge of dancers into the night until the embers of fire fade, limbs tire and sleep sweeps through the hills. They lie in heaps, full of celebration. Young lovers unite in pulsing love. Most slumber down into the welcomed Dreamtime as the moon bathes and wraps them within her shawl of silver dreaming.

Soon the golden Suncatchers of dawn spear down upon the valley of the Boyne. Sunlight stretches, dappling the green rolling hills. A veil of dew sits above the earth. Ritual pipes are raised, realising the fulfilment of the first day of the prophecy. The clans gather and trail the path once again to Dumha Na Ngiall to witness a second alignment of solar magic.

Fionn ruminates on what could be, looking at Síonna with gleaming eyes, envisaging them gnéasnasctha within the chambers of the tomb, glowing with new beginnings. An ealaine cloiche is illuminated once again by a graceful Suncatcher. A measure of silence hangs as each summon their prayers and wishes whilst darkness drinks from the life of light.

Drums return to beat louder as the solar beam eventually emerges from the passage Womb.

Síonna draws the light to her crystal, throwing passionate glances at Fionn. The crystal warms in her hand. The pulse of her heart elevates. Darkness fills the tomb once again after having its union with the light. They stand thinking of the approach of Geimhreadh, Winter, and the cycles of darkness.

As carriers and Suncatchers of the light, they go forth from the passage tomb and assemble. They mount their horses and bring the charge from Tara with them, rambling onwards to the great ceremonial hill of Uisneach.

Chapter 20
Uisneach
Navel of Eriu

The Fir Bolg clans reach the boundaries of the royal enclosure of an Mhi, seeing Cnoc Uachtar Erca spread out in a figure of eight, surrounded by cairns, burial mounds, wells and forts, enclosed by huge boulders of limestone and quartz. The hill pulses before their eyes like an ancient living thing.

Síonna draws the essence to her crystal, thinking of the meeting place where High Kings and Goddesses were bound in ritualistic marriage with the earth and sworn in under the Dlí an Chroí, Law of the Heart, the place where the laws of the land are struck and divisions agreed before the Brehon.

The noble druids lead the clans in the direction of the sun around the Royal Sanctuary, casting incantations, eating acorns and prophesying within the sacred assembly. A flutter of Goldfinches spears by, catching Grandfather's eye.

"Goldfinches beaky pinchers summon mysterious Faery legs to leap into a lizard dance, shaking stinging bums of ancient magic upon the shadows of the Underworld."

Sláine chuckles, hearing his strange riddle as they ride down into the place of power.

Fires are lit. Bark of betony and birch are thrown onto the flames, summoning the protection of the gods. Síonna thinks of all who have walked here before them, the Cessair, Partholón, the Nemid and the Formorian, recalling the tales of their mighty gatherings at the ancient hill.

Grandfather leads them to Aill na Mireann, the rock of power, in the southwest slope of the enclosure. He raises a drone-like voice,

"Ériu. Cúig Cúigí na hÉireann are assembled where all the paths of the Kings meet, as agreed when the five provinces were formed at the beginning. The Earth Goddess waits as we stand upon her navel, asking of her blessing, for prosperity and for the Dlí an Chroí to be struck and initiate Síonna; to be agreed before Brehon and druids, land and the gods who will throw a serpent's dream, shaking her spine to rise to the Wells of the Creator, unleashing a powerful feminine like nothing ever seen before."

His wishing riddle climbs through the silence. Lightning-beings arc through the sky followed by a chorus of thunder and the clans who raise their gods with their roar. Sunrays pour down. The winds rise. They go sunwise again around the ráth and meet at the stone of divisions. Upon the kidneys of Eriu, before the order of spioradálta ones, they draw their swords. The sharp sound echoes over the hill. The blades meet one-pointed as done at Tara.

The tips make connection to the gods, the sky essence returns charging through their blades and bodies to extend over the entire hill. With the great surge awakened, they lower their blades into the ground earthing the charge, rooting while standing as worthy bridges between the two elemental energies.

Before the brehon, ovate, druids, druidesses, bard, ollamh and clans of Eriu, the warriors wait. Síonna's consciousness is suddenly drawn beneath the sod, emerging to a land resembling the Faery meadows-of-the-Sun.

In all her divine beauty, Éire, the Earth Goddess appears bearing a gaze luminously greener and more beautiful than the Earth's clearest lagoon, more beautiful and glowing than the most precious emerald jewel. Síonna falls beneath her enchantment. She is fixated on the golden ringlets that fall to her slender shoulders and the beautiful crown of yellow flowers adorning her head. Her mind races into a spin.

She closes her eyes and when she reopens them, she is standing before the clans with the Goddess at her side like a mystical swan deity. The clans observe her heart-stopping beauty, her eyes tainted yellow from the radiant glow of her crown of flowers. Her presence evokes tears; her mystique, fire in their hearts. A voice of music outpours,

"Great people of Eriu, you gather as have your ancestors before you. I declare before the High Kings, the brehon, ovate, the bards and druids, Síonna, daughter of Sengann, this great warrior of the Fir Bolg has taken her royal seat as is worthy of the title, as Goddess of Eriu."

The drone of their roar is like thunder. The deity then walks around Uisneach as though not touching the earth with her feet, bestowing her blessings upon them. Flowers sprout where her feet touch the sod. Her light spears out, lighting the forests and valleys around her. The elementals acknowledge the moment as bumblebees, butterflies, eagles, hawks and all manner of winged ones suddenly appear, darting through the sky, singing in melodic drones. The horn blowers release with circular breaths a marching trumpas on a collection of trumpets, side-blown horns and mid-range horns.

Wolves and cubs appear running the trails around the hill. Stags stand on a nearby mound clashing their antlers sending the cracking chorus of a rut over the valley as though dancing to the march. Leaves shiver on the trees. Salmon and trout leap from the rivers. Síonna looks to the Goddess to see the waters of Abhna na t-Sionainne suddenly appear upon her white brat as she walks. She senses the image of the river taking her dream over the lands as though racing with her thoughts, desires and wishes.

As the drone of the march falls silent Éire turns to Síonna.

"Great daughter of Eriu, go forth and stand at the centre of your Magic-Wells, spinning your delight over these lands. Invoke my presence when you stand before the Lord of the Underworld and cast the Sleagh Solais with the dreaming of the clans and ancestors of Eriu behind it."

A rapturous roar rings out as the tribes admire the beauty of the two Goddesses, side by side, a wondrous sight, never seen before. They stamp and cheer for the Earth Goddess who suddenly shimmers beneath the sod leaving a faint furrow of her yellow-flowered crown. Síonna glances in awe at the deep blue of Grandfather's eyes. The vibration from the thousands stamping their feet surges through. The tones of trumpets and horns and beating of drums return with their chant,

"Bhanríon Síonna, Bhanríon Síonna, Bhanríon Síonna."

Her mind wanders to when she climbed the ladder of Spirits Saddle and envisaged the cheers of the clans this day ringing out as she ascended each steppingstone. She gulps a mouthful of air, raises her sword and lets out a bestial roar over the valley,

"Éire, our Earth Goddess has spoken. As we are gathered on the navel know that the day beckons for us to face the shadows of the Underworld as the desires of Balor grow. I swear that his wish will not rest long upon these lands."

They erupt, seeing the fire in Síonna's eyes as she sends the challenge,

"Balor, let your eye no longer hide for I stand before you with my invitation: come to the thunder of my people, to the lightning that sears through our blood, to the winds that carry our arrows in swift flight, to the earth singing the charge of our ancient footsteps as we will unleash our swords of truth, to the skies that bear our imaginings. Come to the hungry edge of the Emerald Eye, most hungry for your beasts' heads and thirsty for your demon blood. To the ghostly speed of the Sleagh Solais that will fly and carry with it the light of Eriu. Your shadows will be cast, I promise you this. Come, come darkness. Tar isteach sa ríocht draíochta, ho."

Her battle-evoking words sweep over the hill. A master Brehon stands and declares before them,

"I, Saoirse, bard and brehon, have witnessed with the other orders and now seal the Dlí an Chroí. Síonna, brave daughter of Sengann bears the crown of the white wolf. Amongst us, she now stands summoning the challenge for us to march into battle. Let the fire from this royal sanctuary be carried to the four provinces."

A roar of approval rings out. Fire is carried by a band of rovers to the four directions. Síonna walks to a height in the hill, pushing out her chest and raising the Emerald Eye.

"Before the Brehon, I declare battle upon you Balor, hear our wish. Do you stand with me, warriors of the Fir Bolg? Cúige Mumhan, Cúige Connachta, Cúige Laigin, Cúige Uladh, agus An Mhi, do you stand with me brave warriors of Eriu?"

Veins bulge each side of her throat and forehead. Thundering voices follow her request with a stamping of feet. Sláine steps forth raising his mighty voice,

"Stand together as the blood-bearers of these lands whose rocks are her bones, the earth her flesh and the rivers her veins like the Cuisle do Croidhe flowing with passion within each of us. It surges with the blood from the great ocean of the heart and pulses with the inherent bond we have with these lands. Remember this, we behold the power and living glow in our tributaries and Wells, the inborn life-giving force of nature. Without a living well, life has no source. Brave clans of Eriu, we are the Magic Wells. Now stand as one with our Goddess."

Swords and shields crack whilst they chant again,

"Bhanríon Síonna, Síonna, Síonna, Síonna."

She inhales the heightened charge with one sharp breath and with a long exhale, allows it to fill her with the power of this living thing. She raises the Emerald Eye and casts her intentions upon the edge and up into the tip while recalling the one-pointed structure of An Tiarracht.

"Wizards' wisdom pours from your eyes revealing a sun-magical path to every soul present," Grandfather whispers.

She smiles, gathering the charge before salmon-leaping within, ascending the ladder to the Sky-Wells. Their chant drones over the royal enclosure. She raises the rose crystal, collecting the charge.

Bands of rovers come driving herds of cattle and bulls towards the centre of the hill. Rudraige of Uladh steps up, much to the admiration of the women enchanted by his handsome, youthful looks. He casts his voice,

"Brehon and my worthy brothers, I, Rudraige, offer this herd to my brother Sláine for deeds owed to him. It was agreed and now shall be delivered."

He signals his warriors with a downward arc of his sword. They drive the cattle through the flames, a ritual shielding them from disease and bestowing protection. Satisfied with his new herd, Sláine raises his blade acknowledging the deed.

"Brother, you have gifted strong mighty bulls and cattle as agreed. Our debt and trade end here where all law is struck. Let the games begin."

Warriors gather for the tournaments. Archery, sword fighting, poetry reciting, bataireacht, puck fada, skills of the draíocht-of-the-fingertips and games of divining take place to determine who will take the grand title of an samildánach.

Fionn steps up to partake. He glances at Síonna before competing. He begins with great focus, winning the archery and then faces the strongest warrior of Sláine in swordplay.

With fierce onóraigh, honour, at stake to show the strength of their bloodline, they meet in a great clash. The clans cheer in a circle around them. Fiacha rains down his sword with brutal speed upon Fionn's shield looking as though he may be too strong. Fionn casts his senses outwards, learning the skill from Síonna and captures the warrior's intention at the level of the soul. He senses his lead foot move before he leans onto his toes and lunges forth. Fionn calmly steps aside, lightly touching the tip of his sword redirecting the charge, sending Fiacha into a spin and crashing to the ground. It enrages the mountainous man.

He plunders his blade with all might, only to meet more emptiness, losing his footing and falls face down. It is enough for Fionn to take victory. The wise son of Sengann goes on to win the poetry reciting, the horse racing and the draíocht-of-the-fingertips, showing great calmness and skill that eventually gains him the title of the Samildánach. He proudly raises the crown in the shape of a bull's horn he fills with mead to gulp before a roar of the clans. Síonna's heart misses a beat.

The Tuatha De Bhriain settle many disputes over lands and livestock and agreements that may have been struck between warriors, a simple way between the clans honouring the Dlí an Chroí.

Síonna, Grandfather and the five High Kings hold counsel with the order of Brehon to agree to unite the clans in battle against the Underworld. In assembly, they mark the task by sharing a dúidín. The challenge is sealed over a ritual smoke before closing the ceremony.

With the new claimant to the throne, disputes, trade, proposals, the annual samildánach tournament and the task to battle against Balor's armies settled, a great fest begins. Le suaimhneas anama, agus suaimhneas intinne, with peace of soul, and with peace of mind: dancing and the sharing of wine and mead and games ensue.

A meeting of old friends, sharing of stories, courting and comparing skills of magic, the clans boast of their prowess in battle and courting and their bounty of herds and livestock. They empty horns of poitín and some dance, others shape-shift, while others court. The day has been long and Aisling gathers them slowly. The moon thrusts her silver enchantment through the twilight sky. The Earth Goddess embraces them within her pulsing womb. A world of great magic beneath and a world of great magic above merge in ceremonial otherness!

Síonna ruminates on the day's rituals, recalling the wisdom shared.

"The beast uncoils and climbs the spine, slithery webbed demons tread beneath the shadow of the sun shining of a stalking eye."

Grandfather's riddle follows her into Dreamtime as images begin to stream through her mind like passing clouds. The sorcerers soon visit. Creatures appear surrounded by clusters of shadows and demon hounds bearing shields that seem to roar in battle. She is woken suddenly by the shrilling call of a circling hawk. She leaps from the sod as dawn pours over the valley. She looks to see Sláine by the river, edging his blade and walks to him.

"What has instilled this doubt and fear, Síonna?" he asks, noticing the look in her eyes.

"I have seen in Dreamtime the horrid beasts of Balor, with shields that roar in battle."

"By the passion that surges through these blades as I sharpen them, I sharpen the will of the wolf that drives my spirit and I shall fell every wretched demon beast of the Underworld. They will fall swiftly beneath these eager battle-tested blades, I promise you this, Síonna."

She looks at his scarred face, feeling an awakening of her inner fire.

The High King raises himself and throws his powerful voice over the Boyne, gathering the attention of the warriors,

"Domnu, Gallion and Bolg, clans of the Fir Bolg, the challenge has been returned by the sorcerer of the Underworld. We will stand fearless at the centre of Eriu and meet these faceless beasts. Our lands he seeks but battle he will receive until the last shadow is lit by the solas of our screaming blades, ho. Scream with me and let our war chant reach the depths beneath so that he hears our strength of will. We will not be broken."

A thunderous sound sweeps over the Boyne valley. The warriors stamp their feet. Síonna recalls the words of the monk of Scealga:

"Your vibration creates the outcome; every step is a platform for a new desire. Go to where all events exist and blend with the desire you wish for."

She raises the Emerald Eye, roaring in a bestial voice,

"At Uisneach, at An Mhi, we stand. Gods of war, I call you to charge our blood and summon the gods of the earth to rumble beneath our feet as we march and the ancestors will march with us, ho!"

She screams, arching her neck and with hands outstretched bearing the mighty Emerald Eye and Sleagh Solais. A mysterious sun warms the day. Warriors prepare, sharpening their blades and arrows and test their skills as they sense the eye of Balor glaring.

The three tribes of the Fir Bolg are called to assemble. Grandfather paces before them stag-horned, tapping his lip.

"Battle brings a noble stillness upon the fiercest of warriors as the thin veil of life and death shimmers before them like the double-edge of a battle axe that will gift either life or death."

He raises his Ollamh branch, allowing silence to linger.

"A great pride and passion to defend your lands soars through your veins as though an otherworldly bestial power gives you the bravery to face this foe, fearless like the eagle and hawk who swoop down void of emotion with their wings folded and talons spread to swiftly grasp their prey."

Grandfather summons courage within them, taking them on a journey with his words. Screams erupt. Each King follows the wise Ollamhs' lead giving the clans encouragement.

After Sengann and the nobles take wands of hazel and draw an outer ring of protection around the enclosure, they string hazelnuts on cords and tie them to the wands and place them into the sod, forming a figure of eight and with their intent, seal a magical barrier of power that no beast or demon will cross. Each warrior then approaches the fires in the centre, drawing smoke over their Wells before plunging their naked blades through the flames, cleansing them for battle.

They follow the ritual by walking barefoot on embers, bringing their minds into fearless, emotionless states to gain control for battle. Grandfather turns to Síonna, tapping his lower lip.

"Granddaughter, remember, your destiny was dreamed and is already circulating beyond the boundaries of this world. In these imagining fields, it is already complete. When you lead your warriors tomorrow know that you and your ancestors are inseparable. They stand with you, "as above, as below." Remember, intention is your seed like the salmon who swims upstream to be rewarded with the mystery of a great birth. A feeling-of-the-way can be effortless but remember, challenges forge the will of a great warrior. Become the brave shadow upon the battleground and unlock your power, Granddaughter."

Ríonach curls her tail around Grandfather's leg. He continues,

"Go now and sleep and find your charge whilst listening to the animals, trees, rocks, the earth and the elementals. See lighting. Hear thunder singing a song of ideas. Face the beast that lurks within and sense your solas and that of your ancestors whilst entering the wilderness of your imagination. Fill those rosy, roan cheeks with faery laughter for all the gobbly wonders are witnessing you, waiting, blinking beneath starlit brows where noble fire-beings warm to the cauldrons of your victorious song. Ho, begobbly be the godly so."

She laughs looking into his eyes shifted skywards, dancing in circles while he taps his lower lip, swirling his tongue over his moustache before reaching and tickling her nose with a feather and chuckling wildly.

She whispers,

"Grandfather, our sharing, the aligned destinies that manifest in this world like a silver thread bringing us together to a sacred time of our lives, it truly shines this day. A time most precious I will forever cherish. Ho."

He lays his hand upon her Heart-Well, filling it with a drink of his riddle.

"You-who-knows-no-boundaries, go forth, red-hair, expressing something that they have not seen before, for you carry courage unchanging like the eyes of a hawk honing in on a blossom of flowers held within the grasp of the honeyed gums of a delicious sandstone fox. What do you think, Ríonach? Truly Gobb and wobblied."

He then pulls his chubby lip down and sticks his tongue out, evoking another burst of laughter and turns leaving her to ruminate.

Síonna walks to a shadowed bough beneath an oak, holding onto his precious humour. There she closes her eyes on the world retrieving deep. An unmeasurable amount of time passes before a mysterious voice whispers,

"Great Goddess, take the Grandmothers' Turtle formation and do not break it as you lead your warriors with truth. Fear not the Dark Beast for sorcery can be quenched. Shine forth your brave will from your wandering womb of light and the path will be lit! Stand within the centre of your inner medicine wheel and at the centre of Ériu and do not give up your position there on her sacred navel. They will advance like bees to a hive of the Queen. And there upon Mide, gift them with your heart, your true solas."

A leaf swirls down on her brow waking her. She suddenly hears the mysterious coo of the owl and lunges to her feet, startled to find him hidden beneath a cluster of branches.

"What is your message, winged, and who has sent you?" she asks of the creature, seeing it blended against the bark of the tree, peering with wide yellow eyes and turning its neck from side to side before launching into flight, leaving the sound of its flapping wings upon the still air.

The seductive whisper soon hits her,

"Seek the hazels, Síonna, and the éigse will be yours."

The scar on her forearms begins to sting.

"You must see past the anger and desire of Balor. Look not at his essence but the essence within."

Guidance surfaces. She flees from this place. Frustration boils in her blood. She continues to the river to see the horses drinking.

Neighing, sensing her approach, they pause and she looks into the big brown eyes of Toirneach Bán. Mirrored are the clear waters of the river.

"Flow with a clear mind and all will become as you desire."

The words spring out of nowhere. She places her head upon the horse's neck and stands listening to her pulse and the rustling waters trickling over the rocks.

Observing, she recalls the guidance of the haggard one,

"Listen to Grandfather whilst carrying out service to your people and one day you will have all you desire."

She turns with a new determination towards the enclosure. Ríonach comes leaping.

"Little vix, where have you been?"

She looks north to see bands of warriors trailing in towards the hill. They come from all directions. Horses are puffing. The sound of hooves galloping is a sound that fills her heart with gladness.

Over three thousand Fir Bolg have assembled before nightfall, settling around the fires, telling stories of their accomplishments in battle and spioradálta matters. Síonna, Grandfather and the High Kings meet holding a final council.

They smoke, eating acorns and summoning fís. It is agreed that the plan Síonna received will be put into action after they join the clans around the fires to share it. Grandfather lovingly gifts his insights to the tribes of the other provinces who have just joined them.

"Tomorrow, we face the shadows of our own minds. Death will stalk each one of us. If you fear death, you will fear change but bring life and death together and life will shine. Remember, the only way to live your life is from the point of death!"

Allowing them time for contemplation, he recalls that day when the knife brought him to the verge of death and the gracious gift of detachment he received that has allowed him to gain practical solutions to obstacles throughout his life. He raises his golden branch, thanking the gods.

"Our brother hawk plunges with full speed, fearless and silent upon his prey. Like winged hunters, you must empty your minds of anger and emotions. Move along the path-of-least-resistance and your skills will be swift and you will succeed. I leave you with my final words this evening. If we give our fears away, we give our power away."

The clans erupt into an aroused roar, watching the Ollamh twirl three times, holding his hands outstretched and then bows, sweeping his imaginary kilt back and forth and breaks into a riddle.

"Gods and gobs of war will come but cleverest of all the cleverer will not clash but dance like a great ocean easing around the foe. In victory, the wondrous white wolves will wander and walk amongst us. Come shining, come thundering like the roar of a lizard's tail swinging a serpent's poison and sprinkle sparks of your indomitable souls into the darkness."

Waves of smiles peel their rosy cheeks as he takes a final bow. Síonna stands inhaling the heightened living pulse before suddenly leaping with her sword from the sod. Observing her mighty blade sparkling in the sun, she lands on the sward and lowers her sword and they fall silent for her words of leadership.

"In battle, follow three steps. Send an impulse to the foe. Create tension and then take their balance. That is when you move in for the kill."

She takes a stick of hazel inviting a warrior to demonstrate. He advances. She thrusts an impression into his eyes, making him flinch whilst she moves in, sweeping her hand over his brow and takes him to the ground with a swift placement of the stick just as the wizard of Beginnish did to her.

"Remember, do this emotionless. If fear or anger arises, capture the emotion with a sharp inhale and exhale sending it to the edges and tips of your blades and give it to the creatures alongside their own tensions and anger as though you are splashing them with healing waters."

She crouches and proceeds to draw the plan of the battle on the sod with the hazel.

"When the beasts advance, we must stand at the hearth of An Mhi, within the centre of ourselves. Root into the Mother and upon the kingdom of our ancestors we will form the sacred figure of eight. Break not this formation for demon, beast nor ghost. We will move west on horseback to meet their approach and from there spread wide so that the entire hill is covered. Archers will bide us time to form our positions where we will expand and contract in this figure, moving as though a wave of the ocean. Never stop the flow for those that stand still will fall. In the midst of the battle, Sláine and I will lead the front line east until we separate and dismount and run under the cover of the ridge that will bring us back to the river and there, we will wait for an arrow of fire from the archers, giving the beasts the illusion that we are retreating."

The clans take in her command. She throws her eyes to the horizons.

"I will lead one band back to the centre whilst Sláine takes the East. Sengann South, and Gann South West, Genann West and Rudraige will reign the North. From each position, we will then merge in the centre surrounding them, moving as one in the eight until every shadow is taken from this earth. Each side will shift their positions, sending confusion upon them. With your imaginings, form a border around Uisneach that no demon or creature will enter. We must always protect the navel. Stand with me great clan of Fir Bolg; stand with me future Gods and Goddesses of these lands, ho, ho, ho."

"Ho!" grows into a deafening voice as they beat their fists upon their shields in time with the chant. The war sound echoes to distant valleys sweeping mightily upon the winds. Raising their swords and battle-axes, they raise a druidic war song. When the fire within them calms, they assemble, practising the three steps of the battle skill into the evening. The sun lowers its reddened eye into a starlit horizon and the tribes settle, preparing their minds for the great change that is sweeping over Eriu.

Chapter 21
The Battle of Light and Darkness
Samhain

Cúig Cúigí na hÉireann sounds a drone of horns and trumpets as the sun stretches over the hill. Winter's first snow comes in on the easterly winds. The clans assemble around the fire pits, drawing smoke over their Wells. Sláine watches the march of warriors in numbers he has never seen before. He stands before them raising his gleaming axe, leaving out the voice of the god to motivate them for battle.

"Eager we stand upon this ancient sod where every man and woman will face their own shadows. Wounds will be reopened. Fears confronted. Weaknesses exposed. Strengths will rise as we overcome challenges. Our true merit will be tested to remain untarnished before the forces of the Underworld."

Nodding their heads in silent acknowledgement, Grandfather, the High Kings, druids and bards gather before the assembly. A stillness hangs in the air as the cold front blows in. Grandfather walks to the centre and stands before the flames of the fire with his white wolf robe upon his slender torso, held spine erect. Antlered, he gazes with pride over the army of warriors and taps his lip.

"Clans of Eriu, today, the enemy is not outside of us, it is within. Light the fires of your souls and go forth. Determination is something you may think you will need but you must allow love to enter the determined parts of yourself and the shadows will find no support in your fears and wounds. Do not fear death for if you do, you will fear change in life. Today, change is inevitable. Change is your only source of survival. Match your intent with your will and the spell of sorcery will not settle. Move holding a memory of the most special moment of your lives and the beasts will find no weakness within you."

The Ollamh lifts his bell. The familiar tone climbs, sweeping over the three thousand warriors. He sends honeyed words with mighty conviction as druids burn wood and blooms of furze, sending smoke that curls around his form, giving him that otherworldly mystique. His

Stag antlers reach through the mist, tinted yellow by the flames of the fire.

"Climb the ladder from the lower impulses through the bridge at the heart rising to the Wells of the Creator, spinning all nine and from there, capture the intentions of your foe. You stand over three thousand before me. If you match your actions with your intentions, you will stand as though nine thousand. I leave you with these final words. Nothing, nor can anybody hurt you unless you give them the power to do so! Unless you give them the power to do so. Go forth, warriors of the Fir Bolg, ho."

A rapturous roar follows his heart-raising teaching. Síonna, Cúroí and the five High Kings admire Grandfather's ability to evoke such passion in the warriors that no other can, an act of his great insight. The Goddess steps forth raising the Emerald Eye. A ray falls upon her flowered crown, spreading copper-like through her fire-red hair. She sends the voice of a worthy leader,

"Fir Bolg, we are united in a time of our lives, standing as a great living charge upon the ancient navel. Before the Earth Goddess stand and battle, we will until the last ember of solas falls from our clashing blades. Reign, we promise, so that the flames of our fires will dance in victory. And as our wise ones lovingly remind us, do not let your emotions arise because the mind is mightier than the sword. Live today from the point of death. Bring life and death together and our paths will be shiny and clear. Walk as though life and death are hand-in-hand and lastly, use death as an experience to stay alive today, ho."

The edges of their blades and shields glimmer as they raise them to the sun gods, applauding. Síonna spins her blade. Their eyes trail the arc of the sword until she leaps from the sod, grabbing it in mid-air and spins it three times evoking a strength within their hearts! She grabs it and then stands before the fire, drawing the charge from the earth through her Root and does so with each one climbing the spioradálta ladder.

Sláine raises his eager sword and axe. His war-scarred face is held sharp with focus, crowned with the fierce glaring eyes that adorn his wolf-spirit headdress. Bull-bodied, he stands taking a skull from his shield and takes his blade, cuts his hand, allowing the blood to drip into the skull and calls out,

"Fir Bolg, stand like the dolmens and gallán of our ancient places of power. As my blood pours into this skull of a past foe, drink with me honouring our agreement to face these beasts fearless, with the bravery of something that they have never encountered, ho."

He screams, lifting the skull, drinking his blood before their heightened response as they follow in ritual lancing of their arms, raising their horns and skulls and draining them of the blood before he continues with eyes wildly lit,

"Máthair beannaithe, sacred Mother, behold us on this ancient sod beneath the six powers of the world and guide the pulse of our feet with swift balance as we march into battle. Ancestors walk with us."

He summons a huge sense of pride in the warriors who send three thousand voices of willed passion to the sky.

Each of the kings raises his presence before the eager clans. The wise Cúroí takes acorns from his robe and gives them to each of the kings to chew and prophesize on the great battle. He then takes a bowstring from his back, kindles an arrow in the fire and unleashes it with a swift draw. It soars through the sky taking their wishes ahead of the battle for victory. Assembled in sacred circles, divining, the kings stare into each other's eyes as do the clans, sharing the light traces, evoking greater power behind the wish.

A band of Brehon step up accompanied by horn bearers. They unleash a huge bellow from the instruments signalling the clans to go forth into battle. They begin the battle rituals rubbing water of marigold blossoms into their eyes, enhancing a wondrous sight while chanting incantations to the gods, evoking the ancestors and elementals of nature to bestow them with otherworldly strength.

The noble kings and Goddess walk to the stone of divisions and place the tips of their swords upon it once again, sealing the act of battle before the Brehon and order of Ovate, druids and bards. With the Dlí an Chroí struck, magic enters them from the earth and the sky. Standing between the surge as bridges, collecting, they charge their souls with the essence. After a measure of silence, Grandfather rings his bell closing the ritual.

And the unknown is invited. Blades are raised in one last rapturous roar as Grandfather walks to Síonna's side and gazes into her eyes.

"She-who-bears-sunflower-eyes, I am proud of the light you emanate, of the thunder in your voice. The strength in your will. The fire in your veins. The fís in your eyes. The intent of your loving heart and wisdom spinning otherworldly in those jewel-like Wells of yours. Granddaughter, Goddess of Eriu, remember, nothing, nor can anyone hurt you unless you give them the power to do so; unless you give them the power to do so. Go forth and tread a new path as a true leader, I love you."

He places a kiss on her brow. A tear falls, merging with one of Síonna's, forming a stream of both their tears that run over her freckled cheeks and fall onto her pursed lips.

"Granddaughter, taste the united wish of our souls."

The tears curl over her top lip and trickle into her mouth, tasting their wishful desire.

"The greatest onóraigh in my life is having you by my side, Grandfather. You have shown me the way of the rainbow sage, to sense and see far beyond horizons I thought I would never see."

Tears continue to flow and drop on the sod as she bends down, kissing Ríonach on the nose and with a downward swing of his Ollamh branch, the elders and children follow Grandfather to a beehive on the highest point of the hill.

Síonna trails their walk bestowing blessings of protection upon them, swearing that she will fulfil her task and be united with them soon.

Sláine gestures to the clans and begins beating his chest with his fist whilst summoning a druidic war-chant. A rhythm grows. Voices rise with a stamping of thousands of feet sending tremors through the sod. With outstretched hands, they direct it skywards to the gods. Dawn is in full light. Stars still dapple the red and yellow-blue sky.

The winds lift into a sudden gale. A great mantle of black cloud soon sweeps the colour from the skies. Lightning beings surge through the horizons. Sláine sends a voice of thunder,

"Listen, for the beast has cast his desire earthward. Prepare, or through his wrath, you will find your death."

Síonna signals her army with a downward arc of her blade. They gather into position forming the figure of eight as planned, to expand the symbol over the hill. A howling wind sweeps in, bringing with it a heavy fall of snow.

In the distance, a funnel of black clouds spins downwards at great speed spiralling to the sod. The veils of the dark worlds open and the sorcerer's wish to walk Eriu has begun. Clouds of dust are seen rising afar. The clans observe the darkness of the Underworld churning out beasts, demons and hounds that begin galloping towards them in waves. From the deepest of dark places, they come foreboding to their eyes.

The battle horns and trumpets rise a mighty chorus of drones. Grandfather's wisdom begins to mature in Sionna's mind.

"In order to live, you must die. Use death as an experience to stay alive. Summon your inner crystals when the eye of Balor glares and trust your inwardness. Look not at his essence but the essence that is within you. You have the kennings but only you can unlock the gifts."

She summons a fearless, emotionless state knowing that lust, anger, greed, attachment and pride must be pulled from her being like a poisonous fang bleeding her wound, knowing that by going beyond the impulses she can follow the true movements of her soul. She thinks of the great Breandán Shéamuis Pheaidí Ó Grífín and attunes to the power of sound creating a dán.

"I offer the wilful flowers of my emotions
And fruits nurtured in the orchards of my mind
Summoning the leaping Salmon
To propel our battle-ready beings
And enter the fortress of sorcery
Amongst the company of wolves
Spellbound with a soul-desire
To reach my rightful path
Beyond the impulse
Leading a white steed in a sweltering charge
To where love sings
Where I lay down my blades
Beyond: the fires of the Underworld
And gallop the hills of victory

For I am Síonna – Bhanríon na hÉireann."

She leaps onto Toirneach Bán, thrusting her sword skywards. Her intention is spread upon its gleaming edge, imagining cutting a clean path of truth through the battlefield with Sláine and the High Kings and the tribes of Eriu by her side.

Snowdrifts sweep over Uisneach. The first cluster of beasts and hounds come blazing to rage terror. She watches shadows rush across the valleys as though the storm blows them in on the western winds. The warriors look to see the funnel of darkness spinning, churning out armies upon armies of wretched beasts in the distance.

Síonna screams over the thundering of hooves voicing her wish,

"Kings and clans of Fir Bolg, stand and face the hounds of your own shadows. What we perceive to be evil is but a darkness devoid of the solas of the soul. Remember, if fear arises, cast it to the savage edges of your blades and give these shadows this fear. Battle with me, brave warriors. Take a sharp inhale and pump your stomachs building a steady rhythm, flooding your beings with love light. Now a sharp exhale dropping your rib cages casting out all the fears and tensions with the exhale. As the animals cool themselves after a hunt if you receive a wound summon this empowering action to expel the pain."

A chorus of breaths rises, kindling the fire in their bellies. Sláine raises a brimming horn of mead to his lips and drains it in one huge gulp like a thirsty god. He wipes his mouth with the back of his hand. The warriors follow, draining their horns, warming their blood with Poitín and Uisce Beatha. Their hearts are lit, eyes calmly gaze and they turn like gods of Eriu fearlessly into the lurking shadows.

Síonna sits high upon Toirneach Bán, her tunic rippling each side of the animal's shoulders. The strand of buttercups sits luminous beneath her white-feathered crown. The triskele jewel of Cúroí adorning her arm. Her fire-red hair is glowing like the blood racing through her veins. The protective holly of the Faery is pinned to her breast. Her stone of Emerald reflects the white of the snow. The Golden Relic of Scealga sparkles from the last rays of the sun. She holds the shield of Dovinia to her heart, envisaging skulls to be cracked. The Sleigh Solas is singing, waiting for the destined flight.

As they gather into the eight formation, the voice of her mother whispers,

"Daughter, look into the eye of the star where the pulse of spirit is shining."

She looks to the darkened sky catching a glimpse of the Guiding Star, feeling protected. She raises her blade pointed towards the star feeling the connection and allows the essence to flow down through her body. Events quicken. For a moment the hill holds a sense of silence from the distant rumbling of the beasts' hooves.

Swords are held high. The archers bow to one knee. Inhaling they pull their bows to a bend waiting for the command of the Goddess. Their attention is focused on the silence between each pulse of their hearts. The last of the birdsong halts as the land begins to shake with the oncoming approach of beasts and demons. Animals scurry to the hills as the scent of death sweeps outwards. It is as though the winds know and the very leaves of the trees shiver. Nature is listening, feeling the great disturbance!

Síonna scans the mass of fire-breathing creatures that momentously grow closer and halts until they are within arrow's distance and screams,

"Release!"

Streams of arrows darken the sky. A sense of fear suddenly arrives in the warriors but the sight of their Goddess before them with the sun to her back, the Emerald Eye raised with the shield of Dovinia over her fearless heart, gives them courage.

They summon the breath technique expelling the fear with sharp exhales and allowing strength to fill their beings. Bows bend again, strings sing, arrows go forth like the flapping wings of hunting hawks soaring through the sky. The first line of beasts falls beneath the piercing arrows. Fionn draws swiftly unleashing his skill of the samildánach. Between each pulse of his heart, he lets two arrows soar for every one of the other archers, as though possessed by a godly strength while he tracks the white-feathered crown of Síonna, as she gallops towards the front line.

He envisages holding their hearts together with an invisible string through the separation of battle.

The glittering of armour and blades speckle the hill. Síonna leads like a flame amid the thousands of warriors. The warriors hold a strong fence of weapons ready in a figure of eight. The mighty assembly stands fearless. Some are naked, more are clad in full battle dress. They evoke an emotionless battle-ready state, chewing on acorns of oaks. And the deciding moment arrives.

Light and darkness collide. A frenzy of hatred meets an army holding no emotion, with their task to save their lands and people deeply engrained in their hearts and projected on the edges and points of their weapons.

A thud of cracking skulls and shields rings out like a great stag's rut. Onslaught ensues. Horses neigh and snarl, wildly galloping at full might through the swarm of beasts. Síonna roars over the sound of battle,

"Like the might of a storm go forth for our hearts are bound to the lands of Eriu. Hold that joyous moment and we will surge through them like unseen ghosts."

She leads, swinging the Emerald Eye in an arc and stains her blade with the first blood, swiftly harvesting the heads of several demons!

Crazed beasts roar with a sorcery from fire-red eyes glaring beneath skulled helmets. Rows of savage teeth protrude their huge jaw bones with tongues that hang like serpents, frothing with a hunger for blood. They ravage forth hissing and grunting, casting whispers of sorcery. Some bear skins, thick and dark, like that of reptiles with huge limbs and mountainous torsos of muscle with large webbed feet propelling them at great speed. More are boar-like with huge mouths and hunched backs with claws like swords.

A scent of bleeding flesh soon falls upon the hill. They feel the dark wrath of the Underworld as beasts rage amongst them.

Sláine rides swiftly, unleashing his sword like a god of war with joy glinting from his wolf eyes, cloaked with the experience of battle. His loyal band of Banféinne ride by his side like a pack of wolves. His tartan cloak ripples in the wind curling around his mighty torso. With desire flaming through his bones, he plunders his weapons as though a river meeting the ocean slicing and smashing through them with ease. Demons and hounds charge into the spears and swords of his warriors. The neighing of their horses fills the air.

Sláine buries his blades emotionless. But fire soars through his bulging veins at the sight of freshly spilt blood. He hurls his long-shafted spear and swings his sword in such frenzy, scalps and limbs are cleaved, impaling more skulls for his collection. His brain-biting axe hooks their chins before he lifts them with savage might, beheading them and hurling them through the air.

Síonna observes the cunning skills of his Banféinne, hunting alongside their King like a pack, drawing their foe in by lowering their weapons and as they advance surrounding them in a fury of their blades. She looks at the harvest of spears and arrows plundering through the air, wounding crops of beasts and staining the earth. The warriors set snares and beckon the Darkelve into the traps. The little demon faery come riding boars, their muzzles carrying the scent of human flesh.

Gnarling with fury to taste Fir Bolg blood the boars clash with the warriors' horses. Bones crack. Fire pours from the nostrils of the boars engulfing warriors who run screaming towards the river quenching their burning flesh. In the midst of battle Síonna sees the blades of the beasts over and over trying to cut at the scar on her cuisle do croidhe as though the wound is drawing their attention so that they can effect the sorcery of Balor to flow fresh within her blood. She keeps having to deflect their blows with the shield of Dovinia while harvesting their heads and limbs.

Darkelve and hounds ravage forth but fall merciless upon pointed branches set in the crafty snares. Síonna hears the whistling of spears and the murmurs of death. Demon and man lie wounded. The darkness of death sits upon the sod. She looks to see a restless surge of demons advancing. They cast silken nets like spider webs, capturing warriors for Balor's corpse-eaters to ravage before he wades through the deep snows, casting his lunar gaze, stealing their souls.

Síonna's battle plan is soon put to action. She leads a band of warriors east, tricking the beasts using the same tactics as Sláine's warriors lowering their weapons as they gallop. Once reaching the edge of the battleground they swiftly turn back to the centre. Sláine and the Banféinne retreat eastwards behind the safety of the ridge whilst Sengann goes south, Gann south west, Genann west and Rudraige north giving the demons the sense that they are surrendering.

Sláine takes swarms of beasts in his path. His hair is thickly matted with demon blood. Creatures fall in ruin around him reddening the snow as he hurls his sword with point agleam searing through the foe with an insatiable hunger. He surges through, howling a war-chant lashing through rows of hounds. Ramming his sword to the hilt, he cracks skulls on his shield and the edge of his axe simultaneously. They ride swiftly to the river followed by streams of beasts falling to the plan.

Síonna lifts her sword at the centre signalling Fionn who sees the sparkle of her blade and releases the 'arrow of fire'. All turn their horses with swift pace. From all sides, they return forming the figure of eight encircling what beasts fell for the trick and devour them beneath a flurry of their blades.

More demons swell in with the north winds. A fleet of warriors meets them. Battle-axes plunge forth. Bones are split. Brains spill. Sweat runs down them in streams. Sláine leads the clans with a noble might plundering through lines grasping limbs and heads, slicing veins with his brutal jagged-edged bone knife said to be crafted from the bone of a beast he slew from another world's veil. With warp spasm strength he devours them upon the edges before raining down his battle-axe. Cheek bones crack; thud after thud rings out.

The rhythm of death becomes a song within his vigorous mind, and he dances to its growing pulse. Rudraige swings his two swords with a masterful sense of timing laying a path of death and blood in a full circle around him as he moves in crafty spirals.

Genann leads his clan with oracle divination reading the advancing movements of the demons. Drawing them in by contracting the eight. Once fooled, the warriors expand around them like unseen energy sending blood gushing through the air.

Gann bursts into the foe with fearless precision. Light glints off his chainmail dazzling their eyes as he trounces swiftly. Skulls dangle from his waist as he dismembers clusters of the beasts with his might of war. Sengann tears through the creatures decapitating everything in his path with frightening ease; his enceannach headdress gifting him the elevated vision of the Eagle.

A boiling anger rages across the battleground. Howls of beast and man echo as death stalks. Cúroí, the druids and Grandfather lead the elders and the children in ceremony around a fire chanting incantation of protection summoning great magic watching the carnage pour over the belly of Eiru. Tracking the battleground, they cast protective spells over their Kings and Goddess as they display their dance of death in the thick of the ferocious battle.

Night suddenly falls. The battle has endured the day. The snow leaves a subtle glow on the sward. Síonna uplifts her blazing eyes to see a glint of her Guiding Star, feeling the presence of her mother, hearing her father's voice,

"Go forth daughter, for your strength is boundless."

Under the shadow of night, she lunges into the dark as though into the womb of a dark passage tomb seeing clearly with her Wonder-Eye, acquired through her persistent development in her youth.

The song of war reaches high. She sees Sláine's kingly form dart by, his tartan flowing in the wind as he rages under a break of light with the sun and moon subtly lurking through the clouds. His band of Banféinne are curled around his form battling ferociously displaying their godly skills moving like a murmuration of swallows, bending, adapting, merging and flowing with his movement and with the movement of the surrounding foe.

A gleam of moonlight bursts through revealing the blood-soaked snow and the mass of bodies and limbs that are scattered beneath his feet. Síonna observes him standing like an ancient oak empowered in battle with his legs strongly rooted in the dhúcas of his own land. The hacking and brain-biting rhythm of his sword and axe fills the hill with a clattering sound of death. His Banféinne match the intensity with timely killing rhythms.

Balor races closer outpouring more demons and hounds. His murmuring growl grows in strength. A dark shadow catches the eyes of the warriors who look to the sky to see wretched winged creatures diving. Sounds ring out on their shields as they rain down heavily. Some get through, sinking their fanged teeth devouring the men with a brutal hunger.

Balor's hounds ravage through the wounded, leaving neither limb nor bone. Streams and streams of birds crash down. Fionn and the archers cast a sky full of arrows cutting through them. They fall, impaled upon their spears. Síonna salmon-leaps with blades swinging, decapitating creature after creature, leaving a path of blood shining in the snow as though a river for her warriors to swim.

Cúroí sensing that the clans need to regather, summons his magical mist, encircling the hill. With the defeat of the sky demons and seeing the mist, Síonna lunges deep into the thick of what beasts are trapped behind the wizard's veil finishing those left and gathers with the tribes to rest before another bout.

She walks to the fire bathed in demon blood and plunges her blade through the flames cleansing the juices of battle from it. Those who need healing are brought forth to a laying-of-the-blades. Those that are badly wounded are carried to a beehive where the elders work their leigheas.

Ríonach gallops leaping into Síonna's arms peeling a wondrous smile across her face. She gazes into the vixen's hazel eyes.

"Come my red foxy belly-one with all that joy in your swinging star-trailing tail. We will soon be roaming the flowery meadows of the Valley of the Stags, I promise."

She walks to the beehive. Grandfather emerges to meet her and places his hand upon her heart whispering,

"You are leading with true bravery, Granddaughter, do not fear what is to come for the gifts are aligned within you; action is your flower, wisdom your fruit. As you go forth, remember the words of Sláine, gift birth to a feminine that has never been seen before and keep the charged dance of your inner-state alive!"

"They are trying to reopen the scar-of-the-poisonous-bristles, Grandfather."

"Síonna, remember, the shadow will become your greatest medicine, the Underworld, your allow to reveal your greatest strength. The wound or injury is the place where the light will enter. It is also a place of weakness but only if your mind allows it. Capture the tension that remains on the scar and exhale it onto the tip of your blade. And give it back to them closing the entrance point they seek."

A lightness pours over her brow as Grandfathers suggestion makes sense. She now understands that she is holding on to wound while faced again with the beasts of Balor. She shakes the tensions of battle from her being. In his hands, Grandfather gives fresh sprigs of Rue herb to burn and Catnip and Dandelion root for the warriors to chew and replenish their energy. Síonna walks outside with Ríonach, seeking some stillness and to ponder on Grandfathers teaching.

She sits focusing her attention on the scar sensing with her Wonder-Eye, and catches the opening in her lightbody just above the wound. She sweeps her hand back and forth over it using the draíocht-of-the-fingertips and removes a sludge-like energy, and casts it with a sharp inhale onto the tip of her blade. She then circles the tips of her fingers filling the wound with love light, sealing a protective layer upon it.

Satisfied, she takes her rose quartz and divines. It leads her to a nearby passage tomb where she senses a connection with the Faery. Into a magical spin, her mind flees, and she opens her eyes to see the chubby nose and big, wide, blue-eyed sparkly gaze of Fawnóg.

"Acorns of silver shine in the eyes you bring, wise daughter. Let us now bring our reign upon the hills of Eriu."

He swings his staff in an arc and she wakes to see armies of the Na Sí and Elves led by the mighty Gandal and Uisle emerge with her through the passage tomb. She kisses the rose quartz. And they march onto the hill in their hundreds. Grandfather smiles, seeing the welcoming assembly of little ones.

"A stronghold of Faery with swords, bow and arrow, spears and magical nectar-tipped staffs, what more could a gobbly battle of light and darkness desire?" he riddles, winking at Síonna.

He turns, raising his Ollamh branch, giving insights to the clans before the next charge.

"Tribes of Eriu, close your eyes. Cast your consciousness to where we already stand upon the navel victorious. The shadows have dissipated. Sense and feel that lightness of mind, the joyful pulse of the sod on your naked feet. Look into each other's eyes, faery and elvish eyes also. See a new sun adorning the lands. Nature is singing; hear the song of the rock, of trees, of rivers, of the ocean, and the animals and elementals announcing our gracious victory. Now open your eyes and capture this state. Carry it with you on the edges of your blades when you face the remaining shadows that lurk behind this veil. Go forth, warriors!"

Síonna gazes into his eyes.

"Emerge like an otherworldly swan curled in an empowered sleep awakening; throwing a slashing of wings into the shadows, salmon-leaping with a magic, sweeping a victorious tongue over the navel, singing as a mighty Goddess."

She laughs, allowing it to release every tension before kissing his chubby cheeks and they stand for a moment sharing that knowing gaze before he retreats bowing as he did on Scealga, waving as he disappears through the veil of mist. She turns, battle-ready raising her sword.

The clans and little ones wait for the veil to drop. With a silent spell, Cúroí lifts the mist. Screams of terror and pungent smells soon race in on the winds. They see armies of hounds and demons unearthing from the ground. Síonna swings the Emerald Eye in an arc signalling the clans who race forth into a powerful eight with their shields and swords to meet the onslaught.

The Faery and elves run fearlessly into the giant foe cracking the legs of the beasts at the level of the sod. Blood soon gushes. Limbs fall. Heads roll. The snow becomes a lake of red once again. The ground shakes with the thundering of hooves. Fire bursts from the beasts' nostrils sending warriors fleeing to the waters.

Balor spins his lunar light, drawing inner wounds of those allowing weakness to be sought. Síonna feels a sudden piercing on the scar left by the poisonous bristle and the whisper that has haunted her throughout comes as though a fresh wound is lanced,

"Seek the hazels, Síonna, and the éigse…"

She screams, catching and silencing the whisper with a sharp inhale and exhales the unwanted energy through her body into the earth, and looks to see the expanded wings of the owl flapping over the battleground. Balor's sorcery races through her blood as though he has entered the tributaries of her inner being with his lunar enchantment.

She tracks through the mass of demons and there upon the western horizon she sees the Nine Hags approaching with great pace. Rage sears through her veins but Grandfather's words spring to her mind,

"Nothing, nor can anyone hurt you unless you give them the power to do so."

Recognising her reaction, again she gathers her boiling anger with a sharp inhale, empties it from her mind with a sharp exhale onto the edge of her blade, and stands ready, waiting to finally end their wretched presence on the earth.

She calls over the sounds of battle,

"The Hags, are mine, the Emerald Eye sings for their wretched scalps!"

After a long battle, she summons up a skill of the mind she hasn't used for a long time, a trick that she developed when she was young. She conjures up the sensation of embodying a different age and enters the equivalent of being six, taking on that lightness of mind and bodily freedom in her joints, that youthful charge that is boundless. She gains the extra speed and energy and runs, hearing Grandfather's words again,

"Shine a light on death."

Like lightning, she leaps through the air fearlessly into the middle of the hags. They lunge at the Goddess with fangs and claws pointed. Síonna's form becomes a blur, she moves with such speed, unleashing her new youthful freedom. Her sword cuts through them like an effortless leap of water curling around a rock.

Fionn is fixed on her distant form, seeing the feathered crown like a flame amongst the carnage. He draws his bowstring with two arrows charged for release, protecting each step she takes. The dismembered hags keep returning. Picking up their limbs, they trounce, hissing and growling in fury but fail to lay a wound upon Síonna. She spins into a warp spasm, unleashing her dance of death, crouching, leaping, spinning, and changing level with brutal accuracy casting forth images and impressions of delusion with her magical trick.

Luring them forth to commit whilst she switches direction and her edged blades meet their defenceless forms. They notice the extra speed and childlike way she chuckles and moves, dancing around them.

A sudden thumping of the sod catches her attention. She spins to see a boar of the poisonous bristles unleashing a barrage of spikes which she deflects upon her shield. A timely wave of Nángod arrows spears through. She rolls upon the sod, dismembering the legs of the boars, spinning her shield as she rolls deflecting their continued barrage of bristles.

Elves ride in, thrusting spears. Fionn commands the archers to finish them as the hags close in on Síonna. All nine of them lunge at her at once. She bows to one knee, closing her eyes, drawing her blade in one swift movement embodying that moment in youth when she finally mastered the relaxing of her shoulders to get that sharp power in her swing. She listens to their limbs make rhythm hitting the ground, dismembered they fall but wriggle together again and scramble towards her possessed by the ungodly curse of Balor.

A boar lunges at the Goddess. With her focus fixed on the hags, she feels its presence at the last second and spins, plunging her sword to the hilt as it smashes against her shield, sending her to the ground. The hags rain down their blades capturing the Goddess in a circle of knives. The pointy-nosed leader kneels placing a glittering edge to her neck.

"Where is your brat-like chuckling now?"

Calmness floods her mind recalling Grandfather's words,

"In order to live, you must die."

She summons up that sense of detachment she felt the day when Cúroí plunged his sword into her and she gained that fearlessness of death. She bravely offers her throat to the naked blade and looks to the darkened sky seeing a glint of her Guiding Star, feeling the presence of her mother and father as the hags spit and hiss through frothing mouths, screaming,

"Princess-of-the-red-hair, what has become of you? Bound you will be in the darkest pits of the Underworld, ha, ha, ha."

Fionn draws his bowstring, listening to the beat of his heart – thrum, thrum, thrum. Síonna races up the spioradálta ladder accepting the tension of the blade and enters the Crystal Cave, summoning the light of her soul while conjuring up the stone-dreaming gift of the jolly giant. Fionn's arrows plunge through the air, piercing the hearts of the hags as one slices the blade across Síonna's throat. No blood is drawn. She sharply exhales emptying her body of the tension and springs from the luminous cave, opening her eyes shouting,

"Dúisigh!" sending a wave through her spine and splashes energy like a spit from her Wonder-Eye onto the hag's face.

Lunging to her feet, she sees a cluster of arrows adorned with the potent nectar of the Nángod plundering into the hags as though moths to a fire.

She rolls, pulling her blade from the boar while the hags advance again. She fills the battleground with the words of the earth Goddess,

"Invoke my presence before the Lord of the Underworld when you cast the Sleagh Solais."

Síonna draws the spear of light from her back and without emotion leaps, sending a wave into her shoulder and with a sharp breath hurls it. The magical quartz-eye spins like a star racing through a darkened sky. She closes her eyes and summons her Wonder-Eye upon the tip, seeing with her spirit sight.

With swiftness, the spear plunges through the heart of the first hag and follows through each one of the horrid witches. One after the other they drop to the sod and burst into ash. The spear of solas turns in mid-air. She opens her eyes and leaps with one hand outstretched, grabbing it and placing it upon her back before landing on the sod in a crouched animal stance.

She wipes her face of splattered blood taking a deep breath and roars, leaping from her ground. A whisper falls to her ears as she runs towards the battle,

"Princess-of-red-hair, bound you will be."

She flinches hearing their sickly voices still present on some level.

"You wretched beasts, your remaining trace will be sent to the hands of death."

Gandal and the Nángod observing in the distance, leap around the sod in a dance of celebration.

"Princess-of-the-red-hair, unbound you will be with golden nectar eyes filling the shadows of the beast with your loving light, princess-of…"

Repeating their mantra, the little ones summon a great smile upon her as she watches their Faery dance.

She quickly turns back to the task and races into battle. Balor has gained ground releasing storm after storm of beasts. Demons, hounds and horses of otherworldly strength gallop forth shaking the sod as they plunder through armies of the Faery and elve. Winds ravage through the battleground carrying the rotting scent of death. The sod is ablaze. Síonna runs into the furious mass of demons, swinging her blade, leaping, decapitating everything that moves like an enraged killing beast.

Sláine and the High Kings are holding strong but the warriors on the sides are being wounded. The sky suddenly comes alive. Thousands of ravens pour out of a veil, with their claws and beaks razor-edged, raining down, piercing their defence. Hitting like arrows they wound many. Fionn and the archers respond releasing a skyful of arrows. Síonna gives a signal to Grandfather and Cúroí to work their magic.

Summoning the help of the gods, the shamans feel the hills suddenly echo with a mighty rhythm. Wild horses come galloping in from the south. From the east, a mighty herd of stag thunders through the grassy plains. North come clusters of huge elk. From the west, boars assemble with the horses into a gallop and begin plundering through the beasts and hounds as though in a savage rut. The warriors mount the beasts, thrusting forth their spears and arrows from charged bows.

Toirneach Bán comes swiftly to Síonna and they face the thick of battle. Uaisle gallops by her side on a boar sending his two bataireacht sticks wheeling in vicious eights, cracking skulls on both sides.

Demons and hounds are sent fleeing by the clashing power of the antlers of the mighty Stags and the bull strength of the boars, strengthened with the warriors and Faery on their backs, plunging their weapons through. The fighting has built into a furious battle. Hounds, demons and ravens keep spinning from the source of the sorcerer. Grandfather raises his Ollamh branch to the gods summoning the ancestors.

Fawnóg's kingly form is seen standing on the hill with his sword and wand in hand summoning his Faery magic. A circle of blue sky appears and through it a swarm of bumblebees emerge in great clusters, dropping the potent syrup of the Faery like golden pollen. The Nángod delightfully fill the sky with arrows, dipped in this magical potion.

Síonna observes the bees and arrows sparkling down upon the ravens and demons like a golden mist draining them of power. Carnage ensues. Balor sucks warriors into his dark maze. Sláine and the Kings purge through the dark armies with the passion of Eriu surging through their veins. The sod rumbles as beasts approach from all sides. Sengann raises his kingly voice,

"Our ancestors are coming, behold the tribes of old Eriu!"

The clans see the ghostly forms of the Cessair, Partholón, Formorians and Nemid appear on the horizon, marching naked over the hills. With the scent of victory hooked in their nostrils, their mouths froth. As though the gods walk amongst them, they march holding one task, to rid Eriu of the poisonous eye of Balor.

The Partholón are sallow-skinned with long black hair, tall and mighty and said to possess a masterly command of battle skills. The Cessair came from a land far over the ocean to the east, a golden-haired tribe led by a beautiful silver-haired Goddess emanating a wondrous golden glow around her being. The Formorian are God-like, mountainous men. Some are giants wielding battle-axes and swords double the size of the Fir Bolg blades. The Nemid are seafarers, dark-skinned and tall, lean and chiselled into hardened battled warriors.

They come so vast in numbers they resemble an ocean swell swaying over the battleground. Some are clad in battle dress, the rest run naked. Shields of bronze and iron are grasped within their mighty skilled hands; swords shine double-edged. Spears bear newly-sharpened points that glisten with shafts of light like Suncatchers spearing skywards. Bows are clinched and drawn. A flight of arrows ascends before their march.

A tall, fierce-looking Taoiseach leads them. Battle-ready to nourish his blades, he commands them alongside the Fir Bolg and Faery as their arrows fall with swift direction into the mass of beasts.

Síonna soon witnesses something she has never seen before. The ancestors can only effect play in the battle by using the physical forms of the Fir Bolg warriors. She notices the shimmering form of another blade travelling alongside hers each time she plunges the Emerald Eye into a beast or the outline of a shield folded upon hers. Then she realises that the ghostly ancestors can only work in the physical world through them.

The tribes and ancestors unite with one value, to save the Mother from this sorcery. Just when Síonna thought they had enough numbers to finish the battle, from the hills behind them emerges the mighty Sleá Grianmhar with a band of his warriors accompanied by the clan of Corcú Duibne. Wind-in-his-Hair throws his glimmering blade to the sky to catch her gaze and lights a big smile across her face. They run with huge, leaping steps towards them with their yellow quartz spears and swords held forth.

Síonna's belly warms with their great presence. Clashes ring out as they plunder into the hungered beasts, hacking and slaying. Blood gushes. Limbs are torn and eaten whole by the hounds as thousands keep swarming from the dark funnel. The song of war is loud as many Fir Bolg, horses, stags, boar and elk lie wounded amongst piles of demons spread upon the hill's meadow of death.

Síonna tracks for the faint gleam of her Guiding Star and hears Grandfather's voice,

"Go North, Granddaughter, lead them into the winds of the ancestors. Assemble there and there you must end the reign of this wretched beast. Balor will come and when the signs align you will know when to cast the final imaginings of your people. Ní neart go cur le chéile, there is no strength without unity, ho."

The ancestral clans ravage their way through the warriors into battle. Streams of them pour ghostly upon the dark armies, hacking and slaying, attached to the blades of the Fir Bolg like wind and rain, side by side. Síonna is awed at the magic while passing her hand through one of their shimmering forms. She smiles thinking of Grandfather and Cúroí.

She raises her voice, delivering the plan to move north and looks south over the hill seeing Sengann's Encennach crown moving swiftly through swarms of hounds. Gann's chainmail mirrors the fire in the demon's eyes as he collects their skulls with brutal force. Sláine plunders all in his path fuelled with a warp spasm demonstrating his unique dance of death, his skilled Banféinne beside him holding reign over the east.

Genann is holding the west by her side. His oracle wisdom leads them on a path-of-least-resistance; his quartz-tip staff lighting the way for he-that-has-the-knowing that the mind is stronger than the sword. All move north to join their brother.

Rudraige's mastery of the sword serves him well, holding strong the formation. The Goddess springs from the ground like a crouched doe and tears through the centre of the foe. Sending out her sword and battle-axe simultaneously, she moves in spirals cutting through a relentless surge of beasts, raining upon them with sword and axe swinging in figures of eight. Joined by Uaisle with his two spinning sticks, limbs are crushed. Beasts fall in shock at their speed and the unseen angles in which the blades and sticks fall.

Blood gushes. Carnage covers the snow blanket. Screams of defeat fill the battleground. Síonna's blade finds the main arteries, followed by crushing blows of her shield, breaking bones of skull and spine. The dual-tone of her slaughter-dance is heard as limbs crack like twigs in the undergrowth of a forest floor. In droves, they come to her and Uaisle like shadows seeking light. All that is left in the aftermath are the whimpers of death and the pallor of lifeless ones lying in heaps around them.

The warriors observe her fire-red hair making distance. Blood pours like two walls around her on the field as she befalls everything. The tangibility of her movements gives her the advantage as she crouches, leaps and swirls without tension at great speed holding the important purpose behind her actions, the return to wholeness upon Eriu! Each movement she makes the same ancestor accompanies her, blending his blade alongside hers doubling the effect of impact.

She looks upon the demons forging her success on the belief that they aspire to the meeting of her sword and that she is only there to complete their wishes, leading their souls back to the light. The sod is polluted with dismembered creatures. Skulls lie scattered, dented. Severed limbs phantom-twitch, sending a worrying image to the sorcerer.

The yellow quartz spears of the People of the Sun blaze like stars through the sky, plunging with great accuracy through lines of the beasts. The hill sings of the clashing of swords and shields. Domnu, Gallion and Bolg unleash wave after wave of their ferocious skills now enhanced by the ancestral tribes. Archers fill the sky with continuous streams of arrows. Balor roars in a thunderous voice knowing he is slowly losing the battle. He unearths new armies. Sláine, understanding sound as a source of strength, ravages through their onslaught casting a druidic incantation.

Fawnóg dances with the tip of his staff aglow doused in Faery poison as he sings an Áer, casting spell work. Genann swirls around the little creatures unleashing blades with his shield held high, taking the spits of venom.

The Goddess of Cessair sends a golden light piercing the shields of the beasts, sending them fleeing. Sláine jumps through the air clearing the head of the Goddess and rains his battle-axe down on clusters of them. He screams with blood splashed across his face.

The Nángod take on the Darkelve, thrusting spears and bowing their potent nectar-tipped arrows. Gandal dances in circles taunting them.

"Gandal's eye will sting like a bee of an otherworldly nectar's spell. Come foolishly to our spears, you little oversized lizards," he shouts, stretching his pointy cheeks, sticking his tongue out before flipping upside down shaking his bum and turning again into battle.

The Fir Bolg usher away what horses are left following the command of Sengann as the time has come to finish the battle on foot. They give the impression that they are retreating again and leaving their men to perish.

In the centre, waves of Formorian, Nemid, Cessair and Partholón are gaining ground through the bodily efforts of the Fir Bolg, cutting the webs from bound warriors, driving hordes of the beasts fleeing.

A silence suddenly falls on Síonna. The motion of everything slows. She witnesses demons and warriors raining down their axes and swords, catching the glimmer of light running slowly along the edges of their blades. She sees the droplets of blood separated, sprinkling through the air. Waves of Faery sweep over the battle like an army of ants, she sees them slowly crawl up the beasts' legs and plundering their spears in and out. Elk and stag charge with their antlers forth; she sees each step they take even though they gallop.

Beasts and boars savagely tear at the demons' legs seeing the tips of their teeth puncturing the flesh. And she watches the ghostly forms of the ancestors shimmering behind every movement of her warriors.

Her sight shifts back to see Rudraige losing his swords within a charge and taking his two, knobbed furze sticks tearing through them, swinging like an enraged wind in a figure of eight, leaping, crouching, rolling on the blood-stained snow, breaking bones on everything that moves. Bodies lie around him, spasming.

She looks to Grandfather in the distance, sharing that sacred look as that invisible flame connects them over the battleground. A sudden glimmer of moonlight falls upon her. She feels the urge to howl. She looks to the sky and howls, not realizing it is a charge of lunar sorcery.

She hears the voice of the old shaman White-hair-of-the-cosmos calling,

"Stand in the wheel aligned in its centre upon the navel of Uisneach and set a border that they will not and cannot enter. Upon the Kidneys of Eriu, cast forth your imagining of that of which you are, and that of what you want – become a match to what already exists, a desire that is good for all, ho."

His voice falls silent giving way to another.

"Behind you, Síonna," Grandfather's warning brings her back to the thick of battle to see a spear approaching at great speed.

Moving just as it glances off her brat, she returns the Emerald blade following the arc the weapon travelled and meets the wretched head of a Darkelve cleaving it and forcing dark gunge to pour out.

"Let the demon blood flow!" she screams over the song of war and lunges into the air with blades swinging.

Their clever eight formation draws in waves of the beasts only to be bathed in their blades as they close in from all sides.

Limbs are ripped clean. Beastly roars echo through the valley. Sláine summons light forth from the gods that surges through him to fuse his body with more spasm power. Wolves encircle him, howling. Never tired of slaughter, he runs, decapitating everything in his path. The tribes run into the remaining foe that surrounds the fighting armies.

Balor sends swarms of creatures, but they fall as swiftly to the might of the clans beneath the charged drive of the wolves of Sláine and stags, elk and boar.

The clans are overcoming surges of the beasts. The voice of Síonna's mother sings,

"Look into the eye of the star where the pulse of spirit shines."

She looks to the sky to see the Guiding Star.

The Hunt

The winds calm, clouds lighten. The beasts retreat, the hunting begins! The wolves, elk and boars have driven them back from the hill. Síonna runs through the battleground with bands of ancestors swirling around her form. The others spread out stalking their foe. What creatures and beasts that are left flee crawling into the undergrowth, to hidden boughs like startled snakes trying to shed their visible skins. Scattering in the dark, fleeing from the solas of the warrior's blades that will release them from the sorcery of the Underworld.

Sleá Grianmhar stands upon the navel and roars, with his hands outstretched summoning up the luminous light of the sun, moon and stars that soon fall upon the snow-covered sod. And the warriors begin to track the lit paths, unearthing the beasts with the gleam of their weapons. They watch Síonna in her solemn dance of death, leap around heaps of foe she slays. She leads the clans into boughs and undergrowth as the demons scramble through the hills seeking caves and crevasses to hide in.

The Nángod have finished the Darkelve and assemble with the rest. They hunt, catching the rustling sounds of the beasts in the undergrowth with the might of their elve-hearing. Sláine and the kings track, by the stench of death the demons leave, hunting till every expression of sorcery is quenched of the earth. Cúroí works his magic by veiling the thieving-eye-of-Balor with the magical mist he spins his great fortress with.

The Goddess of the Cessair strengthens his power, unleashing ancient earthly magic. Suddenly two bolts of lightning sear through, impacting Balor on the chest sending a raging fire through the beast. Síonna looks to the distant horizon to see Crom Dubh leaping in a swirling dance, chuckling wildly, casting forth his charged bolts. It summons a thirst in Síonna to complete the task and she gazes through the Emerald Eye of the sword, enhancing her vision divining the whereabouts of the last creatures.

They hunt the last remaining cluster into a circle. The time of the armies of darkness is ended beneath a fury of blades. In a bestial cry, Síonna screams to the sky with her neck arched. Sláine's wolves howl in unison. She raises both hands before the clans and roars with a great passion,

"Samildánach of Eriu, we have felled the last beasts of Balor. Now I will solely face their source."

The clans assemble. Síonna walks towards them drenched in demons' blood and raises her worthy blade to the sky.

"Brave sons and daughters of Eriu, the prophecy of our elders has led us here to where the deepest shadows of our minds are unveiled. Pronounce your wishes and tasks together. Merge them for the greater good, for Eriu and let us give it movement for this shadow is a mirror of what is part of us all. We must conquer our own beasts within in order to give this darkness solas. Remember Grandfather's words given before battle,

"The enemy is not outside, it is within. And nothing, nor can anyone hurt you unless you give them the power to do so. Unless you give them the power to do so."

Rudraige stands up with his two sticks coated in blood and summons the clans.

"Kings of the five provinces and those who reigned these lands before us, Faery of the worlds beneath and warriors of the Magic Wells, we have united to lift these wretched shadows from our lands. Within the darkness, each of us carries a beast. Allow the solas to enter and recall the wise words of our High King of Consciousness: 'Darkness is a place where we haven't yet allowed ourselves to shine in our true light.'"

Sláine stands before them his tartan cloak stained with blood and casts his entrancing voice of war,

"Let us open the final invitation and give thanksgiving. Stand as the most beautiful expression of nature. Attune yourselves to construct something new that did not exist here, a new beginning for Eriu! Stand charged within your glowing Wells for without the Wells we have no source. Move as the pulse of our Mother sings within our hearts like the sweet howl of the wolves, ho."

The Beast Within

The winds lift, collecting their charged voices. Síonna raises the Emerald Eye signalling Cúroí to take the magic mist that veils Balor's eyes. She attunes to her Wells, recalling Grandfather's words,

"Sunrise is a time of death when a maximum of emptiness exists before the Sun God warms the earth."

The Lord of the Underworlds deafening growl races to their ears.

Balor, son of the dark gods finally wills himself to take a physical form, containing every nightmare ever dreamed by mankind; bringing every fear ever felt, every terror ever sensed. The most horrid beast imaginable emerges, glaring from large, black, beady eyes. He steps onto the earth, looming in the distance the height of nine warriors. A pungent smell of death sweeps over the hill. The warriors almost suffocate in the rotting smell of the Underworld.

Síonna sees his form take different shapes, seeing beasts that she saw in her dreams, the most horrid things imaginable. He embodies a terrifying scaled green serpent-like form. His head moves slowly like a lizard. His eyes turn from green to red and then a fierce, luminous yellow, coated with the lunar fire. He scorches the sod around him, grunting wildly. Rows of huge teeth sit jagged upon his beastly black gums as he snarls, showing a long, frothing tongue that hangs, swinging from his hungered mouth.

With a ferocious pace, he begins to hop in mighty leaps, carried by huge webbed feet bearing the same skin as the Beasts-of-the-Growling-Shields that Síonna dreamt of.

Skulls of souls enslaved swing from his waist. Bones stick out of his back giving him an outer protective shell. In one hand a battle-axe with blades bigger than the tallest warrior hangs and the feared lunar sword with its double jagged edge shines luminous yellow held in the other. His third eye glares emanating that piercing light said to be the thieving-eye-of-Balor where one glance is enough to capture the soul and once drawn in, the foe is bound and a serpent skin that cannot be shed grows upon its host.

He raises his weapons, sending his stench of death before him on the winds. Sláine screams over the sound of terror,

"Look from the wonder of your own souls and go forth fearless, ho."

Fionn releases a mighty breath into a horn, raising a battle bellow. Síonna feels as though the melody churns at her root and dances up her ladder, spinning her Wells as she raises her mind, spinning all nine cauldrons at speed while she gives thanks to the monks of Scealga for that final insight. She wills her mind to find the missing charge, trying to enter the Crystal Cave. Her mind races back to when she was suspended, cross-legged on the surface of the ocean in the lands of the

Na Sí. A great sense of lightness comes over her as she raises her consciousness into a one-pointed state sitting over her being. The glow of her inner cave pours out enclosing her physical structure.

With the mighty charge, feeling protected, she opens her eyes and runs leaping in huge steps, feeling lighter than ever before and salmon-leaps higher than she ever did and plunges her magical sword, driving her wish into the point. Balor leads a brutal charge towards her and swings his lunar blade. The clans observe as the weapons of light and darkness meet, sending a deafening high-pitched clash ringing out over the hill.

The impact sends her blade backwards at first but she redirects the point of her blade along the line of his attack, allowing it to travel the path-of-least-resistance and plunges it into his forearm. He flinches as she draws first blood and sweeps his lunar glare down to capture her soul. She raises the shield of Dovinia, seeing the second shimmering shield of her ancestor deflecting the soul-stealing light together. Kindling bravery within her warriors, she screams while rolling onto the sod,

"The sorcerer too bleeds!"

Balor plunges his huge axe down again. She rolls out of the way. It sinks into the ground. Arrows trail the sky. The tribes thrust their spears and blades into the beast. His lunar light captures their eyes, swords clash, blood gushes. Sláine runs with the wolves, the Banféinne and hounds parallel lunge through the air meeting the beast with fierce determination, cutting wounds upon his legs while the wolves, stags, elk and hounds ravage and tear at his webbed feet.

The sorcerer thrusts the butt of his sword out at the High King in a terrible rage. Sláine raises his shield taking the full force that sends him hurling through the air while Balor casts his serpent-tongue in an arc, trapping a cluster of warriors and elves, pulling them into his razor-teeth and dismembering them. Síonna sees the shimmering forms of the ancestors fleeing the warriors, their slain bodies and taking others. Balor then sucks out the warriors souls enslaving them for Sláine to see before spitting their remains over Uisneach.

It enrages the Fir Bolg King. Carnage ensues. The sorcerer's strength and speed are ferocious. Cúroí and the Goddess of Cessair summon more ancestors who plough forward. Balor sends the glare of his enchanting eye sweeping like a solar wind over the sward sending them scurrying beneath their shields.

Fionn and the archers release a continuous stream of arrows causing little effect on his thick serpent skin. Fawnóg raises his staff summoning forth the bumble bees. Swiftly they come, showering the sorcerer in the golden syrup of the Faery.

"Whilst under the influence of love our Mother spins her elemental winds churning a golden pollen of whirly strength from luminous bees who bestow upon the beast a magical nectar," Gandal riddles, watching the pollen fall like snow and stick to the beast's scales, shrouding him in a golden light.

The sorcerer screams in pain.

He leaps, firing handfuls of the golden syrup at the sorcerer. Balor swings his weapons in desperation, whirling into a stampede, crushing warriors around him and sending Gandal fleeing. Síonna crouches, stalking, before leaping in rhythm with the shift of his weight and plunges the Emerald Eye into the back of his thigh, watching the ghostly blade of the ancestor accompanying her sword. As she withdraws it, challenges and impulses from her past suddenly sear through her mind as though contact with the beast brings her down to the lower impulses of the Root-Wells. Images flood her mind.

The golden husks reappear. The music sings beautifully over the sound of battle. Seeing the desire lit within her eyes, Sláine and the warriors quickly surround her and rage upon the sorcerer with great fury. The whisper of mystery also returns but she grasps it with a sharp inhale and on an exhale, leaps from the ground, sending her blade back into the demon, returning his sorcery. Another event opens within her mind.

"Climb the spioradálta ladder," the voice commands.

She sends her mind up the ladder only to be halted again by the whisper, as though a demon snake weaves around her spine stopping her to summit to the Sky-Well. Her yearning for Fionn arises while she continues trying to summon her consciousness. She struggles to regain clarity, seeing the owl hovering over the hill. A sudden call causes her to flinch.

"Síonna!"

She side-steps from the incoming spear and unleashes her blade, cutting it in half. Her clarity sharply returns. "Use death as an experience to stay alive," she whispers.

She takes the rose jewel from her brat, thinking of Ogma recalling all the light gathered throughout her quest, that of the flowers, the trees, animals, the ocean, the earth and the beautiful presence of each of the Rainbow Isles and their people. The plants, the stars, the winged, Faery, Nángod, the ancestors, the rivers, lakes, mountains, the hills and places of power and the sacred state she received upon the Mother Well of Scealga.

With a mighty breath, she evokes the special solas of her dream! The clans witness a wave of energy building around her that climbs up her body, shrouding her with a protective layer of light as though wrapped in the coloured bands of a rainbow. Uisneach wears the sward of blood-red snow. A Goddess emanating such light never seen before stands forth.

"One path it will travel with the clearness of the quartz eye, with the wishes of ancestors behind it. Time will slow for the foe as it speeds to its victory."

Suddenly, all the wisdom weaves together in her mind. She revisits the living links she and Grandfather travelled along the Quest. The trails of the ancient clan lines light up within, like the map of Ogma showing the structure of the Wells. She begins to see each Isle connected by a mysterious thread of light that forms the shape of a diamond.

"Do well with the secret, each announced and whispered to my ear. Now I understand. The Wells must be connected as one."

One wholesome image gathers on her Wonder-Eye. She knows it is time and hears the subtle echo of Grandfather's bell summoning the serpent rainbow Shamans to guide her cast.

"The end depends on the beginning," his guidance repeats.

Balor sends a horrid sound sweeping over the hill followed by ferocious winds that sweep warriors from the earth, hurling them through the air before spinning them to the sod where he throws a thieving-eye-of-lunar-sorcery upon them, enslaving their souls.

Síonna holds the nine-fold bronze shield of Dovinia to her chest as his enchanting eye sears forth to capture her. She summons the rock-dreaming and roots into the sod. Images and teachings flash through her mind.

"Go forth in awakened sleep with your power. Hurl it but never in anger; clear your mind lucid as the mirroring sky. Bring life and death into the middle of the battleground; then life becomes beautiful, Granddaughter, ho. Through this, understand your unique nature and when the moment comes you will know what to do with the crystal and all the light you will collect."

She calls out,

"Duisigi!" and takes the Sleagh Solais from her back bringing tips of both crystals together.

She closes her eyes merging her wish with the light. A magnificent glow pours from the rose quartz into the spear of light, she sees with her eyes closed, knowing, she is now connecting an ancient living thing.

Her eyes spring open. Without emotion, she spins her Wells all at once while bursting into a sprint, finding the range to cast her spear. With the grace of the ancestor subtly holding the spear with her, she takes a succession of quick steps while propelling a wave through her body, seeing the ancestor's shimmering form matching her movement. They leap together, hand in hand around the spear and hurl it with a ferocious swing, merged with a screaming breath to travel before it carrying the power of the wish forth.

Gandal leaps backwards to land on his feet and dance in circles in witness to the magical event. All gazes are fixed upon the illumined point spinning as though a star trailing through the unknown depths of darkness, solving the tasks for all the clans of Eriu. Before it, a flutter of butterflies appears creating a magical flightpath for the spear.

'For you, Daire Domhain and the Milesians," Síonna whispers.

The wishes of the clans glow, one-pointed upon the tip as though passing through the veils of time to arrive at the point of victory that has already been prophesied.

Balor summons all his sorcerer's might. It is as though the sun and his distant shadow that contains all the fears and wounds of mankind are merging above the battleground where only one will survive. Life and death. Darkness and light race through the air, as a balance hangs like a silken thread of a spider holding the prize of an aligned time, for one side to gain reign over the ancient lands of Eriu, the other to be banished forever from the otherworldly province of Mide.

The wishes, dreaming and Aislings of both worlds meet. Síonna trusts the one thing that will determine what the outcome will be, what benefits the greater good of all mankind. She recalls the Equinox ritual at Brú Na Boinne when the Suncatcher shaft entered the womb of the Mother and struck the back stone, summoning a feeling of fire and passion, charged like a beast in the hunt. She roars as Balor casts his spear.

She raises the nine-fold bronze shield to her breast. His spear impacts the centre, sending a concentric ring of lunar light out across the battleground. The hill falls silent. The terrible sound echoes as though nature takes a deep breath knowing that the thin line of life and death hangs within her following actions.

The time of life aligns that binds together the thousands of years of imaginings and prophecies of the druids and shamans. With mighty force, the spear of power furrows along its aligned path amongst the coloured wings of the butterflies and enters the dark womb of the Underworld, burrowing deep into the sorcerer's chest, heart-deep.

Síonna envisages all the wondrous light collected bursting forth from the spear, carrying the special solas of the dream, projecting deep through the veils of fear washing away every wrongdoing of mankind, every impulse of anger, greed, lust, envy, hatred and his unhealthy attachments and desires. She gifts them back to the sorcerer, carrying a clear message: The Fir Bolg will never give up Eriu.

His roar bounces through the hills and rustles through the trees, rattling towards all horizons. The clans observe his towering form stagger beneath the onslaught of arrows. The potent syrup of the Faery seeps into his weakening body and the magic wished by all manifests. Balor's towering form plunders to his knees, sending a huge rattle through the sward. They witness almost in disbelief.

Síonna spins her Wells, entering the Crystal Cave of her mind summoning a great glow around her and draws with her breath a final warp spasm from the earth.

Seeing the ancestor shimmering within the veils of light around her body, she breaks into another sprint. Sláine, the Banféinne and the

High Kings follow her swift trail. Wolves, stags, elk, the Faery and Nángod run side by side like wind and rain as she quickly makes distance from them.

As she runs, she hears music. The warriors are pounding on bodhráns drumming a mighty rhythm in time with her steps. The pipes screech in melodious melody. The trumpets and horns send drones she feels in the very ground vibrating with the warp spasm charge she inhales. The music is like another language to her that gives fire to her will.

She races, swishing through the grass, detached from the fear of death recalling the moment Cúroí plunged his blade into her breast. She advances her white feathered crown sitting like a beacon upon her head, the Emerald stone emanating from the hilt, the triskele torque of Cúroí around her arm carrying the trinity charge of all life, the Golden Relic casting a sparkling spiral as she darts by the clans like a hunting wolf. She runs, her naked feet divining a feeling-of-the-way. Like sword and shield, the ancestor runs beside her.

Her rhythmic breath sharply excels as she propels herself salmon-leaping to a height of two warriors with her intention set in her Sky-Wells while swinging the charged blade.

The clans see the shining arc of steel flash before it quickly disappears deep to the hilt into the beast, followed by his deafening growl. She too roars, pronouncing the name of the Earth Goddess,

"Éire, Éire, Éire, this shadow now holds the special light of our dream."

Withdrawing her blade, she falls to her feet and stands beneath the demon almost drowning in the gushing streams of his blood.

His soul-stealing light sweeps over the land and in one last desperate try, he swings the lunar sword in a downward arc. Síonna draws her shield over her eyes summoning the trick of the giant. His blade bounces off her enforced shield by way of the ancestor as she holds the rock-form. She screams,

"Your lunar blade cuts metal but not stone, beast!"

Empowered, she plunges her blade again into the belly of the sorcerer, recalling the sensation and essence of the sun penetrating the passage tomb. He answers casting his silvery web. She looks to see the silken trap descending and with a swift swipe, she takes the quills of Brian Mac Daire and spreads them with a flick of her wrist, seeing the ancestors hand spread over hers to lance the web into pieces, whilst pulling her blade from his torso.

Shadows swirl out from his wounds trying to attach to some source, but the wounds of fear are closed in the warriors.

Sláine and the kings watch the Goddess drenched in the beast's blood. She springs from a crouched position, spinning her mighty weapon through the air, roaring,

"This is for the Cosmic Juggler, ho!"

An arc of truth shines before her glittering blade as his lunar sword comes down to meet it. Both clash; a deafening sound spears outward.

The Emerald Eye is untouched, protected by the magic hammered, drummed and dreamed upon it by the skilled Gabha.

"Eriu, grá mo chroí," she whispers the powerful prayer etched on her blade and remembers Grandfathers teaching. "Love your enemy and you destroy the enemy within him."

She then summons up one of the most joyous moments of her life when Grandfather looked into her eyes, telling her he was bringing her on this Quest.

Without further thought, she leaps up the ladder into a state of a Creator, and with a swift swing like the spreading wings of a swan, her blade sings through the air. The edge shines of two blades as the clans witness the ghostly ancestor merged with the body of the Goddess. The blade strengthened with the energy of two takes Balor's glaring head with one clean cut. Síonna feels a cutting of threads in her body, as though the lower impulses are cast from her mind, cleaving the head of the beast. She feels she has stepped over the thin veil into the direction of north on the medicine wheel.

The thousands of warriors look on awed as the sorcerer's headless body falls. Síonna falls with him as though she has ascended to the unknown heights, completing her task and is now ready to come back to the Mother to root and merge her being with her victorious pulse as Balor succumbs to his death.

A huge rumble shakes the sod. His torso plunges heavily, wearing a shawl of arrows. Síonna rolls and stands gazing at the slain enemy almost in disbelief. She pulls the Sleagh Solais out, seeing the hands of the ancestor wrapped around it as though a Sun God retrieving his luminous Suncatcher from the darkness of an unknown passage tomb, awakening a new dawn upon Eriu! Souls of those entrapped pour out from the sorcerer's wound. They swirl like dark clouds above them ascending to take another incarnation.

Sláine raises his horn and blows a mighty breath as he did at the beginning of the battle. The pipers, horn and trumpet blowers follow his action. A thunderous sustained tone rises over the hill acknowledging their victory over the forces of the Underworld.

Síonna stands inhaling the charge, before sticking the quartz head of her spear through the snow-covered sward, cleansing the blood of sorcery from it whilst roaring in an entrancing state over the horns. She raises both spear and sword to the sky beckoning the tribes,

"A Dhia os na Déithe, let the shadows of the sorcerer hear you. Scream the words inscribed on this sacred blade, brave clans of Fir Bolg."

"Eriu, grá mo chroí, Eriu, grá mo chroí…" Their voices climb like a singing flock of summer starlings.

Grandfather comes dancing from the hill with his arms outstretched followed by Cúroí, the elders and children. Ríonach races in loops about them. Zara chirps gloriously through the sky. Grandfather takes out two hazel sticks and clicks them together, evoking the entire valley of tribes to click their swords and shields and dance.

They march on the earth, looking at Balor's slain body, lifeless, his eyes frozen, glaring, his tongue hanging limply between his fanged teeth. Yellow blood gushes from his snake-like mouth. His sorcery is dissipating into the charged belly of the Earth Goddess. Sláine beckons Síonna.

The two mighty warriors crouch to one knee and grasp the beastly head. They raise it before a rapturous drone of victorious voices. And just when they thought the sorcery was driven, his tongue comes alive, wriggling with one last phantom surge and wraps around Síonna's forearm, licking the scar of the poisonous boar. She feels a piercing sensation and looks to see his tongue has drawn fresh blood from the wound as many of his beasts previously tried. She feels disappointed thinking she had energetically and ritually closed the wound.

Sláine swiftly severs it with his bone knife. The Goddess unravels the slimy meat seeing jagged-like hairs on its surface coated with her blood and flings it into the flames of a fire lit for the victory celebrations. They then lift the head, dutifully reminding the tribes,

"To imagine is to believe. Walk the path of fearlessness with one foot in life and the other in death. Use death as an experience to stay alive. Cúig Cúigí na hEireann, Teamhrach our actions are delivered and the prophecy is fulfilled, ho!"

They follow her chant, 'Ho!' several times before Sláine completes the task.

"Clans of Eriu, I give you the cleaved head of Balor. Bathe in the fires of victory for the untarnished spark of our souls sings, our glorious kingdom shall never be taken. Our children and their future children will speak of this day with great honour."

The purple-black sky is pierced by a great light. A sense of heightened wisdom dawns as a sun bursts through luminously. A red shroud returns, turning the hill copper. The clans witness Balor's lightbody emerge. It rises in the form of shadows from the many souls he bound to darkness throughout several lifetimes. They lift from his headless body and soar into the sky, free at last. The tribes celebrate, casting arrows and dancing with their swords twirling and laughing and crying. The yellow quartz spears furrow through the air. The elementals sing. Horizons glow aflame with lightning. Animals return, galloping through the valleys. Birdsong chitters.

Horses, stags, boars, wolves, elk and hounds tread the sod. Uaisle, Gandal and the elves leap with them laughing aloud, carrying out trickery, lightening the hearts of those wounded. When the charge settles, Síonna beckons the five brothers of Mac Dela, Sleá Grianmhar, Uaisle, and some strong warriors to follow her to a dolmen.

As though their souls have rolled through many lifetimes to meet at this moment, like masters of mighty magic they stand in sacred union and carry out this great task. A rope is secured to the huge burial slab. With a warp spasm of strength, together, they drag the corpse of the sorcerer to it. Sláine casts a mighty roar,

"To the gods, and deities, the Mother and elementals of Eriu, her ancestors and all in gracious witnessing, let us bury this darkness."

They grasp the huge slab, seeing the shimmering forms of several ancestors gripping it with them. With their help, they lift it with ease and plunge it down upon the dismembered torso of Balor. It sinks into the sod burying him as though he is concealed in a passage tomb beneath the stone of power forever. Síonna turns and sinks her head upon Grandfather's chest, allowing all her emotions to melt into his heart.

Bathed within the soft fur of his wolf skin, she wraps her arms around his waist, weeping. Releasing all the duty and expectation that was placed upon her she feels the pressure melt as cries of victory ring out around her. Her tears seep into his compassionate breast. He caresses her head with his chubby fingers and whispers,

"Granddaughter, as Goddess, you have acquired the gifts and skills that no one before you has endured to receive. It was your destiny to raise the magical Emerald Eye and Sleagh Solais in victory today. Knowable in all the realms of a mystical knower you now stand and Eriu will sing of your gracious deed forever."

She is overcome with tears and then laughter and sinks deeper into his breast, wanting to stay there forever beneath his loving embrace.

Sláine wraps the serpent's head in a hide. Síonna and Grandfather join the clans in the great march to Aill na Mireann where a huge ceremonial fire is lit. They assemble once again around the Stone of the Divisions and raise their swords meeting at the tips repeating the same ritual.

A thunderous roar follows. The wounded pick themselves up from slaughtered heaps and raise their weapons, bearing tired bleeding limbs. Grandfather rings his bell three times circling the assembly. A rainbow arcs down. The healing tinkle trickles to their battle-worn ears soothing their war-stricken minds. He touches the side of the bell muffling the tone as Sláine sends his voice of leadership over the hill,

"Noble ones and tribes, great ancestors, you have stood with us today. Some left their blood and others their souls upon this battleground. We honour the spirit of our slain and the fearless strength of all the hearts who fought with mighty bravery. We have endured the path of darkness. May the path-of-happiness now be worthy, carrying your gracious footsteps home. Your merit in action has saved the precious lands of the Mother, for our way is truly lit, ho!"

He unravels the hide and raises the lizard-like head of Balor before them and flings it into the flames. The warriors merge their final wish with the rising smoke. The flames billow into a great dance and through the same flames emerges the great Goddess Éire. Her otherworldly scent sweeps through invigorating their minds. Her gleaming green eyes awakens the energy of their hearts. Her glowing golden hair lightens the tiredness in their eyes.

She walks to the assembly of kings sending a musical voice,

"Children of Eriu, you have planted the seeds of solas. Our Mother is truly singing, nádúr is in joyful leaping. Go forth and tend to your wounded and prepare a parting ritual for those that are slain. Tonight, gift celebration upon the navel knowing that síochán is restored by your brave actions."

Honouring the Earth Goddess, the archers release a stream of arrows. Like rods of lightning, they dance through the skies and drop to the sod, forming a figure of eight, the symbol of eternity they held throughout the battle, that of no beginnings and no endings, reminding them that this was neither an ending nor a beginning but a continuation with new possibilities. Tears of great joy part their cheeks as the Goddess smiles and disappears into the dance of flames.

They go about their duties, creeping through the carnage of bodies, searching for their slain loved ones. A sense of great sadness sweeps over the blood-soaked hills. Limbs twitch. Warriors bear horrific wounds. Some murmur words of pride as death approaches, embracing the invitation to pass from the world knowing that the seed of the Fir Bolg will live on within their children. Women walk the battleground keening. Grass and trees still burn from the flames of the Underworld.

Many horses lie in death beside their warriors, bringing great tears to those gathering the slain. Some are still alive, neighing, bearing wounds with bones piercing the flesh. With heavy hearts the warriors ease their four-legged into death knowing it is with dignity, helping them across the veils to serve their people in the other worlds.

Síonna whistles. Toirneach Bán and Silent Galloper lead a gallop of horses that circle the hill. The clans stop to watch the sacred dance as they neigh and race gracefully before returning to the Goddess. She canters to a stop and lowers her lightning-streaked head upon Síonna's forehead. Their eyes reunite in silence before she leaps onto her back, searching for Fionn amid the hundreds or so wounded warriors.

She finds him on the western slopes been lifted by two of his archers, bearing an arrow sticking through his thigh but otherwise safe.

"Take him to the summit," she commands, hiding the yearning that tears at her.

She sharply quenches the want to leap from her horse and caress him with her own hands, kiss and stroke his forehead. Feeling his pain, she wants to embrace and heal him with a kiss that would send a warp spasm of her love through his veins like a magical gift. Longing to have him.

"Grá mo chroí, love of my heart, what will we do?"

Tears stream off her jaw as they lift him onto a horse and canter away towards the hill followed by the light of her wounded heart.

What comrades are alive are brought to the stone beehives where the elders knit and splint their bones and wrap their wounds in leigheas, dousing them with the waters of the wells. Wounds are stitched and dressed and their minds are brought to peace and rest by the cure-alls. A laying-of-the-swords is carried out.

The slain are gathered into one big bough. Sláine orders the fires of transformation to be lit. The clans gather around them casting incantations and smoke dúidín. Eating acorns, they summon prayers for the souls of their loved ones to cross over peacefully. Blossoms of gorse and other flowers are thrown with their wishes. Women wail wildly keening in rhythmic voices to accompany them on the path.

An army of ancestors appears to lead the slain into the great light. They watch the shimmering ocean of forefathers carry the slain through the luminous veil. They bow their heads in prayer gifting thanksgiving for the fearlessness and onóraigh of the people who fought with them, for the ancestors past and present. Tears and wailing continue.

Those who fought and need cleansing gather at the river bathing their battle-worn bodies in the invigorating waters. When they return to the hill, elders burn sprigs of Rue, sweeping healing smoke over them and shake bells and beat drums, lifting the sorcery and fears from their Wells and minds. Dúidín are passed. Trails of gratitude-filled smoke rise ascending with their wishes as the stars begin to cast their twilight upon the earth.

The armies assemble to the pulse of one drum and rhythmically pound their shields with the butts of their blades. Walking sunwise around Uisneach three times they sweep the smoke of ceremony over the navel of Eriu and march.

The celebrations begin. Spits roast with boar and stag. Cauldrons of wine, mead, Uisce Beatha and Poitín are full to the brim and are soon emptied by the ravenous thirst of the warriors. Soups and broths warm their bellies. A great fest of victory is declared. Warriors indulge with abundance, regaining their strength while telling stories of their great bravery, seated around the fires. Boasting of deeds in battle, they compare the number of skulls and bones of foe collected. Under the twilight of stars, they make songs and music.

Making new agreements for livestock and lands they play games with the draíocht-of-the-fingertips and wrestle and court the warrior women. The evening fills with the sounds of their celebration. Tests of strength and that of the Samildánach are carried out.

A poc fada challenge is had where Fionn, despite his injury, takes the winning puck driving the sliotar out of sight with a great stick of ash. Spioradálta practises are shared. Night soon falls over the day. A red wispy cloud brings down the final path of the sinking Sun. Eriu is churning with the pulse of new life. The clans dance, ghost-moving and shapeshifting helped along the way with Poitín and other potent brews.

Síonna gazes across the waves of warriors, seeing Fionn glancing from a distance. He stands with the help of a furze stick. That invisible chord of light ghosts from their hearts, gushing out between them like a spring well. She leaves the circle of warriors and walks to the silver waters of the Boyne. Unravelling the crystal, she casts her gaze through the prism seeing the surface of the river. Illuminated by a cast of moonlight, she peels the tensions of battle from her being and offers thanksgiving while thinking of the children, elders and women back in the Valley of the Stags.

Wandering deep, she suddenly hears the soft broken shuffle of his footsteps approaching. Her heart misses a beat. She turns seeing the light emanating from his being as though he is the sun and she is the moon that have circled the sky in different cycles up to now and destiny has finally brought them together to merge into a blissful union and shine wondrously over the hill of Uisneach as Goddess and King of Eriu.

He reaches out taking her hand. His pulse leaping into hers. She wraps her other arm around his waist supporting his walk into the bough where she acquired the vision before the battle. He pulls her into an embrace where she feels his elevated heartbeat fluttering against her chest. Their glinting eyes meet.

She feels the warmth of his breath. She asks,

"Fionn, what about-?"

He halts her words, placing his cupped hand over her mouth. She senses the passion pouring through his fingers. Her legs grow wobbly. He takes her hands again whispering,

"Our hands represent our light. Let us do three things: establish contact; set a task and allow our flow of light to be shared. O' body, we touch another; O' mind, we interact with another; O' soul, we merge our love and shine as one."

They both make a wish, their hands entangled like a union of light between the sun and moon, gifting movement to their united wish. She looks into his eyes waiting for the moist touch of his lips that she has longed for over cycles of many moons. She recalls the time spent yearning for something to happen between them. The soft shells of his nails stroke her cheeks and lips. Her eyes follow his fingertips lift from her face feeling the warmth of his torso slowly pressing against her. They pull back and shed their battle-worn attire. Their skin glistens ghost-like beneath the light of the moon.

She sighs, sinking into the tight wrapping of his limbs. She senses his pulse enter every crevasse of her being, merging in harmony with hers like the spioradálta gift she acquired from the Oileánach. She releases herself of all guilt, surrendering into the flames of his lit passion. Folded together like branches of the rowan, she recalls the Suncatcher shaft of the Sun God at Brú Na Boinne pouring essence through the passage tomb, birthing that living thing as she formed her wish.

Their breaths rise into rhythmic panting and moaning, showering each other in every passion that was painfully held back. They look to the faint light of the fires on the hill, hearing the celebrating voices of their people knowing that their secret is protected. Fionn smears wet mud on her skin making circles over her goosebumps that surface beneath his loving touch. She arches her neck, steering his fingers, placing her hands upon his, running them up and down her body. She grips his hands tightly. They slide into each other.

The womb of the passage tomb slowly kindles. Whispering enchantments to her ear, she quivers beneath his charm unfurling desires within her ghostly heart like two rivers united into a great ocean of bliss.

She defines a position of love. Tears of joy roll over the grooves of her cheeks feeling every wholesomeness of him folding into her being. Her flesh thrills beneath the touch sending a lightning passion soaring through her veins. Their light accumulates. Their hearts leap, meeting in the loving act of gnéasnasctha. Passionate grunts rise. Wildly, like beasts they kiss and moan, stroke and push and pull. Their eyebrows rise and fall with the rhythm of their act. Their eyelids flicker and touch as every part of them meets, stroking and purring with lust, sharing the wild ecstasy withheld.

Their souls merge. Fire and passion flood their veins. Fionn's eyes are fixed in a time that only contains them as they roar blissfully into the night.

A warmth suddenly floods her body. The river of pleasure soars. Their eddies and currents swirl into a gracious union. Fire, sweat, desire and every impulse of desire rise into rhythmic music beneath the naked sky. Their love no longer bound to silence roars in rapture assembly. Síonna lets out a high-pitched squeal, grasping his entwined fingers tightly.

Their bodies tremble like a wave that thrusts salmon through the air. She follows his joyful lust-filled gaze as he lays his head sinking into her pulsing breast, wet from his drooling mouth. And there he rests upon the mounds of the Goddess with energy arresting their beings in the aftermath of their passionate act.

Concentric rings of pleasure continue to pour through them until the grip of sleep lowers them into dreaming. Síonna wanders back to the fortress of Cúroí to see the hooded hag at the door of her beehive casting the same words,

"Fear not for all will not be taken. This warrior is already inherent in your blood."

She is awakened by the cough of a cow and the tinkling sound of Grandfather's bell singing in the distance.

"Fionn, wake up," she shakes him but his sleep is heavy. "Fionn, we must return."

He jumps up startled and quickly dresses with heavy hearts knowing they must part. Síonna wells up. She leaves a trail of tears as they return. Her stomach tightens into a hardening knot.

He grips her tightly, whispering,

"Be strong, Síonna. Something will become of this. One day it will all be right; I sense and feel this. Our love is lit like the steppingstones of your destiny. One day it will be fulfilled. Our paths will lead us to one another again, this I know. And when they do, I will douse you beneath the water of my joyful tears and shower you with blossoms brought from the four corners of Eriu. I will paint your eyelashes with magic faery nectar and braid your locks with buttercups and golden filigree. Your crown of flowers will glow godly upon your head as you take your royal seat and marry me as you have married Eriu."

Frozen within his wishful thoughts their lips seal. Half-formed words are halted by their ever-growing grief and are unable to escape their mouths. Their tongues entangle tightly wishing to never part. Like their fingers entwined, like ivy around a tree, drinking of the same essence praying that the moment would stretch forever. But they know that they must face the challenge and release the grip of their warm tongues.

He takes a teardrop from her cheek and rubs it upon her Wonder-Eye, whispering,

"Within your Crystal Cave, contain the pearls of our hearts and wishfully see our future," he asks of her.

Their fingers slip one by one. Each one feels like melodies with her heart breaking like a drone of a horn dying from the lack of a nurturing breath. He slowly pulls away, separating that living thing birthed until they come to merge again, but they know that this living light bridges their souls forever.

No further words are spoken as the stark silence grips them.

Emerging from the darkness, unnoticed, they walk as though shadows wandering in the night and join the remaining tribes around the fires.

Grandfather divines the event and comes to Síonna with Ríonach trailing his footsteps.

"Let the turbulent waters calm and all the wondrous will shine within your being as a yellow star-like man chants of a wandering sun, dawning a red road of great peace."

He bows before her sweeping his imaginary kilt, trying to summon laughter upon her lonesome being and walks backwards bowing over and over leaving her within the spinning of his riddling words.

Síonna lies by the glow of embers looking up at the gleaming moon contemplating on his words that loop within her tiring mind,

"Let the turbulent waters calm."

She closes her eyes with Ríonach beside her curled like a cloud wrapped around a summit in a dreaming ball.

Síonna's mind races back to the Rowan and she stays there until she hears Grandfather's morning prayer! She approaches his praying up of the sun. He turns, riddling in his usual manner,

"Through starlit wandering eyes you peer like luminous yellow dandelions at a mystical frog spread in a great flight that emerged from the tadpole. He is hunted by a golden lizard-eyed hawk, soaring like the first man who became a whale parting the oceans of consciousness with a quartz eye bearing silver fins spinning rainbows in the worthy wish of man to leap to the summits as Creators, divining victory over one's own fear - that of death!"

Gifting éigse to the new dawn, Grandfather wraps her in his shamanic verse. They return to the clans who are gathering to leave Uisneach. Before they part the five High Kings assemble planning future meetings and then embrace battle-worn with pride after putting an end to the conquest of the sorcerer and seeing the crowning of the new Goddess.

With rapturous roars, they raise their blades one last time. Sláine sends his praise before them,

"Go forth to our kingdoms knowing that we have slain the shadows within until we meet again. Síonna, worthy Goddess, we thank you for leading our armies with your brave fearless heart. Upon your continued path-of-happiness we wish you blessings, ho!"

Gandal and his band of elves release a stream of arrows lit with fire that swerves and swivels, forming another figure of eight as they did for the Earth Goddess. They leap on the sward flipping in their usual humorous manner, sticking their tongues out and circling their eyes evoking great laughter. As the clans part to mount their horses, embraces are tight. Tears are shed for their lost loved ones. Joyful words outpour saying farewell to the Faery, Elves and the ancestors. The kings cast a final blessing upon the sacred hills and lead their tribes from the royal enclosure with their wounded strung between the horses on logs.

As they canter from the hill, Grandfather senses a presence and looks back to the eastern horizon to witness the most glorious flock of swans glide down. He knows a mystical event is in motion and rings his bell alerting the others, pointing his golden branch to the hill. They turn and witness the spioradálta spectacle unfold.

The bull-dreaming prophecy foreseen manifests. The sacred swan shape-shift into a pack of white wolves. Silent and awed they observe the nine wolves, nine representing the Magic Wells. The clans watch the wolves walk three times around Uisneach, stamping their feet in a march and back to the centre to where they stand mysteriously gazing back at the tribes.

"The white wolves will walk Uisneach. It is so as the prophecy was spoken," says Grandfather.

The wolves begin to dance on the earth, acknowledging the sacred task fulfilled by Síonna and the clans of Eriu. The tribes then look to see a lone hawk appear, hovering above the wolves. A tear rolls down Grandfather's cheek knowing that it is the shape-shifting spirit of an elder that has crossed the veil. He rings his bell three times more, honouring the journeying soul and turns, leaving the wolves in sacred space and signals the clans onwards each to their own province.

Chapter 22
Return of the Goddess
Valley of the Stags

Our sages and tribe journey endlessly through the day and through the night with the task of reaching the Valley of the Stags for the first light of dawn. They canter down the green path as the sun is taking command of the last of the twilight from the night sky. The elders and children eagerly waiting run to meet their onward march. They swarm around Síonna, throwing petals and the waters of the wells honouring her noble status.

Great celebrations await. Fires are blazing. The spits are rotating, sizzling with game. Cauldrons steam. The horns call everyone into assembly beneath the old oak. They embrace their loved ones and the wounded are carried to Turtle roundhouse, where the elders apply their medicine. Many hugs of joy and sorrow are had after hearing of those slain. Women of those lost wail and wail to the gods.

Sengann beats his sword against his shield gathering their attention. Aibhlin stands by the king's side and delivers word that came from the Rainbow Isles,

"White-Hair-of-the-Cosmos has crossed the veils."

Síonna lowers her head. Tears well up as she reflects on their visit to the sacred Isle of the Cosmic Juggler.

Grandfather thinks of the hawk, soaring over the wolves and lights his dúidín, offering up a wish-filled smoke for the wise sage's journey to be lit. The clan gather in prayer around the fire-pits sharing a smoke, offering it to the wise elder and those slain and for the wounded to soon recover. The warriors warm around the fires speaking of the occurrences in battle, sharing praise of she-who-slain-the-beast.

They soon have their fill of brews and potions and celebrate the hard-earned victory of being united with their loved ones. In dance, they surround Síonna holding their harvest makers, forks, spades and cultivating tools ritually honouring her transition and the transition that is to come as the hibernating cycles of Geimhreadh approach, a time to give way to the darkness to further shed what shadows prowl and to rest and renew.

After the dances, they sit with the children by the fires, listening to their newly crowned Goddess tell of her great feats.

"The smell of death purged across the land as I closed my eyes pouring the light from the crystal into the tip of the Sleagh Solais, summoning the solas of the dream. An ancestor shared my presence and with a wave of love thrusting me forth like a flower enchants a bee, I salmon-leapt with the shimmering form of my ancestor alongside me, casting the Sleagh Solais. It spun and spun upon a path guided by a flutter of butterflies and burst heart-deep into the beast of the Underworld! Balor's horrid form fell. And as prophesized by our ancestors, the Faolchú Bán appeared before our eyes. The wondrous swan then took the form of the most beautiful wolves. We watched them walk around the navel where a mysterious hawk appeared and a rainbow fell in arcs over the hill."

The tribe celebrate into the early hours until the embers of the fires quench with their tiring minds into a worthy sleep.

Enchantment

Winter soon takes its place within the cycles of nature. Daily hunting and foraging for wood occupy the warriors' days, preparing for the cold snows to deepen and for the nights to grow longer to be spent around the roar of flames as everything around them will soon fall to hibernation.

Síonna bathes in the reverence she receives for many moons but within, she knows that her role as a leader is not yet complete. She begins to shy away from gatherings, feeling an ever-returning yearning for the senses that she experienced, seeing the glittering golden husks of the hazel. Hearing the sweet music, so enchanting. Thinking of her secret with Fionn, she longs for a life of truth. On the second day of her return, she passes his wife at the centre of the enclosure sharing one glance that passed that ghostly truth between them.

She finds herself secretly observing the women with their babies blindly drinking from their breasts. How their tiny fingers clutch their nipples, sucking, sucking as the women laugh heartily, sensing that undeniable bond between Mother and child. A soft leap of the heart reminds her that she is longing like a bee amongst flowers denied of the golden nectar. She desires to bear his children and sit amongst those same women of the Turtle Roundhouse, feeding and nurturing as a Mother should, her own clan. Her wish is soon granted as she feels life forming within her womb, and she begins to wear loosely fitting tunics to hide the ever-growing bulge in her belly.

The terrible whispers of the sorcerer come back to haunt her. The desire for power surfaces and grows. Balor visits her again in Dreamtime luring and enchanting with promises of the éigse.

Chapter 23
Samhain
The Path-of-Danger Between Light and Shadow

The ritual fires of Samhain burn bright. Bloodletting beneath the full moon is carried out. Bones are cast into the communal fire as the tribe chant druidic incantations, wearing masks, warding off roaming demons of the Underworld. A feast of the dead with a burning of blood is carried out for the shamans know that the world of living becomes entangled with that of darkness. The veils dissipate. Drumming their ancestors around the warmth of fires, the clan leave food and Mead, Poitín and Uisce Beatha for wandering spirits.

Autumn equinox soon reaches into the cycle of Geimhreadh. An Cailleach casts her sleepy darkness over the lands, as animals slumber into the enchanting spell of hibernation. Owls-of-omen soar the skies hunting and lurking in the boughs of idle minds looking for lost souls. The veils peel open in the dark trails of the people's thoughts. Darkness grasps the sky within its hand each day as though crushing the sun from its familiar path.

The shamans see the strength of the sun declining, knowing that Balor will be unearthed. They also know it is time for the salmon to return to their sacred spawning grounds, birthing new life. River currents eddy with challenges and obstacles like the scales of the young salmon that remain brown until they reach the ocean where their silver colour grows sparkling upon new gracious skin. Grandfather observes Síonna, knowing that she too must overcome the growing challenges that surface upon her Goddess scales. He worryingly senses her yearning to shed her old skins, replacing them with something otherworldly.

Síonna walks to Abhna na t-Sionainne hiding the secret that is tearing her within, not realising that Grandfather knows her shadows as well as her layers of loving light. He turns, hearing her approach. She melts into his embrace wanting to reveal everything but instead enjoys the moment of his heart-warming presence. She arches her spine drawing in her belly, hiding her secret. He wastes no time and lets his teaching unfurl from his honeyed tongue.

"Granddaughter, to do any of this work successfully you must find forgiveness. Remember, non-forgiveness is a limitation to be thrown away at all costs. Do not waste your energy on the unforgiveness of yourself and others. And don't spend your time trying to get out of things that didn't exist until you created them."

She takes a deep breath. His stream of wisdom continues,

"We renew as we sleep. If we did not sleep the night fire of the moon would begin to burn us. The stomach is the 'sea of water', the Goddess of life. Like the peeling waters of the womb, the currents spin an earthly bank that race silver, dreamed over Eriu as a new worthy King takes birth. Sparkling salmon's tail waddles forth in a spin of emotion churning bubbles of regret leaping to new spawning grounds lost in a world beneath a lucky star, fading to a sight that cannot see the signs."

He pauses for a moment, allowing the riddle to seep through. She grows pale-faced hearing him refer to the 'sea of water' and the Goddess of life, and of a future king taking birth.

"Granddaughter, do not stray too far outside the path even though a leader will walk paths that others cannot!"

He allows her to churn his words around her mind to search for the deeper message. Releasing his embrace, he kisses her on the brow and whispers,

"Granddaughter, go now and receive power while sleeping and remember no one can hurt you unless you give them the power to do so. Repeat with me. Unless you give them the power to do so."

She thanks him, throwing a big smile double-edged with her worry and walks with a measure of tears, carrying his voice to her roundhouse, wrapping it around her as though a band of a rainbow while looking back several times at his erect form praying by the river. Feeling a huge heaviness grow within her breast, she closes the door and falls into a night of broken sleep. The shrilling call of the owl wakes her before dawn.

She looks out to see him sitting high in the twilight sky. She glances around the sleeping valley, silent, feeling the pulse of another world's heart drumming an enchanting rhythm within her, knowing that it is her time to shift, to heal and to grow into that of a true leader. She thinks of the noble title she beholds, of Grandfather and her secret lover, of the children and elders. The guilt of leaving surfaces.

The whispers of those wise words stream to her ears,

"To move forward the wish is important. Possibility is always waiting. Potential is moved with action. Travel close to the path and encounter the events you need. Give life to a new time and make a prophecy. You do not have to follow the predetermined paths."

She sharply inhales her doubts and spits them like a shadow onto the earth. Soon that guilt fades. She gathers her belongings and lays them on the hide of a deer. She takes her white-feathered crown and places it at the door of her roundhouse.

Drawing with a stick of oak, she leaves a symbol of eight and whispers his words,

"When two spirits meet, we are upholding the blessed privilege of our birth upon this Earth. This splendorous love is our unifier."

Closing her eyes, she divines while placing her hand upon her heart, whispering,

"Grandfather, forgive me, I love you. I must follow a feeling of my own way seeking the-path-of-happiness to fully express my individuality as a leader. You of all clever Rainbow divine knowing should understand. Help and guide me and I will return and stand by your side bringing with me another world's magic."

She crouches to one knee kissing the green sward imagining kissing Grandfather's glowing brow and whispers, leaving a crystal of her riddling tongue in the earth for him.

'Under the tenderness of your wing
In the silent fluttering of your Spirit
Ennobled and humbled: a blossoming grew
Hewn from your soul
Words
Honeyed
Knowable
Kneaded a worthy Goddess.'

Tears gather on her freckled cheeks. She walks to Toirneach Bán resting her forehead upon the horse's neck listening to the animal's pulse and gathers her own, envisaging them cantering together into a mystical land where her wildest dreams are manifested. She lifts her head looking into the horse's mirroring eyes. Her tears roll over the animal's cold nose.

"I will return, my spirited friend like the lightning being that runs so swiftly through your body. I will return. I promise."

The horse bows his head leaving out a lonesome neigh.

Síonna turns and creeps from the enclosure like a stalking fox making pace from the Valley carrying a returned heaviness upon her breast. Ríonach trails, dipping her nose into her every footprint. Dawn starts to sprinkle the valley with light. Grandfather wakes, sensing change has taken place after a night of vivid Dreamtime where he saw Síonna standing before the well of another world's veil with a sorcerer's enchantment lit upon her eyes.

He walks to her roundhouse to see her door opened. He quietens his mind sensing her intentions, seeing the figure of eight drawn into the earth with her flowery crown resting in the middle.

"Oh dear," he whispers and crouches, spreading his hand, feeling-her-way. A tear gathers in the corner of his eye and falls onto the white feather.

His mind flashes seeing her wearing the crown, battling upon Uisneach like a flame amid the thousands of warriors. He watches his tears roll down the silken plumage of the feather sparkling with the first light and summons a wish,

"Gods and deities, she has been called forth; guide my

Granddaughter with the spread of your hands, with the whispers of your winds for she carries a wandering womb that swells with the essence of a new life. Allow her to see the borders of the path-of-happiness and stray not from the feeling-of-her-way, ho."

He gently rustles his bell three times summoning his wish. Síonna trots further from the enclosure as though a wild wolf hibernating within her has awoken into a wondrous hunt. The forest comes alive around her. A rainbow arcs to the ground bringing her mind to Grandfather. She conjures up the loving state of gazing into his cornflower eyes. Feeling the sensations within her heart that only he summons with such humbleness. Silencing his great influence seems to become a far-off veil that she cannot summon as she struggles with the true purpose of her desire.

She enters in consciousness through each Well, bringing the doubts and fears from the Root to the heart trying to gain understanding and clarity.

"Be kind to yourself, Síonna, yellow pearls sing from the mermaids of your hazel eyes."

His words keep fluttering through her mind. She hears his soulful laughter while seeing his eyebrows leap in a playful dance. Sticking out his tongue, rolling his ever-sweet wisdom to her ears. How he twirls his moustache with his chubby fingers, bowing before leaping into his familiar kilt-lifting dance. Tears stream down both her cheeks.

She misses his company as though a part of her very being is missing. Resting her head upon his warm breast. Gazing into his arresting twinkling eyes. The sound of his riddles. His boyish smile and chubby rose cheeks parts evoking the joys and wonders of the world around him. Ríonach suddenly jumps and bum butts her with her front legs.

"What's wrong little belly?" she asks. "Do not fear, all will be fine. Now come, for we have new paths to wander."

She hears a yelping sound and looks to see a flock of Snow Geese spread against the reddened sky with their black wingtips in a rhythmic flow. Their pink legs dangle sweeping through the infinite mantle of clouds like stars.

A sense of confusion arises. She takes the rose quartz asking for direction and voices of the wise come,

"As Goddess, you are now a leader, one who is at the front and followed. You can walk paths that are closed to others who would not venture there, as they would consider the task impossible. As a leader, you create conditions for others, set tasks and determine the direction to move so that they will seek and follow. One who leads is the centre of light, the Well and source of the Fir Bolg. Your glow unites those around you. The light trace you leave will create live time, which is life creativity, as your womb is now growing with such life."

She ruminates on the message, placing her palms on her belly feeling the movement, she is torn between the truth that grows within and the sorcerers desire from outside that is driving her. Grandfather's riddle floods her troubled mind,

"Always remember, with power, comes responsibility. Wobbly legs will wander. Let the dance be your wonder spinning the mind of man away from the beast, away from the foe of thought who binds a silver skin, weaving a song of enchantment in the rivers beneath a life-giving Well."

She feels a sudden kicking in her womb. Her mind races to the rowan entangled in blissful gnéasnasctha with Fionn, asking,

"Oh, grá mo chroí, what have we done, Fionn?"

An overwhelming sensation floods through her veins. She hears the voices of her mother and father. Tears flow as she tries unbinding the pain knotted within. Outpouring her sadness and loneliness and confusion she yearns for Fionn's sensual touch. To look into the cauldrons of his blue eyes to hear him whisper again the promise of love he swore to honour on Uisneach. She too longs for Grandfather's continued reassuring love and guidance.

Feeling the life communicating within her womb, she makes a wish,

"Eriu, a new living time of life is coming, let us create a special solas for the dream. East, I will go and give the wings of movement to something new."

She gathers her emotions with a sharp inhale and gives motion to her journey on the exhale with Ríonach fast on her trail.

Over rolling hills, valleys and bogs they ramble to come to a forest that seems lifeless like the forest-of-the-hags. Divination tells her to ritually bless the path and she spreads her awareness around her like a spider spinning a web and steps fearless into the forest with her hand lightly rested on the hilt of the Emerald Eye. Silence falls beneath the dark grove of trees. A sudden wind sweeps over the floor of the forest sending leaves twirling in spirals.

Just like on Scealga, she senses something approaching recalling the words of Cúroí,

"When there is a disturbance, you will feel it."

She summons the age trick again embodying a younger version of herself, feeling her breath pour the youthful sensation through her hips and knees allowing her to move with a renewed lightness over the earth while silencing her mind. Tracking the forest, she picks up every sound, swivelling leaves, tweaking trees, animals foraging, subtly breaking every movement down when a stalking figure enters her outer vision. She sees a mother wolf with a pack of young who are observing the actions of their mother, learning the precise skills of stalking and herding.

Síonna watches them darting back and forth as though trying to confuse her with movement as she threads at a safe distance.

The mother holds her tail high signalling her leadership. Síonna watches the beast backtracking over the path that she previously walked and begins scent rolling upon the prized discovery, coating her fur in Síonna's smell. The cubs follow, rolling on the path before she excretes an odour informing the young to spread out and scent-mark their territory, homing in, going through the various stalking processes.

A clearing in the forest gives her a better view of the pack. The mother is white with streaks of grey running through her back. Her yellow eyes glare and she shows a mouthful of her clenched teeth to Síonna. Two larger fangs protrude over her gums that trickle with saliva. The six cubs are a mix of black and white, almost grown into the developed stage of young adults. She knows she must hold steady and strong and not be forced into a run.

A wind whistles through the trees as though signalling the beasts to advance. The pack howl in unison in a ghostly chorus sending a shrilling fear to surface on her spine. She quickly captures it with a swift inhale and splutters it out with a long exhale, relaxing further despite knowing their howling is a call for assembly and the hunt is on.

Their deathly chorus drowns her in the threatening sound. She senses the forest suddenly come alive. Shadows fill empty spaces. Trees whisper shuffling their leaves. Huge beetles suddenly unearth, emerging with pinchers the length of her sword. Long, hairy legs propel them at great speed across the forest floor. The veil of darkness has opened again! Balor's beasts advance. The same pungent smell that doused Uisneach sweeps through. The trees begin to sway. Eyes appear in their trunks, glaring. They cast out branches of claws and thorns.

Shadows and shapes blur past. Hounds and boars and bands of Darkelve come blazing, carrying that wretched stench of death. Tides of them race, craving for her flesh. That cold, horrid scent of Balor sweeps through the ghostly woods curling up her nostrils. She spits the fowl taste from her mouth and moves with Ríonach at pace with her blade singing and the shield of Dovinia ready to crack skulls.

A thunderous growl rises. She looks to see a second pack of male wolves lurking in the black of the forest, eyes glaring, advancing in a crouching stalk.

"The mind is mightier than the sword," teachings come just when she needs reminding.

A sense of bravery stirs within as she builds a steady breath, shedding what fear arises and freeing up her limbs with the youthful charge to move swiftly. She plants an impulse firmly in her mind to reach the end of the forest and exhales any doubt onto the edge of her blade.

Shadows cross her path.

The horrid beetles make distance on her. She allows them into hand-to-hand space and turns emotionless, driving her blade in great arcs, sending claws and limbs scattering. Ríonach scurries up a tree as she finishes the cluster of the creatures and turns, gathering pace.

The wolves carrying her scent begin to trot as their growl tares before them sending the command to close in for the kill. Nine of them spread out in an arc around her and the haunting whisper returns. Above the dark canopy, she sees the white wings of the owl appear.

Knowing she has slain the beasts once, she will do it again; Grandfather's voice reaches through,

"Síonna, I sense the Wells of Wonder are bubbling beneath the earth, waiting for a wise leader to drink from their source and anoint a people with a new dreaming and imagining. Do not walk in somebody else's dream of you. Quest, and you will find."

She drives forth, propelled by her rhythmic breath, seeing the shafts of sunlight break through the canopy in the distance.

The wolves gallop into a furious hunt with the Darkelve on their backs. The beasts make ground closing off the path from all directions. Síonna turns and before her eyes are the nine hags with the boars of poisonous bristles by their sides. Their delirious screams of laughter fill the forest as she casts her voice,

"I killed you wretched creatures already but now as Goddess of Eriu I will delightfully gift you your second death."

She salmon-leaps through the air with the point of the Emerald Eye held forth as though a star blazing through the dark of the forest. Heads fly, dismembered limbs scatter over the undergrowth. A warp spasm of strength sears through as bristles of the boars and arrows pound a piercing rhythm on her shield. She cuts through everything in her path, sending the Darkelve fleeing.

Packs of wolves and beetles pounce to the hags' rescue. The elves cast a stream of arrows; Síonna deflects. She grasps the Sleagh Solais, and with a mighty breath releases it, running behind its furrow of light as it plunges through the beasts. She leaps, grabbing it, hearing the voice of the jolly giant,

"Síonna, rock-dreaming is a powerful state of observation."

She takes heed and grabs Ríonach, summoning the gift and transforms and stands as though a mountain, motionless, witnessing the sudden confusion on the faces of the hags and beasts.

"Some new tricks just for you, wretched ones. Ha, ha, ha."

The Goddess sends her voice loud while filling the forest with her laughter much to the anger of the hags.

A silence ensues as she plans a way out, watching the hags and beasts approach her with great hesitation. The wolves crouch sniffing. Quietening her mind, she hears the teachings of Breandán Shéamuis Pheadí Ó Grífín,

"Recall the most joyous loving experience, summon that aligned time of life and go forth fearless."

She summons that joyous moment when Grandfather gazed into her soul on the hill of Tara.

"Dúisigh," she sharply calls, sending a wave through her spine and springs from the ground with Ríonach on her back leaping over the creatures.

As she sprints, she releases the Sleagh Solais that pierces through a cluster of the horrid things and picks it up with swift hands hitting the sod running towards the light of the other valley. She leaves beasts, hags and ciaróg in her blazing path. They try cutting her off from the sides, darting in for the kill, but she flips a great height, forcing clusters of them to collide.

Running, holding the state-of-happiness, demons and spiders and arrows sweep effortlessly after her. She runs towards the veil of sunlight breathing in fast bursts, propelling her body swiftly when an army of Darkelve lunge from the undergrowth advancing from the border of the forest.

She is about to plunge into them with the Emerald Eye and senses movement from behind. She swiftly turns seeing an axe spinning through the air that darts by her towards the remaining Darkelve. Gandal is standing in the distance with his hand raised saluting her as his axe is followed by a stream of Nángod arrows led by the mighty Uaisle.

"Run, Síonna, run and do not stop. We will dance a merry death with these excuses for elves," the brave Uaisle calls out.

She casts a great smile, raising her blade and turns, building into a sprint towards the veil and takes a huge leap clearing the army of Darkelve. She takes one glance back seeing the shower of Na Sí arrows advancing on Balor's army.

As she makes pace, she hears the screams and the clashing of swords and shields as the brave elves battle. She gains distance before coming to rest in a bough beneath an oak. She feels a certain tiredness carrying the extra weight within.

"Ríonach, we made it. If Grandfather could only see us now. Thank you, dear Gandal and Uaisle and all your elvish wonders, ho!"

Leaving out a huge sigh she kneels, placing one hand on her heart, the other upon the earth and breathes heavily bringing waves through her body, releasing tensions connecting her pulse with the heartbeat of the earth. She places her forehead onto the ground, making that sacred connection with the Mother.

After some rest and eating of herbs and other edibles she could forage, onwards she quests. Descending a huge hill, she enters a flowery valley. A musical lowing of cows fills the air and grass blades glittering of dew feel cooling to her feet.

A shuffling of mackerel clouds reveals a rainbow that bridges the two horizons. She feels a sense of aliveness as a leader making decisions for herself, for her own spioradálta worth. She takes her crystal and draws the essences around them into the precious stone asking,

"Guide me and gift me with the signs."

Her eyes are led to a subtle trail that eventually leads them through woods that meet with a mantle of green meadows.

A forked path sits before it. One leads east, the other north. She looks at the surrounding horizons gathering her whereabouts.

"I am still within the boundaries of the lands of Sengann, a few days out from the Valley of Stags heading east towards the kingdom of the mighty Sláine."

A flight of swans flies north bringing her back to the mystical flock over the Fruitful-Breast-of-the-Mother,

"O' Scealga, sanctuary of my soul, how I long for the pulse of your great suaimhneas."

Her eyes trail the gracious flight of birds until they fade into the distant horizon. A sudden flapping of wings catches her attention. There, soaring east is the mysterious owl. A wind rises, rustling leaves around her feet bringing the haunting whisper to her ears,

"Seek the hazels, Síonna…"

Her heart races in thunderous beats. Desires rise.

Torrent rain comes suddenly in charged bursts. Lightning-beings light the horizon. Thunder gods rumble over the earth.

She senses a great power return. Ríonach retreats to where the divide of the flowery meadow meets the forked path. Winds whistle ghost-like. The sun's red shawl darkens as strange clouds suddenly shadow the moon. She leads them down the eastern path feeling that sense of enchantment. She dips her eyes, ruminating. When she raises them, she flinches, drawing her sword as a crone bearing the head of a raven stands before her on the path.

Flames kindle around the hag's form.

"Piseog, spell," Síonna whispers, holding her blade lightly ready to behead the creature on first advance.

"I have come as the veils are thin, Red-hair."

Síonna recognises the voice. The hag raises her hands, removing the red-beaked headdress revealing her face.

"She-who-walks-between-light-and-darkness, what brings you?" Síonna asks.

"I bring again this message: All will not be lost, Síonna."

The flames brighten and the crone vanishes through the veil, leaving the path empty.

"What does she mean, all will not be lost?" she asks, stopping to one knee asking herself over and over and ruminates on the day's teachings that day in Cúroí's fortress.

She collects flowers and wraps ivy around the base and places it upon the earth asking for guidance.

"A Dhia, os na Déithe, cabhraigh mé, God before the Gods, help me. All shall not be lost as I now follow my dream. I now will it and project it and see it complete as I leave this Burla ghuí, flower bundle, upon the Mother. Show me a stream of light in order with my wish, for I walk fearlessly as a leader to the well of promises."

Chapter 24
Connla's Well
The Otherworldly desire

"Síonna-in-a-cholaidh, carrier of the dream of ancient stories, telling of a wandering spioradálta being where paths appear and disappear, enchanting, romancing. A longing spills emotions and wants, leading you from the-Path-of-Happiness - a spiralling river flows, asking of your worth as though a rainbow sits upon a golden horizon waiting for us to arrive with all the imaginings of the task manifested within the merit of our actions. Linger not on turbulent waters where emotions spin a web of sorcery for there you will be caught within currents that merge with your weakened footsteps, furrowing a path-of-danger."

Grandfather's many riddles circle her mind as she struggles with the battle between delusion and enchantment, slowly extracting the hidden warnings from his unusual weaving of words, as Balor's sorcery slowly seeps to her soul. She senses a disturbance around her. The animals suddenly scatter. The birdsong falls silent. Beautiful music trickles to her ears. Enchanted again, she recalls the moment she tasted the hazel in Aisling and the graceful feelings that filled her senses. She looks to the sky to see the Guiding Star faintly glittering, realising it is fading! A stilled state falls upon the forest.

At the Valley of stags, Grandfather, Sengann, the druids, the elders, shaman and druidesses gather in the Turtle Roundhouse to ritually reaffirm the purpose of Sionna's actions. The bloodletting of a white bull douses the altar at the centre of the enclosure as the Ard Druí leads a wise Ollamh through the ceremony, eating raw meat washed down with the broth of the animal's bones. The Ollamh is then wrapped in the slaughtered bull's hide to sleep and receive the signs.

He enters Bull-Dreaming while the elders and druids chant incantations, encircling his roundhouse, chewing acorns, holding wands of hazel summoning the gods and deities to give him vision. The Ollamh awakens beneath the full Moon and gifts the message,

"The gods have spoken. Síonna is in the motion of her wish. We must honour and respect this. On this night, an eclipse of the moon will shadow the Sun God from the Earth. This will be an event that will test the strength and wills of mankind. We must cast prayer on our straying daughter. There will be endings and beginnings. The shadows of the Underworld will freely walk the paths. The sun, stars, fire, light and lightning will all sleep behind the veil of darkness. A new moon will bring a cycle that will align with the Earth and with the sun. We must hold strong and remember our purpose on this land and not put limitations on Síonna's free will! Guidance we can give her but we cannot change her final decision, ho. It is now spoken."

Grandfather quietens his mind and wills his consciousness forth, merging with her breath, passing his wisdom through the cycles of nature around her to awaken her. Accompanied with a steady pulse of a drum, the wise ones cast forth the light traces of their Wonder-Eyes merging to her path bridging a light between them. But Síonna knows that no draíocht nor druidic spell will change her decision now.

Ríonach circles her. A howling of wolves brings the mind of the Goddess back to Uisneach lying naked beneath the moon with Fionn, dousing passion upon each other. To the solar alignment of the passage tomb. To the thunderous chanting of thousands of warriors at the victory ceremony. To raising the Emerald Eye around the Lia Fáil with the High Kings and to that eternal gaze of knowledge shared with Grandfather. The beauty of the Rainbow Isles, their tribes, and the values and teachings of each Well that she received, seeing the wise faces of those who gifted her! Being initiated at Tara with her white-feathered crown raised before the clans. The otherworldly beauty of the Earth Goddess and the mystical walk of the white wolves.

"Mother of all Goddesses, cabhraigh mé, cabhraigh mé, cabhraigh me," she whispers, asking the trinity of the gods and deities for help while rubbing her belly that grows and churns with a great movement.

The inner promptings halt her for a moment but beneath, the Áer of Balor sings loud.

"I feel hurt in her words and wounds in her desires," Grandfather whispers in the Valley of the Stags.

Síonna looks to see heavy clouds darken the sky. The moon moves between the Earth and the sun emanating the light of change. Fog descends upon her path. A voice comes,

"Beware of the mist that is eclipsing your soul."

She looks at the borders of the moon wearing the orange glow of the sun. The sweet music enchants. A silver gleam falls lighting the steppingstones. She senses for a feeling-of-the-way.

With her will set on the task, she trails onwards, following the flight path of the owl that leads her to the manifestation of all her inner desires. There in a bough in all its delusionary majestic presence, lit with a wondrous solas as she saw in her dreams, stands the hazel tree over Connla's Well! The forbidden powerful sight that has haunted her throughout her quest, radiating so wondrously to her veiled eyes.

She looks to the rounded leaves shimmering and flickering around the nuts, thinking of the sought-after éigse. They sparkle wondrously, so silken in their golden husks. The otherworldly lunar light on the well's surface captures her in a timeless spell.

"The Well of Connla so beautiful and mysterious just as you appeared and sang so sweet in my nightly Dreamtime," she whispers, with a burning desire upon her tongue to taste the otherworldly nuts and acquire what she believes is rightfully hers, the otherworldly éigse.

Her fingertips itch to clinch around the nuts' silken skin and sink her teeth, tasting that power yearning to be the wisest in all Eriu.

Tales of the elders return, telling of the forbidden place where only those with lost souls foolishly roamed, or those brave enough and who dared to venture. She screams,

"I am those brave enough! A leader entering paths that are not available to others, paths others dare not tread. Such is this truth, for I am Síonna, Goddess of Eriu, and this is my Aisling."

Lightning crosses the sky in vast, jagged arcs. A great source of something she hasn't felt ripples forth from the well as she recalls the three steps to the wish but her sorcery-veiled eyes are fixed on the sparkling jewels, enchanting more beautiful than anything of this world.

She's fully taken by the mystery when a sudden approaching of hooves distracts her. She looks beyond the borders of the path to see stags, horses, wolves, elk, boars and animals running in a furious stampede. The neighing of horses rings out. The elk and stag charge at each other in a ferocious rut, clashing antlers sending a chilling cracking sound through the forest. She feels the trembling through her Root.

Sensing with her heart she knows it to be a sign of danger for elk would never clash with stag. She feels a hopping of her heartbeat in all places of her pulse.

They bark and cry and neigh, sending shrilling calls evoking shivers to race up and down her spine. Ríonach curls her tail around Síonna's leg startled by the visit, and they suddenly come to a stop and all face her, taking one glance and turn, galloping away as though carrying her final chance to see beyond the sorcery back to the Valley of the Stags.

She allows the unsettling event to pass and looks to see Ríonach cowering away and whistles,

"Ríonach, what is it? It's fine. I am going forth to create new traces of light so that my descendants will follow a path of the leader that will be void of the mistakes that I made. Come my little jewel-eyed vixen and after I grasp what is mine, we will return to the Valley of the Stags, I promise."

She desperately tries to hang onto Ríonach as though unconsciously knowing that she is her last link of hope, despite being overcome with the sorcery. But she summons her will back to the task.

"I seek the individuality in my spirit to bring the unmanifest into possibility. With purity within my heart, speech and actions, I stand beneath the constellation of stars as Grandmother Moon has taken the sun before dusk. And now as she boldly shadows the sun, I close the borders of doubt and go forth walking into the lore that others fear, into the dark, for the way is lit!"

She hears the words of her teachers whispering one by one,

"Learn to put aside emotions when the path of destiny faces you. Now that you have felt the greatest fear, your mortality is clearer. One day, you will have all that you desire."

The golden sparkle of the hazels captures her like a spider slowly weaving her into its webbed lair. The steppingstones grow brighter. Balor's lunar force draws her to a future event where the great promise waits. Becalmed, she walks to acquire a consciousness of the all-wise, that of the Rainbow Head like Grandfather, and embody the Rainbow Body, and powers and qualities that she had buried when she lost her parents.

The powerful sorcerer finally achieves his worthy catch. The long hunt he rigorously endured manifests as he lures her in through the 'cuisle do croidhe'. Síonna surrenders to the otherworldly charm. The golden leaves of the hazel shimmer and drop upon the path. She looks to see the light intensify as the moon's reddened face emanates the lunar charge from the surface of the well.

A rainbow suddenly arcs down bridging the path with the well. Everything rainbow brings her to Grandfather and she whispers,

"Grandfather, please forgive me. I must seek my own way now that I am a Goddess, a leader upon the path-of-happiness."

Thinking of him brings a spring of hope. She feels the impulse of his presence and in honour of the guidance he bestowed her with throughout her life and their quest, she wills her consciousness through each Well, recalling the values beginning at the Root, transforming weaknesses into strength, fear into survival. The Navel: lust and guilt to pleasure. The place of Jewels: shame and pride to willpower, dreams into jewels. The Heart: grief and loneliness into love. Honey-Mouth: lies and betrayal to truth. The Wonder Eye: delusion to insight. Crown: attachment to pure energy. The Soul: timelessness as a Creator and finally to the Spirit seeing the white light of Oneness with all creation. The dúrún, profound secret.

She bravely steps through the rainbow from one world into another. Grandfather senses the sudden heaviness in his heart. His image grows in her mind. She closes her eyes as though seeing him standing before her against the blazing sun, adorned in his full Stag headdress. When she opens them, an unmeasurable delight pours over her being. She stares in disbelief seeing his shimmering form on the path. She looks to his cornflower eyes, glittering. His moustache is copper from the lunar glow. Tears of joy run over the crevasses of her cheeks. They gaze, sensing, knowing without a word, without touch, engaging in the essence that streams between them like an invisible chord that can never be severed, sharing all that is needed to share.

Grandfather respects her wish and her summoned boundary. Síonna honours his innate understanding to allow her the 'Saoirse', freedom, in her choice and actions. They stand as though the course of the sun and moon has stopped in the sky, as though the stars have dimmed and nature takes a deep breath to allow them this sacred time.

What seems like a long passage ensues until a sudden sensation of heaviness grows upon her chest, seeing Grandfather's luminous form begin to fade.

A glorious rainbow sweeps him from the sod leaving a furrow of his great light to her wistful eyes. Reaching out to grasp his fleeing presence, she calls for him to return as though knowing with him goes her last chance to turn from the sorcery and go back, roaming the beautiful hills of the Valley of the Stags together. She quietens her mind and ascends through her Wells to enter the cave of illuminations, but the entrance is veiled by what looks like the skin of a hazelnut. She hears the teaching of the Cosmic Juggler. "If you truly enter the Crystal Cave without desire or expectation, only then will you come to know and acquire the true éigse of this world, and that of the other worlds."

A salmon suddenly leaps through the veil like the blazing star the Faery King magically summoned. Suddenly she finds her mind taken to the cave at the Valley of the Boars seeing each of the ancestors etchings illuminated by the magical Suncatcher. Like relics she carried throughout her life within her mind they vanish one by one like each sign within Grandfathers words and those of the sages. She opens her eyes and the well recaptures her gaze.

Balor wastes no time and casts his thieving eye from the mirror of the well, quickly luring her back beneath his charm. She turns with a heavy heart spellbound and walks oblivious with what determination surfaced, broken. Her ears become entranced by the sound of the sweet music. Her gaze grows fixated on the glowing husks.

And by the way of her wound when Balor wrapped his tongue around her scar upon Uisneach, licking his intent of sorcery into the very depth of her being and truly sown the taste of his seed, she goes forth fearless unbeknown of the danger.

Gazing at the mystical nuts hanging in a timeless state waiting for the hand of a brave sage to pluck them, she walks the remainder of the glowing path. The forest stills. The winds fall silent. She whispers,

"I will be as though a flower that becomes a fruit that ripens to speak a honey-mouth of other worlds magic that has never been heard before. Buds of wisdom will bloom upon my tongue. Words honeyed like new pollen I will cast over Eriu that will manifest great magic with a command of éigse never revealed before. I promise you, people of the Fir Bolg."

She steps beneath the hazel and glances upon the surface, the moon turning her eyes red with desire, summoning a whole new level of yearning within her! Words come,

"The signs are on the surface."

She takes one last look over the path to see Ríonach in the middle with her nose cocked, standing on her hind legs, staring beady-eyed.

"Everything will align, my little vixen. Do not fear little-belly for the path of a leader is to be fearless."

Grandfather and the assembly of sages send a final attempt to steer her mind from the path-of-danger, giving their wish to a flock of swallows who go forth. A fog lifts and swirls around the well, veiling the surface. Síonna looks to the sky to see a glinting sparkle of her Guiding Star break through the gloom of darkness. Shining one last time she hears the pleading voice of her mother,

"Look into the eye of the star where the pulse of spirit is shining and to the smile of heart where the rhythm of the earth is beating. And when spirit calls, choose the path that awakens your heart, daughter."

A glorious moon, star and sun appear rustling through the shadowed sky. Wisdom from the quest trails through her stricken mind.

"When you stand along the dark path, evoke this state of sun, moon and star and the correct expression of your soul will emerge; it will shine on the surface of your being and you will not seek or be enchanted by another world's light when you possess the required glow. And say to yourself, I am in a state of pure light in the time of my life, summoning the special solas for my dream, ho, remember, Síonna, remember."

At the Valley of the Stags, Fionn takes a horn and blows a mighty circular breath sending a drone upon the wind-whisperers, following the flight of swallows, carrying the ritual intent of all in the Valley of the Stags. Soaring through the valleys, over hills, through the dark forest and down into the valley of the well, the birds swirl around her chirping to her ears the full might of the clan's wish.

They startle her. She hears the magical tone of the horn within the flapping of their wings, trying to bind her in a protective veil. Fionn lowers the horn with a heavy heart knowing that he must take more action. He whistles for Toirneach Bán who races forth. The king's son leaps upon the lightning-bearing four-legged and lets out a roar,

"I will find you!" and races from the Valley of the Stags.

Following the double set of prints, he charges forth holding the promise that he made upon Uisneach within his mind. Síonna's womb kicks again and again. She wraps her hands around her ever-growing bulge. Tears sprout. Confusion arises. Grandfather and the shaman's message hit her strongly. The Ollamh's words lovingly linger on her mind,

"Nothing, nor can anyone hurt you unless you give them the power to do so; unless you give them the power to do so."

She can see him wording the warning and knows that she is giving her power away but she also believes that she will receive a new power beyond that which she never experienced.

Grandfather and the elders bow around the fire knowing that they have now done what they can and must allow her to deal with the consequences of her own choices!

She feels painfully stretched between worlds, between the voices of her elders and the voice of the sorcerer whispering and the beautiful music of the enchanting tree. The owl-of-omen swoops down casting a barking, keening sound that startles the swallows. A sudden gust rises. She watches the stream of messengers flee and accepts her choice lowering her gaze upon the well.

A hazel drops, breaking open, revealing a rich purple stain that colours the scales of the glittering salmon who feast on them, gifting the dark red freckles to their silvery skin that sparkle beneath the lunar light.

Síonna stands with yellow pearls of sorcery shining from both eyes. Empowered, she announces,

"I am no longer who or what I was. I now detach from all past hurts to offer service to my tribe by creating a new Time of Life. I go forth as a living leader unveiling my inherent powers and the wisdom of all éigse will be mine and mine only!"

She takes the rose crystal from her brat and spins it, gifting movement to her wish. It leaves her flicking thumb. She trails the sparkle that halts mid-air as though stopping with the whole world for a moment to breathe as she recalls the day Ogmu gifted it to her and seeing Grandfather's eyes flicker with a love so wondrous. Tears sprinkle from her eyelashes and fall onto the surface of the well scattering the red moon into ripples.

She reaches out to grasp the crystal but it slips through her fingers. A drop of her blood seeps from the wound left by the poisonous bristle. Her startled eyes follow the glowing furrow of the crystal followed by the little red bubble of her blood. It falls, breaking the surface of the well and is gulped beneath leaving bubbles on the surface that her blood soon stains to her disappointed roar,

"No!"

Her voice echoes like the pleading voices of her people. And there through the very juice seeping from her cuisle do cruidhe, the eye of Balor steals her gaze. During her madness, she takes the fearless imaginative leap with the desire of a sorcerer's dream enchanting her, knowing that the only senses that are missing are touch and taste. The great yearning seals her decision.

She reaches for the hazel, everything stills as though time stretches like in a dream. She grips the golden husk between two fingers and plucks it from the silvery branch. With a draíocht-of-the-fingertips, she caresses the silken skin, divining. Her head goes into a spin as sorcery seeps into her Wonder-Eye, sealing the desire deep, breaking the hazel skin veil and flooding her Crystal Cave. She takes the otherworldly nut to her mouth and bites into everything that mankind said was forbidden.

Her teeth slice through with ease. A bitter taste runs up her tongue, a bitterness more powerful than the most potent Poitín of the lands.

A great sense of empowerment sweeps through her. With fire in her gaze, owl-eyed she announces,

"Something new within me is created and my clan line will reap from the magic that will flourish through my Goddess words and actions. Hail the light of the gods for I go forth with the time of life assigned to me. Unravelling the limitations from my mind, I capture the favourable light as a Druidess, a sage and now a Goddess. A new time is born for I am Síonna, a leader worthy to receive the magical éigse."

Within her illusionary empowered state, a horrid sense of weakness suddenly cuts that imagined thread of power from her mind. Feeling the bitterness swirl down her throat, around her belly and seep out through her Wells, it's like a snake of another world's realm shaking dead scales from its body. Desire, emotions, pain, envy, anger, lust, greed, attachment and every lower impulse of the Root-Wells rush to her mind! She throws her startled eyes to see the well wildly bubbling and the prophecy comes to fruition.

A great salmon suddenly leaps through the lunar-lit surface as she just foresaw in her Wonder-Eye. Observing its magnificent flight at first, she then senses the sudden danger knotting in her belly as the sacred fish sheds her silvery scales. Watching in horror as the skin detaches and is carried on the winds towards her.

"A skin that can never be shed," the stark voice rings out as events of her entire life suddenly flash by.

Everything stills as it did on the battleground for a moment. She hears every riddle Grandfather gifted and the warnings within them screaming within her mind.

"A new King worthy born, as salmon's tail waddles forth in a spin of emotions churning bubbles of regret, leaping to new spawning ground lost in a world beneath a fading lucky star, pale to a worldly sight that cannot see the signs."

Every desire floods her veins as the mysterious scales soar in the air, sparkling and the realisation sweeps over her that there is nothing she can do to prevent it.

The scales attach to her fingers and toes and rapidly crawl up her limbs, spreading all over her with great pace, enclosing her in Balor's otherworldly skin beneath the red glow of an eclipsed Sun. She recalls the lore as the hidden truth is revealed,

"Once the pool's surface has been broken, the spell of the sorcerer will be sealed."

A dark veil dims the bands of the rainbow as though quenching what light is left in the world and from the surface of the well glares the sorcerer's eye. His terrifying words reach her ears,

"You now wear a serpent skin that cannot be shed, daughter of Sengann. Oh, so vulnerable and weak. Where are your gifts and your white-headed Rainbow Ollamh now? O' Grandfather, what has become of your little jewel, the great princess? She-who-slain-the-beast now wearing the silken scales of the Underworld, the skin of every shadow and sorcery feared by mankind that can never be shed."

His horrid laughter sweeps through the valley. A storm rises. A terrible reality has gripped her in a merciless claw. Her legs grow heavy and wobble. Her heart misses a beat. Her breathing paces as the beast she thought she-had-slain lures her deeper into his lair. She desperately tries to reach the Crystal Cave within her mind, but darkness is all she meets. And the feared inevitable occurs. Losing her footing with the weight of her new skin, she topples into the pool.

Like the prophet foresaw. The hazelnuts entangle, twisting and matting her long flowing hair like the eddies and currents of the pool. The water begins to stir her around and around. She screams and screams his name,

"Grandfather."

The mirror of the well's surface has been broken. The terrible beauty of the Goddess shimmers and pulsates across the pool, driving into the red earth, throwing up banks on either side. The nine-rivers-of-Eriu emerge into an angry spin forming into one magnificent river. Each river wraps around her torso attaching to each of her nine Wells. And from the ever-growing trauma, her waters burst. "Grandfather." She screams again, asking for his help.

Grandfather receives a terrible pain in his chest, knowing that she's now entrapped by the sorcery until a way is sought to rescue her from the shadows of her own desires. He closes his eyes with his hand held on the sun disk envisaging through his Wonder-Eye the rose quartz and fills it with his wish. The gemstone collector-of-light sitting on the bottom of the well suddenly emanates a protective glow that encloses her womb as she breathes in quickened spurts within the swelling waters of the river.

Fionn rides swiftly and sees the distant figure of Ríonach staring into the river. Tears stream down Síonna's horrified face as she pushes and pushes, grunting and screaming in the depths, recalling the night they shared beneath the Rowan. A shoal of silver fins surrounds her, weaving a crystal dance like spinning magical webs, binding her tightly, spinning and churning the waters as she surrenders onto the gravel bed like a salmon to spawn.

One last heave and a huge gurgling sigh fill the waters, followed by the wondrous muffled cry of a baby. A new time of life is gifted as salmon and Goddess merge in the spawning pools, birthing!

The solas of her dream of all that she collected and nurtured are manifested as she looks at her son, enveloped by the light of the crystal in the otherworldly pool.

"A warrior already inherent in your bloodline, oh crone of Cúroí, this is what you foresaw and secretly warned me?"

She gazes into his turquoise eyes, seeing the same gaze his father holds. She desperately reaches out to embrace her newborn but the currents swirl and spin and spin, enclosing him in a circle of eddies that break the 'srince' the sacred cord of all connections between them.

His pale-skinned little form, with limbs wildly dangling, searching for his mother, is swept to the surface like a beacon wrapped in the light of the crystal emerging to an unknown world without her, glowing like the Creator's idea denied of that first embrace. Like the salmon who stop feeding when entering freshwater, they die, renewing the cycle, leaving their eggs to fend and survive and carry their living lore into an unknown world.

Denied that bond, that sacred first suckle she screams, recalling the women in the Turtle Roundhouse feeding, as she watches him float from her grasp and screams and screams again, crying out his name into the churning waters. She is uncontrollably pulled beneath by a ferocious current and swiftly releases the Sleagh Solais, the nine-fold shield of Dovinia and the great sword of the Emerald Eye as a trace to track her whereabouts.

Síonna looks to the surface to see a flutter of butterflies and three bumblebees swirling around each other, bringing her to ruminate on the values they represent, those of the Goddess and of inner transformation. She reflects on the motion of her actions, the cycles and the progress that has brought her to this moment crowned as Goddess of Eriu, where she has stepped like the caterpillar, from the old into something new, into the direction of east on the medicine wheel taking the flight of the butterfly to the promise of an otherworldly wisdom, to arrive in the centre of the wheel embodying the all-knowing. But the sad truth of the illusion roars within like the keening voices of the women that day she lost her loved ones.

Shoals of salmon circle her banished being. Her red hair twists and entangles as though further wrapping her within her own desires. The curse is in motion as each of the nine-rivers-of-glow merges. Words of every sage hum to her mind,

"Linger not on turbulent waters where emotions spin a web of sorcery, for there you will be caught within currents that merge with your weakened footsteps, a path of danger."

Realizing the signs were always there within Grandfather's riddles, and the teachings of all the sages along the Quest, she knows that she failed to take heed and embody them to a level where she truly would gain control over her sense-pleasures.

"Through your red locks, it flows
Spread it as a Goddess upon the map of your soul
And take it with you wherever you roam
For the wizened will can feel-the-way
Through paths so clear: but be aware
The well of wonder can sometimes fool
Mirroring the eye of Balor's pool.'
"Grow not, scales of regret, Red-hair of Sengann."

"So many signs and I did not take heed, O' so foolish," she wails in rhythmic bursts as the teachings of all the wise ones race through her mind.

"Síonna, I sense the Wells of Wonder are bubbling beneath the earth waiting for a wise leader to drink from their source and anoint a people with a new dreaming and imagining."

Her tears merge with the great charge of currents as she gulps his words with great regret knowing that the dark dread of Balor has finally captured her.

Her bodiless voice whispers regret after regret, wounding herself further, drenched in her desire. Her pride hurts. Her sorrow bleeds into the flowing waters. And the nine-rivers-of-Eriu spin into a great surge.

And Síonna, Goddess of Eriu, is entrapped in the spell that can only be broken by a chosen one whose will and heart are pure and desireless of power. And there, she begins another voyage thrown and captured in an infinite regret, another Quest into the unknown as the river swells outpouring a white-silver blanket upon the lands. Amid the churning eddies like a flower starved of light, she races across the lands of Eriu with the sacred river that forever bears her name: Abhna na t-Sionnaine.

She looks back at the little glow of life she gave birth to floating to the surface and calls aloud,

"My godly son, Conán, Mac Dela-Síonna. Go forth and reign as Ard Rí of Eriu. Reflect the movements of your blessed soul within your actions. Seek Grandfather and he will reveal to you your father. Conán, find a way to break this spell for your way will be lit!"

She screams his name over and over, seeing his face eddying away with the flowers of her regrets. Just when she thought everything was lost, a sparkle of joy unfolds. A Suncatcher blazes through the surface where she sees the white streaked sandstone fur of Ríonach's forehead, her hazel eyes gazing in the distance, and the grief-stricken face of Fionn appearing beside her. She watches his hands dip down, churning two crystal furrows on each side of Conán's naked being and pulling him from the surging waters. She screams as a torrent current takes her away at great speed.

She looks back to see the Emerald stone and the Golden-Relic-of-Scealga sparkling on the riverbed alongside the rose crystal and sends words climbing through the currents,

"Grá mo chroí, Fionn, agus mo Conán Mac Dela-Síonna, find a way."

Críoch

Grandmothers dreamy voice brings their journey of wonderment to its end.

"Children of the Fir Bolg, so wondrous are your owl listening ears and beautiful Dreamtime divining minds, accompanying our sages on every trail through light and shadow throughout their great Quest of the Magic Wells. As you hear the faint pulse of my drum, will your consciousness back through the clan lines, back along the paths of thought arriving to open your eyes before our transforming fire, bringing with you the wisdom, lore and gifts that we have explored through the adventure. Open your wishful eyes, little ones.

"Before our dance of flames, we will now gift críochnaitheacht, finishing, to our story until the next cycle of a full moon when we will gather again in this place of power and fulfil another passage of the story and learn about the great Conán Mac Dela-Síonna, warrior son of our brave Goddess. That's for another time. As we go forth creating, remember that we are the dreamers carrying the living links, those prophesying and manifesting our worlds into being.

"Let us honour Síonna's quest one last time by climbing our spioradálta ladders. Close your eyes and ascend the silver thread of time from the lower into the emerald and up into the bliss of white violet that spins above your heads, realizing all the wisdom you embody as though gifted the very éigse from the salmon's pool.

"Free of desires, free from the grip of the past, of time, remember the ancient memories of your ancestors. Hear their tasks. See their dreams and wishes, swimming the lakes and rivers of life for you are the Creators, the gods, and deities that understand all that is sacred.

"Reveal the source to others as you summit the ladder, hearing the true laughter of the world. Now draw your eyes into the beautiful caverns of your Crystal Caves. Submerge your beings within these cauldrons of luminosity. Dwell here for a few moments and meet the sacred seeing everything with clarity, merged into one wholesome image. Now journey back and open your eyes, my little dreamers and let's take a deep breath as we did at the beginning.

"Allowing our bellies to fill just as the magical ocean swells. Let the air trickle out like the swell falls as though the great giant of the Rainbow Isles has waded through the ocean to blow a breath of stars, he plucked from the sky over our enclosure granting us our every wish for we share that living thing that sings within each of us.

"I hand each of you an acorn. As we chew, let us make a wish for Síonna and her kingly son, Conán Mac Dela-Síonna for his future way to be truly lit!

"Déan trócaire ar Dhia, Gods have mercy. O' body, we touch another; O' mind, we interact with another; O' soul, we merge our love and shine as one. Such is our truth my beloveds.

"As a well's bubbling spring is lit by a shave of blazing sunlight, reaching down to depths unknown, becoming a source for new life, we must endure darkness to know our strengths and rise again, spreading wings of realisation that the Creator is within the Uisce, water, from which we drink. This is so, for we are the Leigheasóir and children of the Fir Bolg. Ho!"

About the Author

Malcolm James Griffin, is an avid practitioner of the shamanic healing techniques of the Celts, the shamans of the Amazon and the Andes. He is a keen poet and musician. He has embodied a lifelong learning of martial arts, bioenergetic medicine, plasma science and GANs technology, and engages in an ongoing pursuit of the Elevation of the Soul through the enlightenment teachings of the draíodóir.

Acknowledgements

First and foremost, is my spiritual Rainbow Headed Ollamh, Allen Ernest H Martiensen, my inspiration, grá mo chroí, this book is because of you.

You opened my heart at 101 Terry Street, dissolving the chains of my conditionings and attachments to see the Souls Way; to walk the path of unconditional love.

To my parents James and Eileen, my brothers and sister, and to all in Spike for your love and support.

Granny agus mo shinsear

To mo chairde worldwide.

My heart dancing thanks to the wizardry of Sergey Avdeev, for your otherworldly humorous riddling and Translighter Codes to the Soul.

My gobbly gratitude to Professor Joseph O'Connor, Donal Ryan, Giles Foden, and the 12 Apostles for your belief in my storytelling, your, help and support, and friendship, and to the two golden Elve helpers who helped make this possible.

To the wizards of Systema, Vladimir Vasiliev, Lev Ivanov, Alexander Koslov, Emmanuel Manolakakis, Alex Kostic, Ivan Popov, Zettler Twins, Konstantin Komarov, Alexander Andreichenkov, and many more for the power breath of life.

To Yang Mian, Master Zhen Hua Yang, Shaolins Yan Lei, Dim Maks, Russell Stutely, Fire dragon, Eamonn Cambell, Rising Sun, Paul Frenchy tutu McCaughey, and to all the martial masters for helping me to create a labyrinth of skills.

To Mehran Tavakoli Keshe, for your Crystal Cave plasma Zues, star knowing.

To the shamans, John Moriarty for your soul bog-wisdom. Ernest Veter, Joey, and everyone at the Temple of Light for the siddhis. Alberto Villoldo, Sun Bear, Wabun Wind, Crazy Horse, John (Fire) Lame Deer, Sitting Bull, Eckhart Tolle, Deepak Chopra, and the great gobbly Dreamtime sage of all-knowing: Allen, the Australian Rainbow Head, le buíochas for the Solas Anam.

To artist Desmond Kinney and Professor Mícheál Ó Súilleabháin, for their combined vision in creating the Síonna Mosaic at the University of Limerick that kindled the Suncatcher of this story in my mind.

To you awakened reader for choosing this book. May you acquire the Ollamhs golden branch.

To my publishers, MTP, Keith Abbott, and all the team for your belief in the book.

My editor, Caroline Mylon, has immersed herself in the mythological world of Eriu, much grá from the cauldron of my heart for helping to shape the manuscript.

To the great Maisitheoir, Dómhnal Ó Bric, for your draíochtúil imaginative weaving creating that illumed living image, containing the essence of the Quest.

Mathew Flaherty, and John Ahern for the teanga dhúchais.

To Aibhlín and Pádraig Corkery, for gifting me a wondrous window to the Rainbow Isles at 9 Dún An Óir, where the Magic of the Wells took manifest.

Siobhán Prendergast, le buíochas for your insightful literary help.

Last thanks and grá mór to Brian J O'Connell, Anam Cara, and to our beauteous four-legged Goddess of Chorca Dhuibhne, and Baile na Loiscneach, Ríonach,

- what a wonderful life.

Available worldwide online and from all good bookstores

Printed in Great Britain
by Amazon